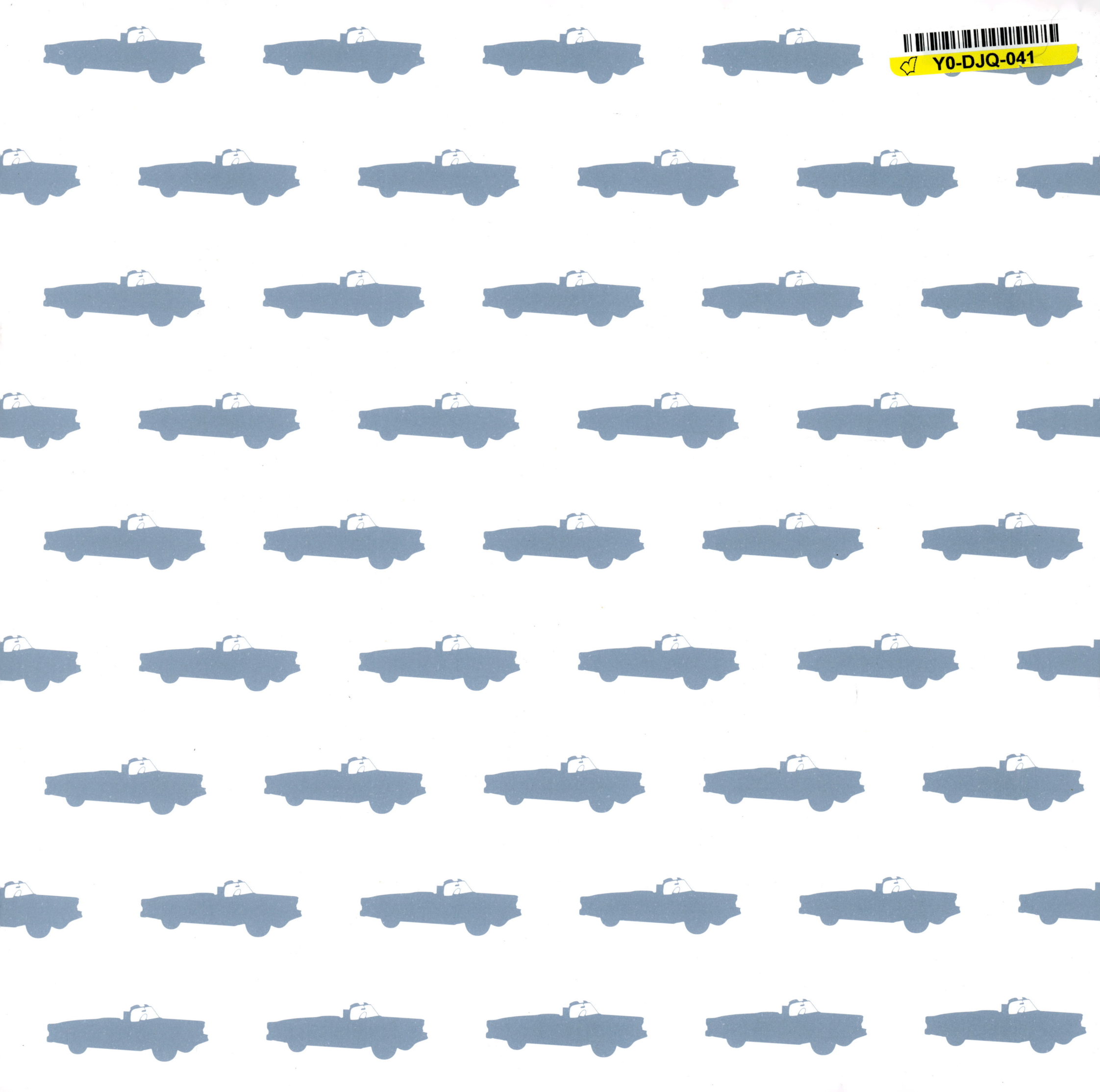

GREAT AMERICAN CONVERTIBLES

pil

Publications International, Ltd.

Copyright © 2003 Publications International, Ltd. All rights reserved. This book may not be reproduced or quoted in whole or in part by any means whatsoever without written permission from:

Louis Weber, CEO
Publications International, Ltd.
7373 North Cicero Avenue
Lincolnwood, Illinois 60712

Permission is never granted for commercial purposes.

Manufactured in China.

8 7 6 5 4 3 2 1

ISBN: 0-7853-6872-8

Library of Congress Control Number: 2002112004

Special thanks to the owners of the cars featured in this book for their enthusiastic cooperation:

Dean and Deborah Tuggle, 1930 Oldsmobile F-30; *Sam S. Chastain,* 1933 Ford Cabriolet; *Thomas E. Lyon,* 1934 Pierce-Arrow Salon Twelve; *Don and Sarah Spieldenner,* 1938 Oldsmobile L-38; *Robert E. Hannay,* 1939 Cadillac Series 90; *David Holls,* 1941 Lincoln Continental; *John Kepich,* 1941 Packard 120; *Joseph Leir Memorial Auto Collection,* 1942 Dodge Custom; *Richard Kughn,* 1946 Mercury Sportsman; *Harry Nicks,* 1947 Cadillac Series 62; *Robert N. Carlson,* 1947 Chrysler Town & Country; *Larry Klein,* 1948 Buick Roadmaster; *Arthur J. Sabin,* 1949 Frazer Manhattan; *Peter's Motorcars,* 1950 Oldsmobile 88; *Norman Frey,* 1951 Chrysler New Yorker; *Cal and Nancy Beauregard,* 1951 Lincoln Cosmopolitan; *Rex Barrett,* 1951 Nash Rambler Custom Landau; *Deer Park Car Museum,* 1953 Oldsmobile Fiesta; *Chicago Car Exchange, Inc.,* 1954 Hudson Hornet Brougham; *Gary Thomas,* 1954 Packard Caribbean; *Gary L. Walker,* 1955 Buick Century; *Greg Gustafson,* 1955 Cadillac Series 62; *Jim Cahill,* 1955 Chevrolet Bel Air; *Gary Richards,* 1955 Mercury Montclair; *Cappy Collection™,* 1956 Ford Thunderbird; *Cappy Collection™,* 1956 Lincoln Premiere; *Robert J. Pond Automobile Collection,* 1956 Packard Caribbean; *Bill and Rita Malik,* 1957 Chevrolet Bel Air; *Ralph M. Hartsock,* 1957 Chrysler New Yorker; *Michael Gallagher,* 1957 Ford Fairlane 500 Skyliner; *Brent Walker,* 1957 Lincoln Premiere; *John W. Petras,* 1957 Oldsmobile Super 88; *Cappy Collection™,* 1958 Continental Mark III; *Cappy Collection™,* 1958 Edsel Citation; *Eldon Anson,* 1959 Cadillac Series 62; *Mervin M. Afflerbach,* 1959 Dodge Custom Royal; *Neil Swartz,* 1959 Ford Thunderbird; *Beau Day,* 1959 Pontiac Bonneville; *Charlie Wells,* 1960 Edsel Ranger; *Sean J. Machado,* 1960 Dodge Polara; *Steve Thompson,* 1961 Ford Galaxie; *Contemporary & Investment Automobiles, Inc.,* 1962 Dodge Polara 500; *Mike and Kay Maxson,* 1963 Chevrolet Impala SS; *Larry Wood,* 1963 Ford Falcon Futura; *Keith Thompson,* 1963 Plymouth Sport Fury; *Doug Moysuik,* 1963 Studebaker Lark Daytona; *Fraser Dante, Ltd.,* 1964 Pontiac GTO; *Chris Davis,* 1965 Chrysler 300L; *Randall Skulemowski,* 1965 Ford Mustang; *Mick Cohen,* 1965 Rambler American 440; *Jeanne C. Finster,* 1966 Chevrolet Corvair Monza; *John Adamek,* 1968 Mercury Park Lane; *Robert Beechy,* 1969 Plymouth Road Runner; *Lewis H. Hunter,* 1969 Shelby GT-500; *Carol Spagenberg,* 1973 Buick Centurion; *Milt Jenks,* 1973 Mercury Cougar XR-7; *Jim Miller,* 1975 Chevrolet Caprice Classic; *Tom Berthelsen,* 1975 Oldsmobile Delta 88 Royale; *John Phillips,* 1975 Pontiac Grand Ville; *Cappy Collection™,* 1976 Cadillac Eldorado; *Buick Public Relations,* 1983 Buick Riviera; *Mitch Lindahl,* 1986 Ford Mustang GT; *Buick Public Relations,* 1990 Buick Reatta; *DaimlerChrysler Public Relations,* 1996 Chrysler Sebring JXi; *Chevrolet Public Relations,* 1998 Chevrolet Corvette Pace Car Replica; *Ford Public Relations,* 1998 Ford Mustang Cobra; *Pontiac Public Relations,* 1999 Pontiac Firebird Trans Am 30th Anniversary Edition; *Panoz Public Relations,* 2000 Panoz Esperante; *DaimlerChrysler Public Relations,* 2000 Plymouth Prowler; *Chevrolet Public Relations,* 2002 Camaro SS 35th Anniversary Edition; *Ford Public Relations,* 2002 Ford Thunderbird; *DaimlerChrysler Public Relations,* 2003 Dodge Viper; *Cadillac Public Relations,* 2004 Cadillac XLR.

The editors gratefully acknowledge the work of the following photographers for their contributions to this book.

Vince Manocchi; Bud Juneau; Nicky Wright; Milton Kieft; Nina Padgett; Gary Smith; Dan Lyons; Jeff Rose; Doug Mitchel; Sam Griffith; Scott Baxter; Phil Toy; David Newhardt; Thomas Glatch; Jay Peck; David Temple; Richard Spiegelman; W. C. Waymack.

CONTENTS

page 6
FOREWORD

page 8
1930 OLDSMOBILE F-30

page 10
1933 FORD CABRIOLET

page 12
1934 PIERCE-ARROW SALON TWELVE

page 14
1938 OLDSMOBILE L-38

page 16
1939 CADILLAC SERIES 90

page 18
1941 LINCOLN CONTINENTAL

page 20
1941 PACKARD ONE TWENTY

page 22
1942 DODGE CUSTOM

page 24
1946 HUDSON SUPER SIX BROUGHAM

page 26
1946 MERCURY SPORTSMAN

page 28
1947 CADILLAC SERIES 62

page 30
1947 CHRYSLER TOWN & COUNTRY

page 32
1948 BUICK ROADMASTER

page 34
1949 CADILLAC SERIES 62

page 36
1949 FRAZER MANHATTAN

page 38
1950 OLDSMOBILE 88

page 40
1951 CHRYSLER NEW YORKER

page 42
1951 LINCOLN COSMOPOLITAN

page 44
1951 RAMBLER CUSTOM LANDAU

page 46
1953 OLDSMOBILE FIESTA

page 48
1954 HUDSON HORNET BROUGHAM

page 50
1954 PACKARD CARIBBEAN

page 52
1955 BUICK CENTURY

page 54
1955 CADILLAC SERIES 62

page 56
1955 CHEVROLET BEL AIR

page 58
1955 MERCURY MONTCLAIR

page 60
1956 FORD THUNDERBIRD

page 62
1956 LINCOLN PREMIERE

page 64
1956 PACKARD CARIBBEAN

page 66
1957 CHEVROLET BEL AIR

page 68
1957 CHRYSLER NEW YORKER

page 70
1957 FORD FAIRLANE 500 SKYLINER

page 72
1957 LINCOLN PREMIERE

page 74
1957 OLDSMOBILE SUPER 88

page 76
1958 CONTINENTAL MARK III

page 78
1958 EDSEL CITATION

page 80
1959 CADILLAC SERIES 62

page 82
1959 DODGE CUSTOM ROYAL

page 84
1959 FORD THUNDERBIRD

page 86
1959 PONTIAC BONNEVILLE

page 88
1960 DODGE POLARA

page 90
1960 EDSEL RANGER

page 92
1960 FORD GALAXIE SUNLINER

page 94
1962 DODGE POLARA 500

page 96
1963 CHEVROLET IMPALA SS

page 98
1963 FORD FALCON FUTURA

page 100
1963 PLYMOUTH SPORT FURY

page 102
1963 STUDEBAKER LARK DAYTONA

page 104
1964 PONTIAC GTO

page 106
1965 CHRYSLER 300L

page 108
1965 FORD MUSTANG

page 110
1965 RAMBLER AMERICAN 440

page 112
1966 CHEVROLET CORVAIR MONZA

page 114
1968 MERCURY PARK LANE

page 116
1969 PLYMOUTH ROAD RUNNER

page 118
1969 SHELBY GT-500

page 120
1973 BUICK CENTURION

page 122
1973 MERCURY COUGAR XR-7

page 124
1975 CHEVROLET CAPRICE CLASSIC

page 126
1975 OLDSMOBILE DELTA 88 ROYALE

page 128
1975 PONTIAC GRAND VILLE

page 130
1976 CADILLAC ELDORADO

page 132
1983 BUICK RIVIERA

page 134
1986 FORD MUSTANG GT

page 136
1988 CHRYSLER LeBARON GTC

page 138
1990 BUICK REATTA

page 140
1996 CHRYSLER SEBRING JXi

page 142
1998 CHEVROLET CORVETTE PACE CAR REPLICA

page 144
1998 FORD MUSTANG COBRA

page 146
1999 PONTIAC TRANS AM
30TH ANNIVERSARY SPECIAL EDITION

page 148
2000 PANOZ ESPERANTE

page 150
2000 PLYMOUTH PROWLER

page 152
2002 35TH ANNIVERSARY
CHEVROLET CAMARO SS

page 154
2002 FORD THUNDERBIRD

page 156
2003 DODGE VIPER

page 158
2004 CADILLAC XLR

page 160
INDEX

FOREWORD

Convertibles aren't as numerous as they used to be, but they still exert a timeless magic. Though difficult to define, the appeal is part environmental, part visual, and part fantasy.

For example, sunroof sedans and T-top coupes may let in the breezes, but they're still essentially closed body types. In a convertible you can be virtually one with nature, feeling the wind in your hair, the sun on your face, or the coolness of a shady lane while viewing the passing scene with no obstructions except a couple of windshield posts. Of course, the experience loses something if you're stuck behind a bus on a gray, chilly day in, say, downtown Chicago—but then you can always raise the top and roll up the windows. By the way, it's those two features that distinguish a convertible from a roadster, which typically has clip-in side curtains and a top not permanently attached to the body.

Which brings us to aesthetics. Somehow, a top-down car almost always looks prettier than a counterpart sedan or even a coupe. Maybe it's the "lighter" look that results from not having a roof.

Or perhaps it's the promise of adventure that comes from lowering the top and throwing caution to the winds.

Advertising has long played on that promise. In a convertible, after all, you can be exposed not only to the elements but the public gaze, ready to see and be seen come what may. Glamorous Hollywood stars drive convertibles, presidents parade in them, college homecoming queens ride down Main Street in them. It's exhilarating to be so "accessible," and ads still drive home the point that driving a convertible is the next best thing to being a celebrity yourself, an instant ticket to admiration, even romance.

Image notwithstanding, the convertible story is pretty much the story of the automobile itself. Indeed, the earliest "horseless carriages" were mostly convertibles, built like open horse-drawn buggies with bodies comprising a wooden framework covered in fabric or leather.

That was enough for a time when cars were expensive playthings and too cranky for trips longer than a Sunday drive. But cars were fast made reliable and cheap enough to become daily transport for millions, and buyers began demanding sturdier bodies with "all season" comfort. Thus the rapid rise of steel construction and the popularity of closed body styles in the 1920s. By World War II, convertibles were no longer significant to the auto business, a situation that prevails today.

Still, "ragtops" were not forgotten, becoming more practical thanks to steady engineering improvements. Tops, for example, are not only far more durable than they were in the '50s, but seal much better too. Many even have heated glass rear windows instead of flimsy plastic that most always turned cloudy. Power tops? Available since the late '40s, though still not universal.

What does remain universal is the enduring appeal of American convertibles from grand '30s classics to the high-tech wonders of the new century. To appreciate why, look no further than the pages of this book.

1930 OLDSMOBILE F-30

Only 233 F-30 Special Six convertible roadsters rolled off the line in 1930, enticing shoppers who did not yet feel the impact of the Depression. Dire days lay ahead, but Olds had a long history of survival.

As the sting of economic pain began to be felt in 1930, Oldsmobile—established before the turn of the century—ranked as the oldest surviving American automaker. Like other manufacturers, Olds Motor Works had begun by producing open cars, starting with the curved-dash runabout. Soft-topped bodies continued to dominate the market in the Teens.

By the Twenties, closed bodies were taking over. Open models—roadsters, phaetons, and convertibles—turned into the fashionable leaders of each product line.

At a glance, Oldsmobiles differed little from a dozen other makes. Nearly all automobiles still featured straight, upright lines. Only by looking more closely could the unique features of an Oldsmobile be discerned, as compared to its GM cousins. A new instrument panel went into 1930 models, and the windshield adopted a mild rearward slant.

All Oldsmobiles used a six-cylinder L-head engine, displacing 197.5 cubic inches and sending 62 horsepower to a conventional three-speed manual transmission—long floor lever, of course. "Syncro-mesh" would not arrive until 1931.

Convertible roadsters came in all three price levels: Standard Six, Special Six, and Deluxe Six. Rarest was the $1070 Special Six (shown), with only 233 produced. Oldsmobiles could be equipped with either wood or wire wheels. Dual-sidemounted spare tires and a rear-mounted trunk were fitted to upper models.

Conservative styling actually helped Oldsmobile weather the Depression better than most companies, as did some daring technical moves later in the decade. After ranking ninth in the industry in 1929, sales sagged in 1930; but so did those of nearly every manufacturer.

1933 FORD CABRIOLET

In its second season with V-8 power, Ford offered a long list of body styles and trim levels—none more appealing than the Cabriolet, flaunting a rakish new profile.

Four-cylinder Fords made their final appearance in 1933, but V-8 models got all the attention. Ford's "flathead" V-8 engine had debuted in '32, shoving aside the popular four-cylinder Model A and reaching past Chevrolet's six-cylinder cars.

Now, stylists—directed by Edsel Ford, Henry's only son—tucked that V-8 into a more stylish machine, with a jauntily slanted grille and windshield. Sharp corners were rounded, and the hood mated with the windshield. Wheels shrunk to 17-inch size for a lower stance. Streamlining was in vogue, and Ford determinedly followed the trend.

Engineers redesigned the Ford's frame and injected an extra 10 horsepower into the V-8, for a total of 75. Hot rodders later grew to love that flathead engine, praised for its power by none other than bank-robber John Dillinger.

One of 16 V-8 models, the Cabriolet cost $585. A total of 7852 were built, plus 24 that used the four-cylinder engine. Model-year volume rose by 100,000 cars, but Ford trailed Chevrolet in total sales.

1934 PIERCE-ARROW SALON TWELVE

One of Pierce-Arrow's main rivals was gone by 1934, and the other was about to issue a medium-priced model. Could this one-time potentate of the automotive road survive much longer?

Known in the 1920s as the three "Ps" of American motordom, Packard, Peerless, and Pierce-Arrow vied for shares of the high-end market. By 1934, Peerless had left the automotive scene, Packard was going strong—and Pierce-Arrow faced financial woes.

Pierce-Arrow had been owned by Studebaker since 1928, but the latter company filed for bankruptcy in spring 1933. Receivers were ordered to sell off Pierce-Arrow, which was purchased by a group of bankers and businessmen from the Buffalo, New York, area. Somehow, they managed to give the '34 models a total restyle, more streamlined than before.

Only 287 Salon Twelve cars (Model 1240A) were built in 1934. Weighing in at 5072 pounds on a 139-inch wheelbase, the convertible coupe sold for $3395. That body style also was available in the Deluxe Eight series for $400 less. Displacing 462 cubic inches, the V-12 engine made 175 horsepower, as opposed to 140 (maximum) for the straight-eight. Pierce-Arrow also sold a few larger-yet Custom Twelve models.

Sales continued to sag, and the Pierce-Arrow firm was losing money rapidly. After a futile attempt to merge with Auburn, they filed for

bankruptcy in August 1934. Despite a slashed workforce, Pierce-Arrow managed to hang on through 1937, but then gave up shortly after the '38 model year began. What many considered America's most eminent marque—with a history dating back to 1901—had become extinct.

Pierce-Arrows were built in Canada as well as the U.S. The convertible coupe pictured here was the first Pierce-Arrow to roll off the Walkerville, Ontario, line in 1934.

1938 OLDSMOBILE L-38

Rumble-seat ragtops and sidemout spares were old news by 1938, but Oldsmobile still offered both—plus a forward-thinking transmission with no clutch pedal.

The Depression seemed to be lifting in 1938 when the stock market snapped, creating what Republicans gleefully called the "Roosevelt Recession." Sales slumped throughout the American auto industry—especially at Oldsmobile, which turned out half as many cars as it had the year before.

The '37 Oldsmobiles had been heavily redesigned, so the '38s were little changed. Still, all models sported more prominent grilles flanked by new "catwalk" trim in the inner front-fender aprons. Back for a second year was the "Automatic Safety Transmission," a clutchless manual gearbox presaging fully self-shifting Hydra-Matic in 1940. For '38, AST was newly optional for six-cylinder Oldsmobiles as well as Eights. Unchanged were Lansing's two L-head inline engines: 95-horsepower 230-cubic-inch six for F-38 models and 110-bhp 257-cid eight for L-38s.

Each line again offered a convertible coupe, but this was the last year for Olds droptops with rumble seats and optional sidemount spare tires. Both features were by then out of fashion with buyers—and out of production at most other automakers. It's odd that Olds was so slow to drop them, considering its growing renown as General Motors' "innovator" division.

The L-38 convertible coupe pictured here is one of only 68 with the factory sidemount, this out of 475 cars total. The six-cylinder version managed 1184 copies in all. Unlike later years, however, ragtops are not the rarest '38 Oldsmobiles. Though integral trunks had become popular for closed body styles, Olds also persisted with passé "trunkless" sedans. These, too, would vanish after 1938 and very low production in eight-cylinder form: just 200 of the four-door model and 137 of the two-door.

Typical of late-prewar GM cars, the '38 Olds dashboard was rather "Buck Rogers," but put most instruments and controls directly ahead of the steering wheel. Such affairs may look quaint to modern eyes, but they were real "hep" at the time.

1939 CADILLAC SERIES 90

Just seven Series 90 convertible coupes with the V-16 engine were built in 1939—a hard sell by then, compared to Cadillac's smooth-running V-8.

Massive, mighty, and defiantly magnificent. Those are just a few of the words that might be used to describe one of the last Cadillac V-16 convertibles. Riding a lengthy 141-inch wheelbase, this convertible coupe tipped the scales at close to 5000 pounds.

The open-roofed Model 9067 flaunted its enclosed, sidemounted spare tires and reaching-ahead hood ornament, the latter of which sat atop a burly barrel-shaped grille and still-separate headlamps. But the main attraction lay beneath the hood: a 431-cubic-inch V-16 engine making 185 horsepower. Like Cadillac's companion V-8, the V-16 engine featured dual carburetors, as well as separate water pumps and distributors for each cylinder bank.

All that bulk to transport a pair of passengers—for a $5440 price at that—might have seemed excessive in the late Depression years. And so it was. After all, Cadillac also offered convertibles in Series 61 and 75, with a marvelous 140-horsepower V-8 engine. A Series 75 convertible coupe could be obtained for a mere $3380, and 27 of those were built.

Only 134 Series 90 cars were produced this year, divided among a dozen body styles. But these mighty machines were on the way out. The V-16 lasted only into 1940, a final relic of a more glorious era of motoring.

1941 LINCOLN CONTINENTAL

One of the most stunning automobiles of all time, the Lincoln Continental started life as a personal car for Edsel—Henry Ford's only son, and president of the company. Flowing lines and a V-12 engine helped the Continental Cabriolet set a new standard in stylish motoring.

Think "classic," and one of the cars you're likely to envision is the original Lincoln Continental. Dozens of other models have been assigned that designation by the Classic Car Club of America, of course, but nearly all are from the 1920s and '30s. Most classic cars are rarely seen, but despite their relatively small numbers, plenty of people have spotted a Continental on the street, as well as in movies from the Forties.

Continentals were produced in coupe and convertible form from 1940 to 1948, extending into the start of the postwar era. Yet, they earned—and deserve—full classic status on the basis of their trend-setting, timeless design.

Styling was conceived by Edsel Ford, based on the Lincoln Zephyr and executed by E.T. "Bob" Gregorie. Edsel wanted his one-off convertible to be "thoroughly continental," including the use of an externally mounted spare tire. In the 1950s, when outside spares became popular add-ons for more prosaic makes, they were called "Continental kits," borrowing their name from this Lincoln.

Each year, Edsel Ford wintered in Palm Beach, Florida. For the 1938-39 vacation season, he wanted a one-off convertible to drive around the area. Response of his neighbors and friends was immediate and enthusiastic. Just about everyone who saw the car thought it sensational.

So did the folks who saw the production version, which arrived for 1940. Reaching beyond stylish, this car turned heads wherever it went.

Only 404 Continentals were built in 1940, but the total rose to 1250 in 1941. Just 400 Cabriolets went on sale that year, priced at $2865. The rest were closed club coupes.

New pushbutton door releases for 1941 added to the car's distinctive allure. Continentals held a 292-cid V-12 engine, rated at 120 horsepower. Many were equipped with the new Borg-Warner overdrive unit.

Lincoln also offered an attractive regular convertible, but only the Continental deserves to stand among the finest automotive designs of the Twentieth Century.

1941 PACKARD ONE TWENTY

While some makes offered one or two convertibles, Packard had eight in 1941. They ranged from the modest six-cylinder One Ten to the rakish, rare Darrin Victoria. If less opulent than some of their ancestors, Packards still exhibited grace and dignity.

Status was Packard's hallmark from its inception in 1899. But after 1935 it became easier to "ask the man who owns one," as Packard ads instructed, with the popular, more affordable One-Twenty series now in the line. By 1941, they also offered a six-cylinder One Ten series, giving less-affluent families an opportunity to drive a Packard. Still, the hierarchy was obvious: One Ten, One Twenty, One Sixty—and ultimate One Eighty.

Convertibles were highly-regarded members of the Packard family. Soft-top coupes in 1941 ranged from the $1195 One Ten, to the $1407 One Twenty, twin One Sixty models, and a Custom Super Eight One Eighty.

The convertible shown here was an aberration: essentially a One Twenty, but with One Eighty trim. Twenty-five were produced, to be offered as prizes in a contest for Packard salesmen. This example was purchased by actress/ballet dancer Vera Zorina.

Packard rebodied its full line for 1941, but the modifications were subtle. Headlamps now sat in front

fenders. Floors were lowered, and motor mounts enlarged. An oil-bath air cleaner was installed. In the One Twenty series, Packard's straight-eight engine displaced 282 cubic inches and developed 120 horsepower. Three-speed column shift was standard, but buyers could pay $37.50 for the "Electromatic" clutch, which disengaged via manifold vacuum when releasing the gas pedal.

1942 DODGE CUSTOM

Pearl Harbor made Detroit's 1942 a very short year, but Dodge was not alone in offering its brashest, shiniest cars ever.

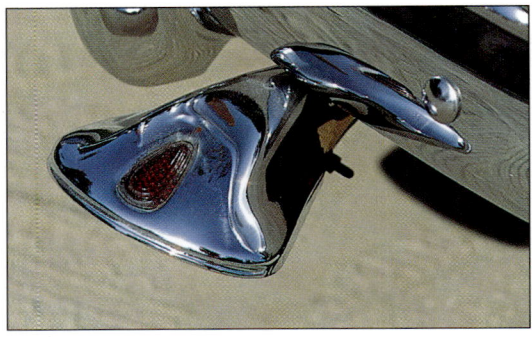

Detroit's 1942 model year was cut to barely seven months by America's entry into World War II and the government-ordered halt of civilian car production in February. Yet while any '42 model is a rare prize today, Dodges were more numerous at the time than some other cars, volume totaling some 68,500 units. Just 1185 were Custom convertibles, which sold for $1245.

Like other Chrysler Corporation cars, the '42 Dodges wore a heavy facelift of their new-for-1940 bodies. Custom and price-leader DeLuxe models returned with broader front fenders and a lower, more horizontal grille that bulged in the center. Customs again offered optional rear-wheel skirts, now with chrome moldings to match added brightwork on front and rear fenders. The Custom dashboard (still symmetrically arranged) was just as dazzling. In all, the '42s were the shiniest Dodges ever—until Washington ordered chrome reserved strictly for war use. Dodge and other makes then switched to painted moldings, creating the even rarer and now highly prized "blackout" models unique to 1942.

There was little unique mechanically about that year's Dodges, which continued with a trusty but dull L-head six dating from 1934. Displacement, however, was upped by about 12 cubic inches to 230, where it would remain until 1960 and the old soldier's belated retirement. Horsepower rose from 91 to 105, but Dodge in 1942 was still some years away from being a "performance car" in any sense.

1946 HUDSON SUPER SIX BROUGHAM

The early postwar years ushered in a booming seller's market where even rehashed prewar cars sold like crazy. Hudson prospered with the rest of Detroit, but built very few convertibles.

World War II deprived Americans of new cars for nearly four years. Once peace returned, the public rushed to replace their aging clunkers with any newly minted wheels available, even if they were just rehashed prewar designs. And most 1946-48 cars were precisely that, because manufacturers had been too busy with war work to do much about postwar models. Even so, the high pent-up demand created an unprecedented seller's market that benefitted most every Detroit automaker. Not until 1950 did supply finally catch up and make freshly designed cars really necessary.

Hudson was no exception to this pattern, issuing modestly revised '42 models for 1946-47 and selling every one it could make. There were fewer choices, however, as Hudson axed lower-priced offerings to concentrate on more profitable Super and Commodore Sixes and Commodore Eights. Differences from '42 involved a more complicated "face," minor interior touch-ups, and higher prices (the result of postwar inflation). Engines remained at prewar power levels: 102 horsepower for the 212-cubic-inch L-head six, 128 for the 254-cid straight eight.

Early postwar Hudsons were smooth and solid but rather staid, even the Brougham convertibles. For 1946 these comprised an $1879 Super Six and a $2050 Commodore Eight, both on a 121-inch wheelbase. All told, Hudson built only 1177 ragtops for the model year, most being Super Sixes like the one shown here.

1946 MERCURY SPORTSMAN

Anything seemed possible in the heady optimism of the early postwar years, so why not a woody convertible? The Mercury Sportsman was a grand idea, but it just didn't sell.

Most Detroit automakers didn't bother with new designs right after World War II. In the frenzied seller's market of the day, warmed-over '42s were more than enough. Still, some companies thought they could do even better business by offering something that rivals didn't—like a convertible with structural-wood bodywork. Thus was born the Mercury Sportsman.

Chrysler had glamorized the woody wagon with its prewar Town & Countrys, and this likely inspired off-and-on thoughts of woody convertibles during the war at Ford Motor Company. Many ideas were floated, but only the Mercury Sportsman and a similar Ford Super DeLuxe model made it to showrooms.

Both Sportsmans wore solid maple or yellow birch framing and mahogany insert panels. The framing was not only structural at the rear, but beautifully mitred and varnished to lend a welcome touch of class to familiar 1942 styling. Otherwise, the Sportsman was like any other '46 Merc: 118-inch wheelbase, antique transverse leaf springs at each end, 239 flathead V-8 with 100 horsepower, and rather busy "big Ford" looks. Trouble was, the Sportsman's wood required lots of hand finishing, and that made for a steep price: $2209, nearly $500 more than Mercury's all-steel ragtop and $200 more than the Ford Sportsman. That was a tough sell, so Mercury moved just 205 Sportsmans, too few to continue the model beyond this one year.

Somewhat better sales gave Ford's Sportsman a three-year run: 1209 copies for '46, 2250 for '47, and just 28 for the abbreviated '48 model year. But whether Mercury or Ford, these convertibles are highly valued today, not only as rarities but for their unique elegance. At a time when dark clouds hovered over the future of Ford Motor Company, the Sportsman provided a hopeful ray of sunshine.

1947 CADILLAC SERIES 62

Cadillac offered only one convertible in 1947, but it was no less glamorous or desired than its predecessors. For many Americans, a droptop Caddy was the ultimate way to say, "I've made it!"

Cadillac in 1947 was poised to become America's luxury leader. Unlike Lincoln and Packard, which persisted with Depression-inspired medium-price cars, Cadillac returned to pure luxury to prosper in booming postwar America. Soon, Cadillac pulled even further ahead of rivals in both sales and prestige.

Open Cadillacs had long been glamorous dream machines, but unlike the numerous convertibles of prewar times, only one was available in 1947. Priced at $2902, some $350 above the similar '46 model, it was the costliest member of the sales-leading Series 62 line, which then accounted for some two-thirds of Cadillac volume. "Pontoon" styling, new for '42, was making its final appearance, and Cadillac's smooth 346-cubic-inch L-head V-8 was in its next-to-last year. As ever, optional fully automatic Hydra-Matic Drive was a big sales point and increasingly popular. Adding appeal to the '47 droptop were newly standard "Hydro-Lectric" power windows, which joined leather upholstery and other no-cost amenities to help boost production from 1342 in '46 to a healthy 6755.

1947 CHRYSLER TOWN & COUNTRY

The Town & Country convertible added much-needed glamour to a staid group of early postwar Chryslers. For impact and sales alike, it was king of Detroit's non-wagon woodies.

Chrysler sold more non-wagon woodies than anyone in 1946-48, most being convertibles. Granted, there wasn't much competition: just the Ford/Mercury Sportsman convertibles and Nash's surprising Suburban sedan. But Chrysler's ragtop Town & Country led the parade not only in sales but in combining sporty elegance with vault-like solidity, smooth-riding luxury, and loads of glitter.

The T&C was also sold as a four-door sedan through mid-1948. Most used the six-cylinder Windsor platform, whereas all convertibles rode the longer New Yorker chassis with its 135-horsepower 323-cubic-inch straight eight. Chrysler had planned a whole line of T&Cs, including a roadster and what could have been America's first hardtop coupe, but only a handful of these were built as prototypes. The four-door attracted 4050 buyers, making the T&C convertible, with production of 8380, one of the few cases in modern automotive history where an open model outsold its closed counterpart.

Chryslers hardly changed between 1946 and '48, all being distinguished by a dazzling "harmonica" grille and bulbous lines. Still, the droptop T&C was a real "looker" with its structural ash wood framing on bodysides and rear deck. Inserts were genuine

mahogany through mid-'47, then realistic Di-Noc decals. Interiors were impressively furnished with wood paneling and leather/Bedford cord upholstery. Alas, the price for such opulence was high: $2743 in '46, $3420 by '48, figures that placed them squarely in Cadillac territory.

The T&C convertible returned in Chrysler's all-new '49 lineup, but was far less special. After a 1950 hardtop, Town & Countrys were again strictly wagons. Since then the name has graced a steady stream of Chryslers—many wearing elaborate pseudo-wood decoration—but none match the majesty of the glorious 1946-48 originals.

1948 BUICK ROADMASTER

Buick's 1948 styling wasn't new, but it still looked fresh. And there was an innovation for Roadmasters, including the convertible: Buick's first fully automatic transmission.

Buick completely restyled on the eve of World War II, so its design was technically just a year old when civilian production resumed in late 1945. That means its cars still looked fresh, so it's no wonder that sales went nowhere but up.

Although there were far fewer Buick models than in '42, the 1946-48 lineups again included convertibles in the mid-range Super series (124-inch wheelbase) and top-line Roadmaster (129). Both used smooth straight-eight power—a 248 and a 320, respectively—and engine tweaking for 1948 increased horses to 115 and 150. But the big news that year was Dynaflow automatic transmission, a $244 option exclusive to Roadmasters. Though not as responsive as Hydra-Matic, Dynaflow proved so popular that Buick had to double planned installations. So equipped, a Roadmaster ragtop sold for $3081—rather pricey then. Still, most of the 11,503 built probably got the new automatic—and definitely got a lot of looks.

1949 CADILLAC SERIES 62

Thanks to a brilliant new V-8, Cadillac's Series 62 convertible was even more an object of desire in 1949. It also had tailfins, the new ultimate in Detroit styling.

In the words of a later era, Cadillac had it all together in 1949. The previous year introduced all-new styling with tailfins—startling at the time, but soon widely imitated. Now Cadillac offered two more firsts in the luxury class: a brilliant high-compression overhead-valve V-8, and an equally predictive "hardtop convertible" model, the Coupe de Ville. If anyone doubted Cadillac's supremacy in the high-buck field, they were silenced in 1949.

The Coupe de Ville appeared in the mainstay Series 62 alongside Cadillac's sole convertible. At $3497, the new hardtop cost $55 more than the soft-top, but was just as rakish and glamorous. Though hardtops would ultimately dominate Cadillac sales, the convertible was more popular in '49 at 8000 units versus 2150. Either way, Cadillac's new 160-horsepower 331-cubic-inch V-8 delivered smooth yet lively acceleration. It was also lighter than its L-head predecessor, so handling improved as well. No wonder all '49 Cadillacs are still so highly prized by collectors.

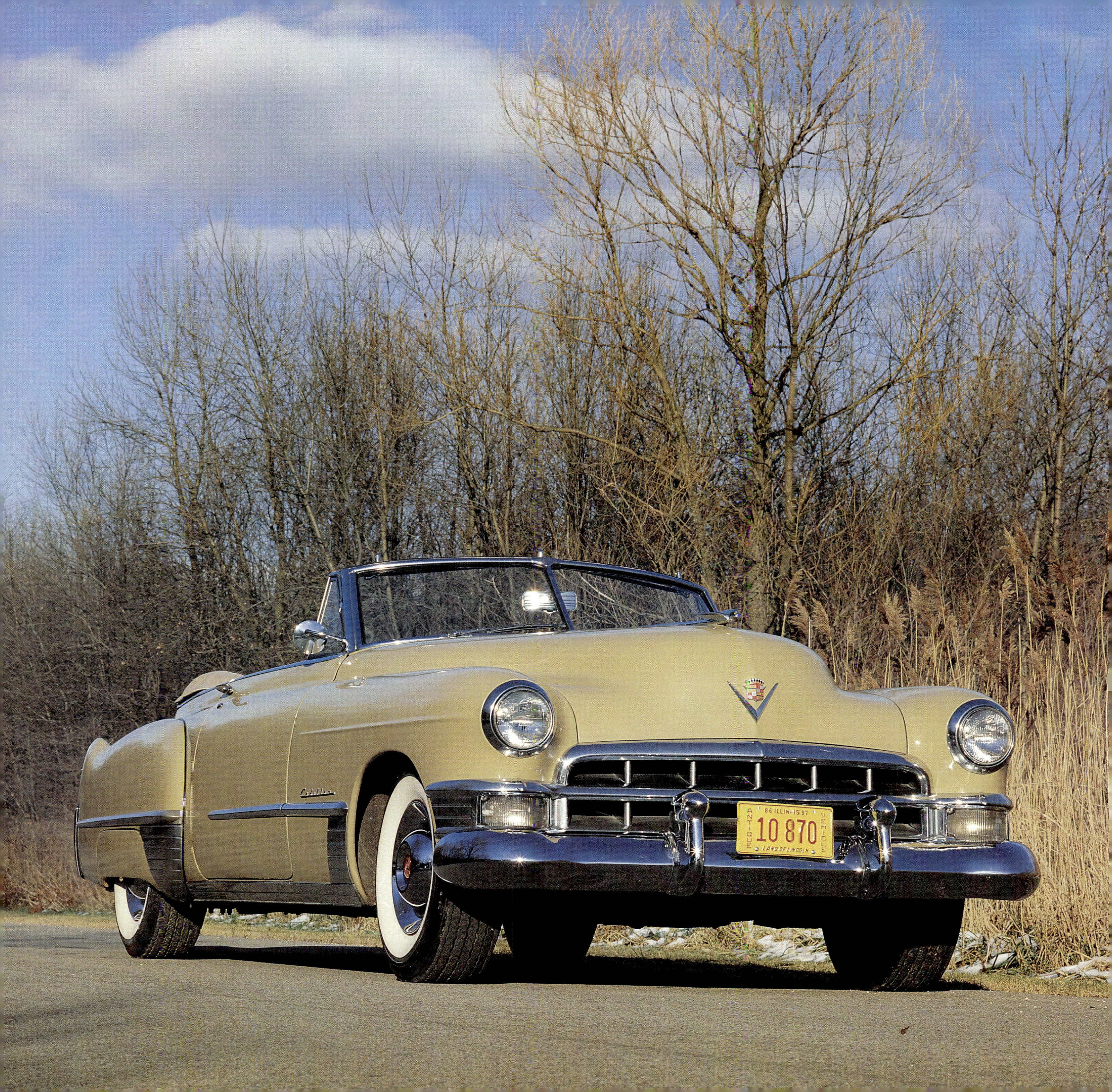
10 870

1949 FRAZER MANHATTAN

America's first postwar convertible sedan was a hurry-up job by an upstart independent maker suddenly in need of some new sales magic. Unfortunately, this '49 Frazer wasn't it.

After pumping out scores of World War II Liberty ships post haste, Henry J. Kaiser decided to pump out cars—by the boatload, he hoped. But though his new six-cylinder Kaisers and Frazers did well enough in 1946-47, sales dropped sharply once updated Big Three models appeared with all-new postwar styling and more power. The upper-medium-priced Frazer, named for Henry's partner and industry veteran Joe Frazer, was hit particularly hard. But rather than heed Joe's advice and come back with all-new 1950 products, Henry ordered higher production—and wound up with acres of unsold cars.

Among them was a new '49 Frazer to attract showroom crowds: America's first postwar convertible sedan, created by simply snipping the top from a four-door sedan, the only body style K-F had. Offered only in upper-level Manhattan guise, it wore the same facelift as other Frazers (highlighted by a shiny eggcrate grille), but rode a heavier—and costlier—reinforced frame that only further taxed the 112 horsepower of K-F's 226-cubic-inch six. Structural concerns prompted the use of fixed side window frames and B-posts with glass inserts, so this wasn't even a "full" convertible.

It was, however, luxuriously furnished and equipped with niceties like self-shifting Hydra-Matic Drive. Alas, that only contributed to a lofty $3295 price in a year when a Cadillac convertible cost but $150 more. With all this, the Frazer just couldn't sell, and only 70 were built through 1950. Another 131 with a heavier facelift were built for '51, after which Frazer was consigned to history.

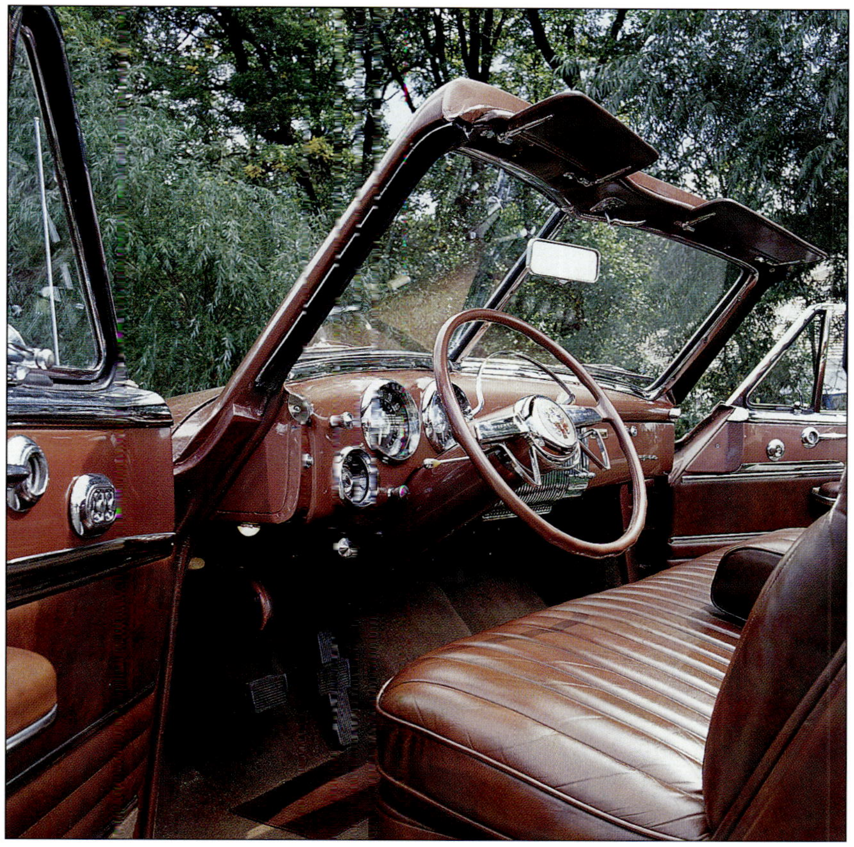

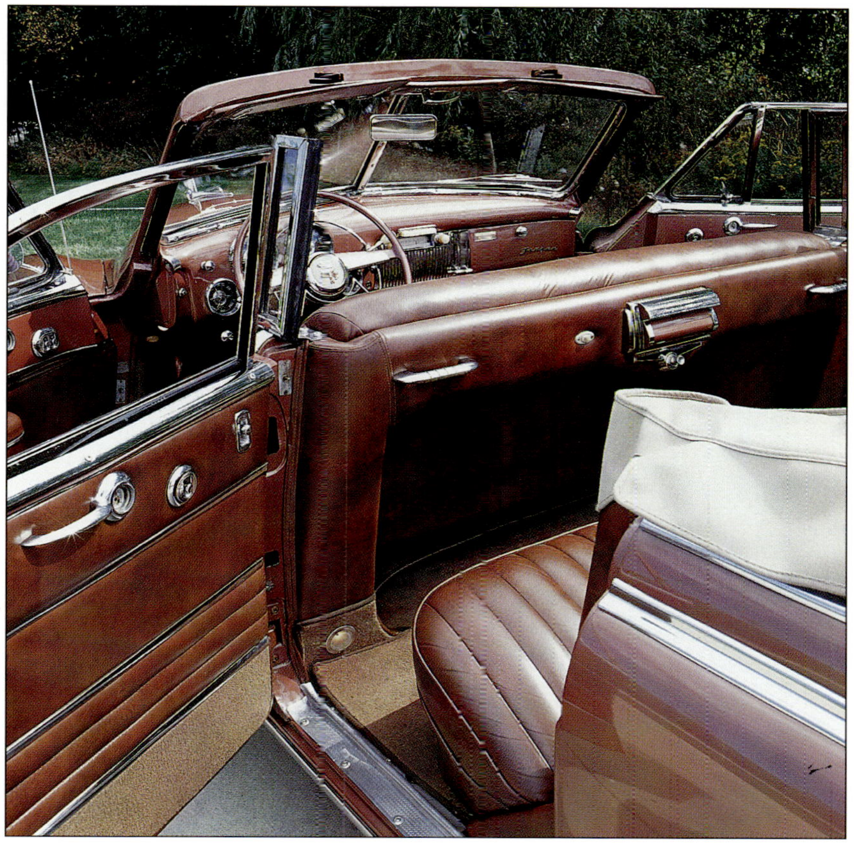

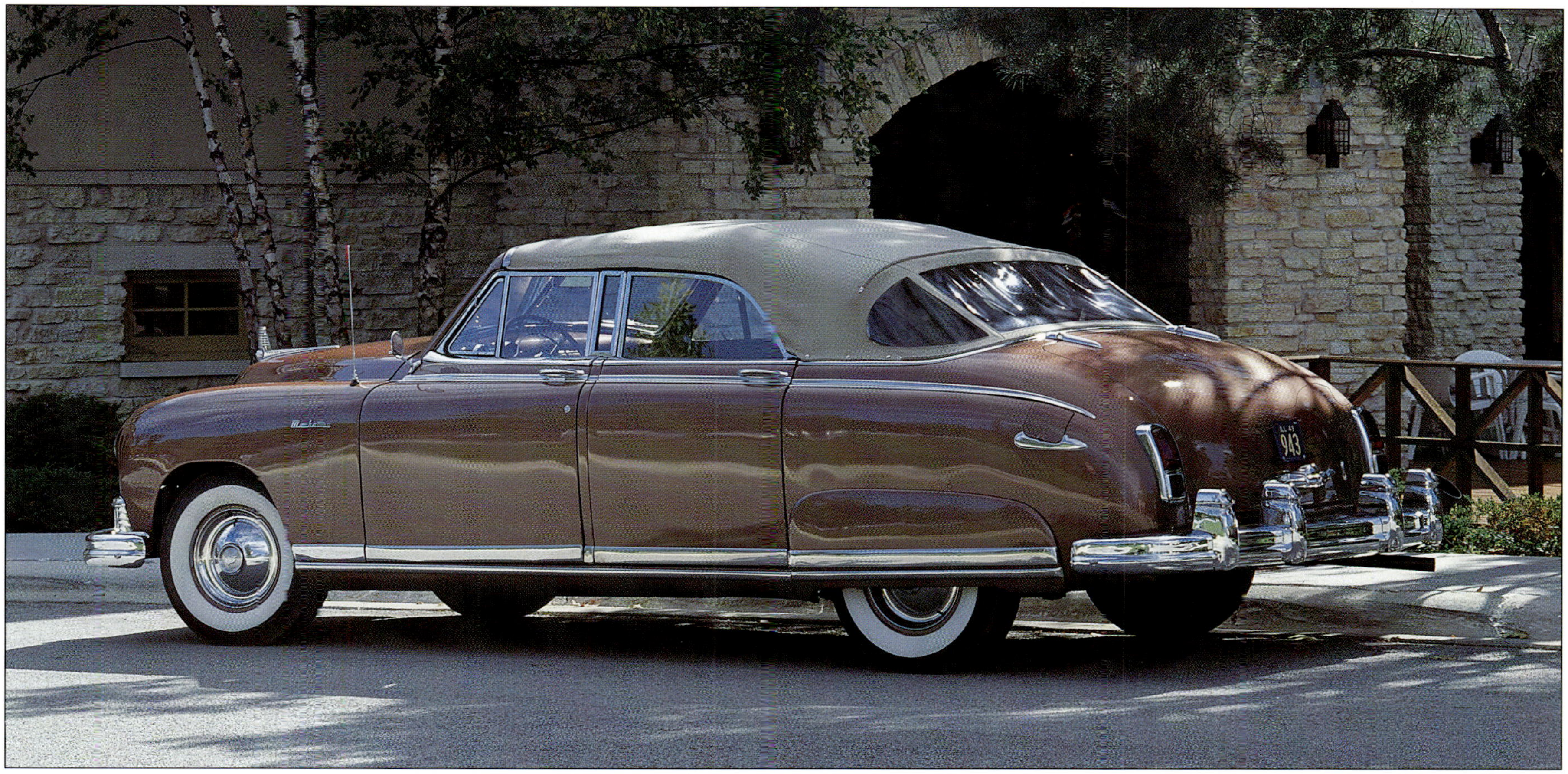

1950 OLDSMOBILE 88

A dashing convertible that goes like a rocket? If that was your dream, Oldsmobile had your car in 1950: America's only "Rocket Action" ragtop.

Oldsmobile created America's first "factory hot rod" in 1949 by combining its new high-compression Rocket V-8 from the big 98 series with the smaller, lighter platform of its six-cylinder 76 models. The resulting 88 was a sensation on road and track—especially in dashing convertible form.

Though designed independently of Cadillac's larger new 1949 V-8, the Rocket, too, was an efficient lightweight engine with great tuning potential. Even with mild 7.25:1 compression, this 303-cubic-incher initially delivered 135 horsepower, giving the 88 a 22.5:1 power-to-weight ratio—outstanding for the day. With that, the 88 brought to thousands of buyers the kind of performance once reserved for high-priced cars—or home-built hot rods.

Oldsmobile's popular Futuramic styling was little changed for 1950. While other 88s offered standard and DeLuxe versions, the convertible came in only one well-dressed model attractively priced at $2294. Olds built 9127 for the model year. Hardtop variants dominated the racing circuits, Olds claiming both the NASCAR crown and class wins in the Mexican Road Race—"Rocket Action" indeed.

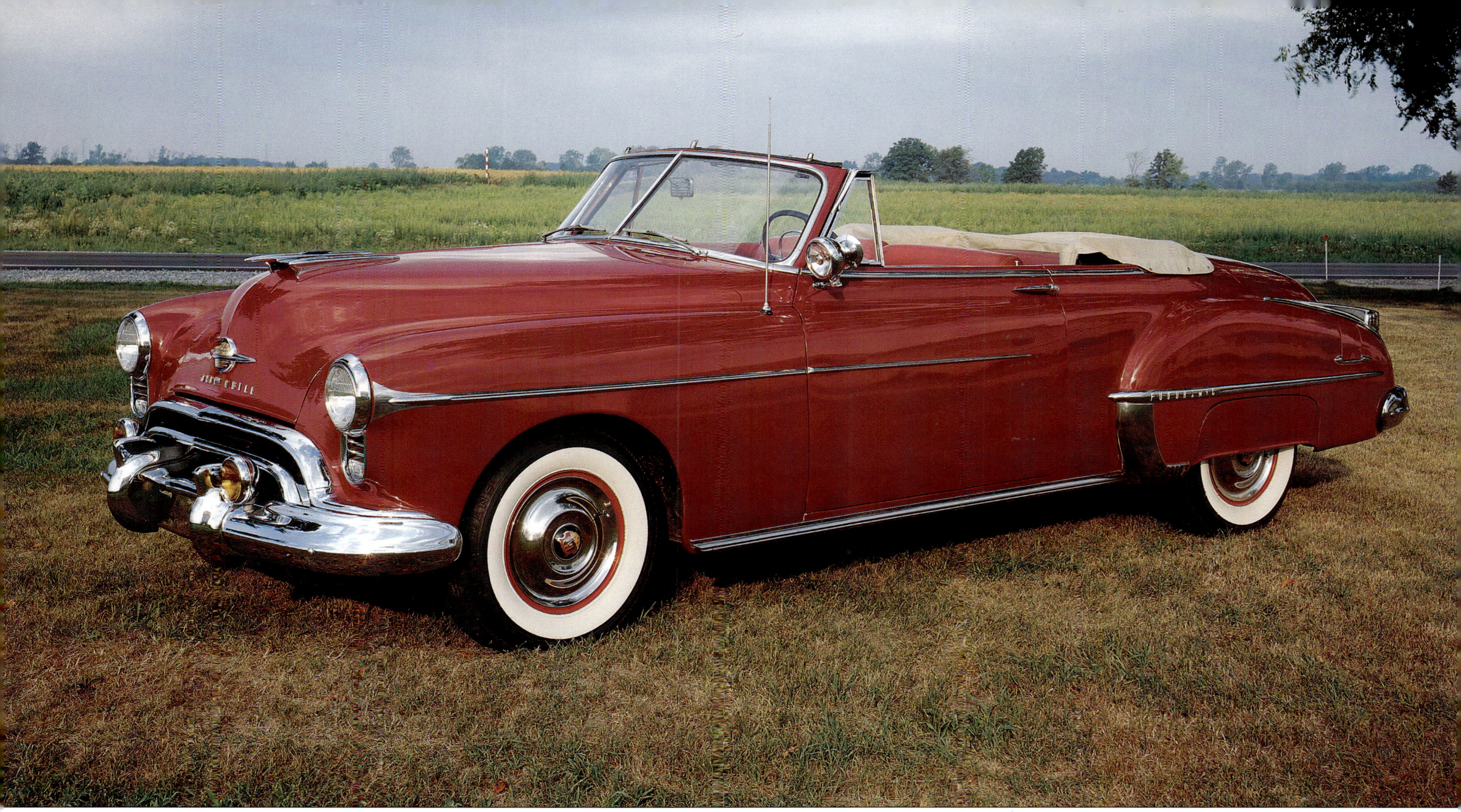

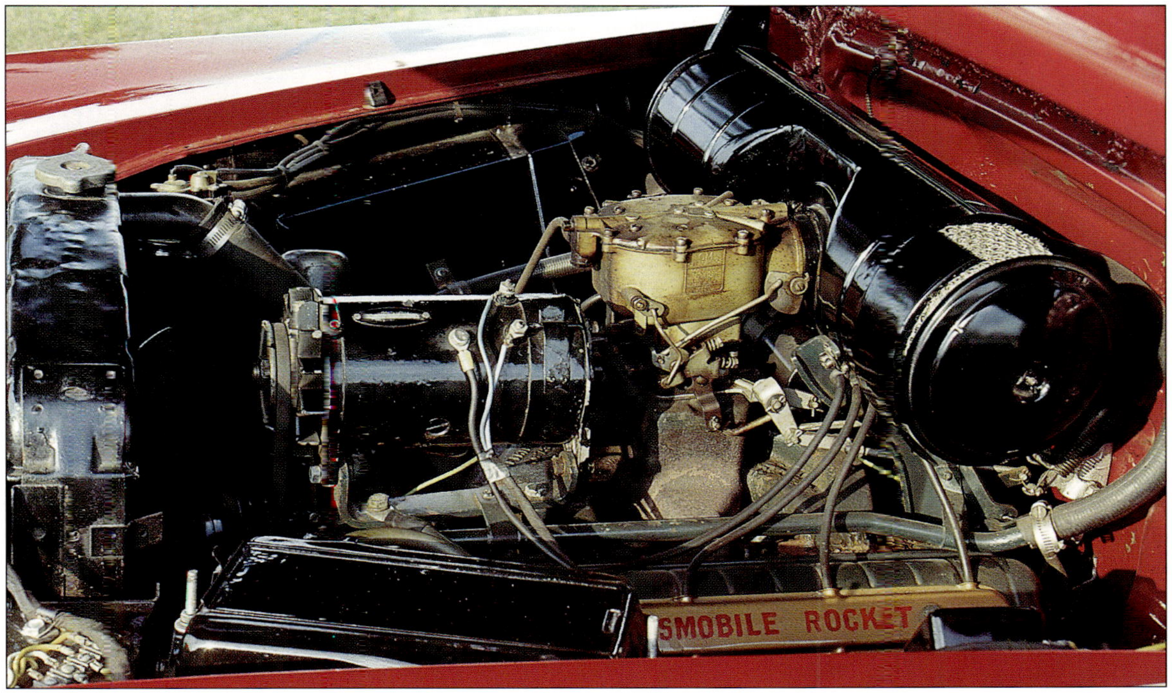
SMOBILE ROCKET

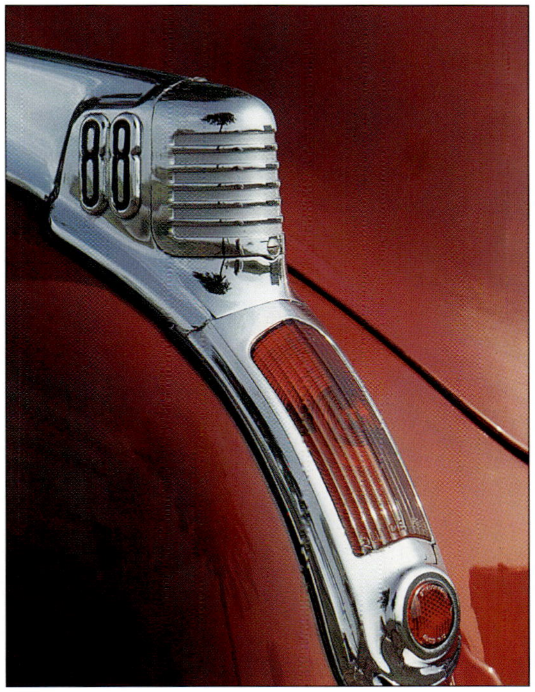
88

1951 CHRYSLER NEW YORKER

A "horsepower war" was raging in Detroit when Chrysler unleashed the famed hemi-head FirePower V-8. With that, Chrysler convertibles offered more wind in the hair per mile than most any other ragtop around.

American car buyers happily endured a "horsepower war" in the 1950s. Oldsmobile sounded the gun with its 1949 Rocket V-8, but Chrysler's new 1951 "Hemi" was a shot heard 'round the world.

Though not a new idea, the Hemi—named for its combustion chambers' half-dome shape—produced more horsepower per cubic inch than any other engine around. In initial form it made 170, 10 more horses than Cadillac's contemporary V-8 of identical size, and even minor modifications could easily yield 300. But though a New Yorker convertible paced the 1951 Indy 500, the Hemi wasn't raced much before mid-decade because the cars it powered were large and lumbering. And Chrysler did little to change that, its 1950-54s being mainly brighter, smoother renditions of its square and stodgy new '49 generation. (So little change occurred for 1951-52 that Chrysler didn't even keep separate production tallies.)

Chrysler paid the price as sales steadily declined to crisis levels by 1954. Government-mandated production curbs during the Korean War didn't help. Nor did inflationary pressures that boosted the New Yorker convertible's price by $700 for '51 to a lofty $3916. As a result, sales were just 2200 in 1951-52. The cheaper six-cylinder Windsor convertible managed 4200.

But even when handicapped by sluggish semi-automatic Fluid Drive transmission, the FirePower Hemi redefined performance for the medium-price field in no uncertain terms. Of course, it also speeded up air flow through the hair of Chrysler convertible drivers. Indeed, a Hemi ragtop perfectly symbolized the "sky's the limit" optimism of the age.

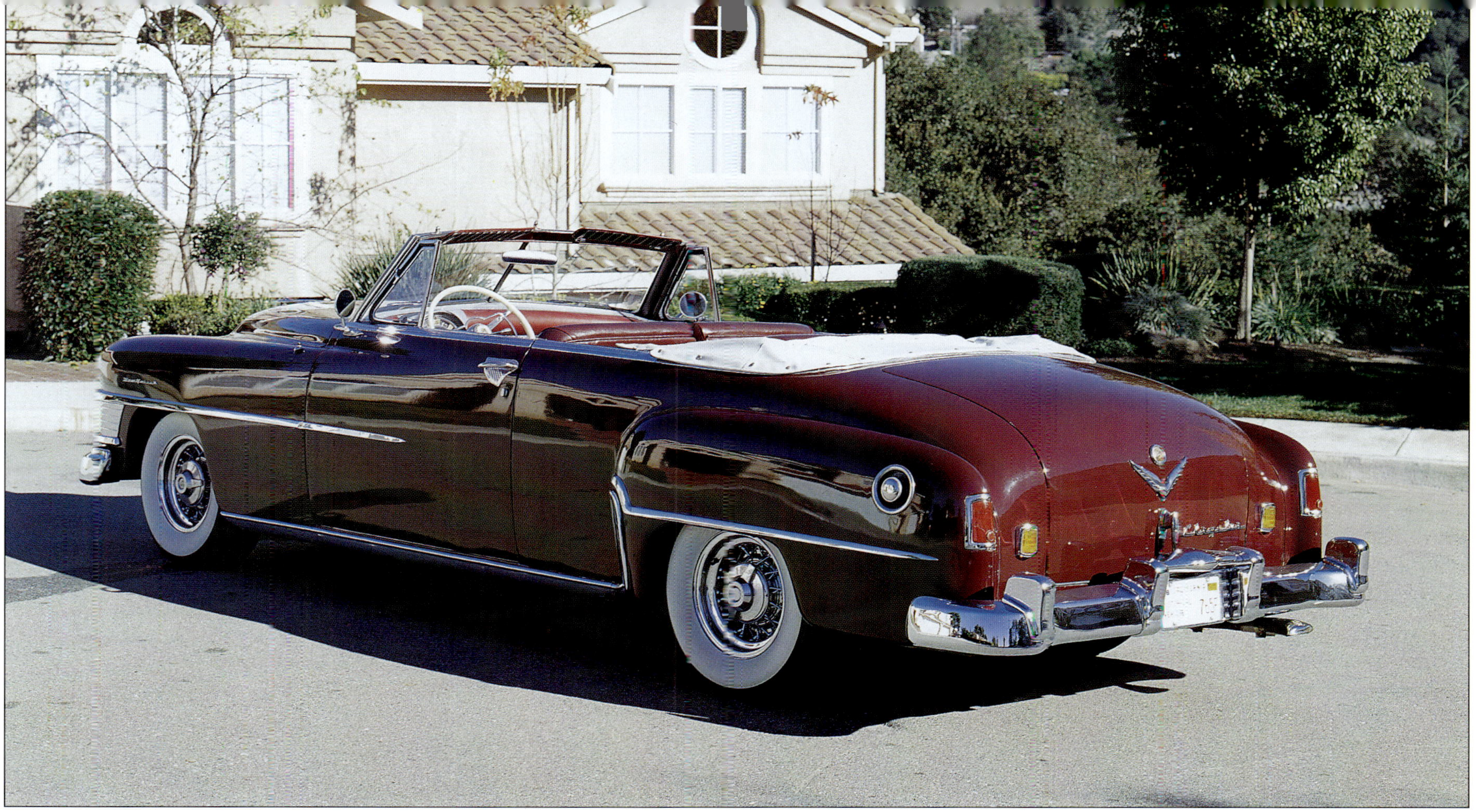

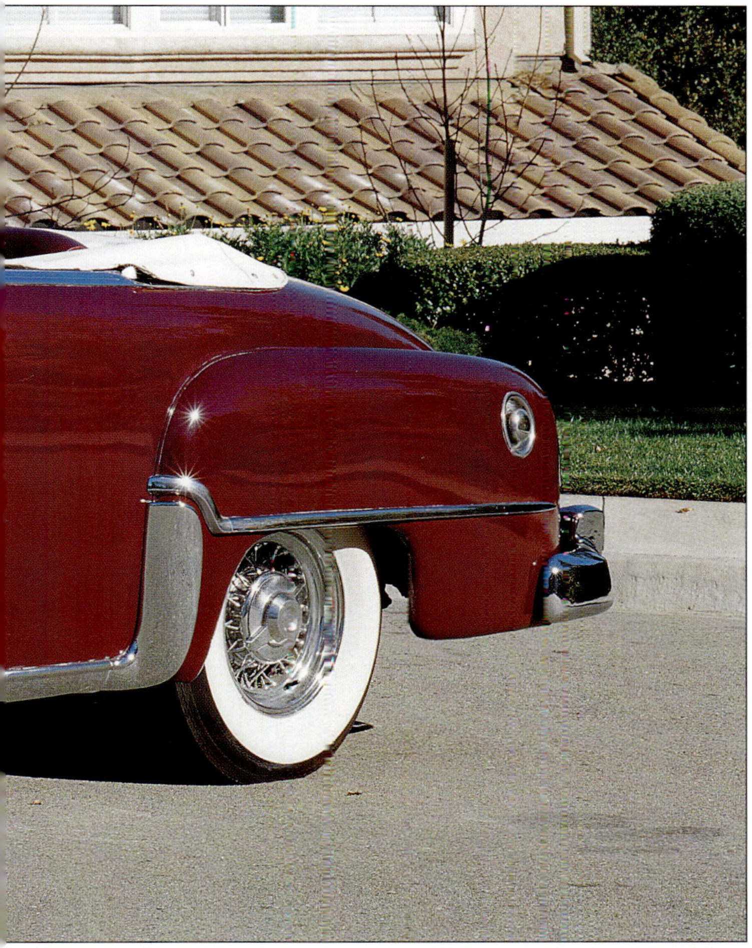

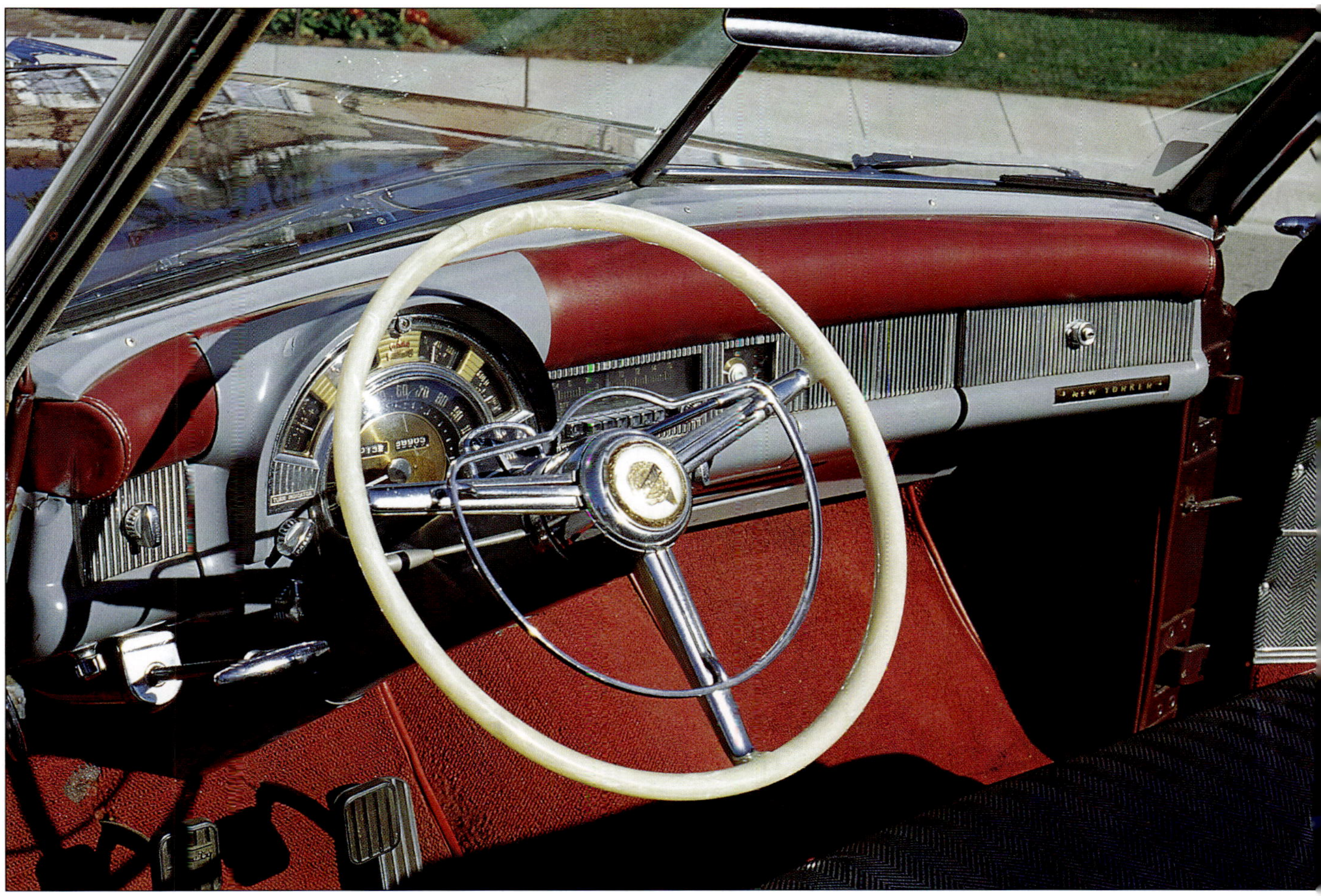

1951 LINCOLN COSMOPOLITAN

Though highly prized today, the "bathtub" Lincolns weren't that popular when new. But the top-of-the-line Cosmopolitan convertible was mighty impressive—and frequently seen at the Truman White House.

The 1949-51 Lincolns were an odd mix of old and new. The latter included Lincoln's first fully independent front suspension and optional self-shift Hydra-Matic Drive (hastily "imported" from General Motors). On the other hand, Lincoln gained no prestige by trading its aging V-12 for an old-concept 336.7-cubic-inch flathead V-8 borrowed from Ford trucks. And though Lincoln's smooth but massive "bathtub" styling was new, it was clearly the stuff of the early '40s, not postwar thinking. The '49 Lincolns thus sold reasonably well, but the similar 1950-51s managed only some 25-30 percent of their volume.

Still, the "bathtubs" were no less solid, refined, or luxurious than prior Lincolns, though new "junior" models were much like contemporary Mercurys, thanks to some cost-conscious platform sharing decreed at the last minute. The "real" Lincoln of these years was the 125-inch-wheelbase Cosmopolitan, which included a line-topping convertible. For 1951 it cost a hefty $3891, which partly explains why only 857 were built.

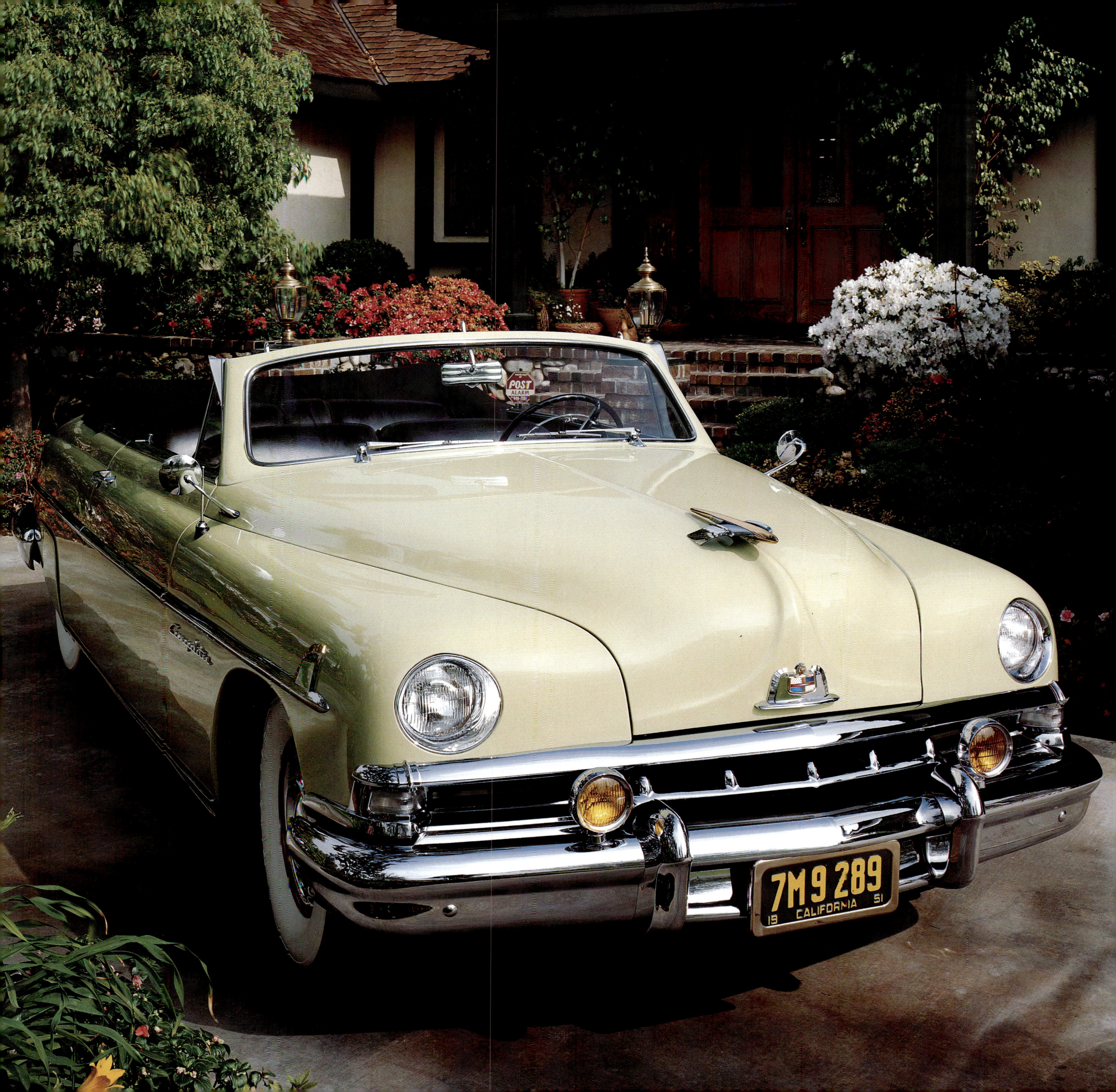
POST
ALARM
7M9 289
19 CALIFORNIA 51

1951 RAMBLER CUSTOM LANDAU

The 1951 Rambler Custom Landau was the perfect car for a style-minded go-getter on a budget—like ace reporter Lois Lane.

If you remember the old *Superman* TV series, you may recall Lois Lane driving a Nash Rambler like this one. It was an apt choice for the *Daily Planet* reporter: easy to park, thrifty with gas and, in 1951, quite affordable at $1933. And that was for the grandly named Custom Landau convertible, distinguished by a cloth roof that furled like the door on a roll-top desk.

The Rambler also looked tubby in the way of period big Nashes, but it was America's first successful compact. Nash president George Mason loved small cars, and he made sure buyers liked Ramblers by insisting on big-Nash features like rattle-free (if rust-prone) unitized construction, Weather Eye heater, and a dull but proven 172-cubic-inch L-head six with 82 horsepower. Early Ramblers even had the same skirted front wheels as big Nashes, which only made for super-size U-turns for Lois when chasing bad guys on the crowded streets of Metropolis.

Though two-door wagons were the most popular early Ramblers, Mason was quick to add a trendy hardtop coupe for '51. That would have suited Lois too. But then, she couldn't have lowered its top to catch Superman's eye from on high.

44

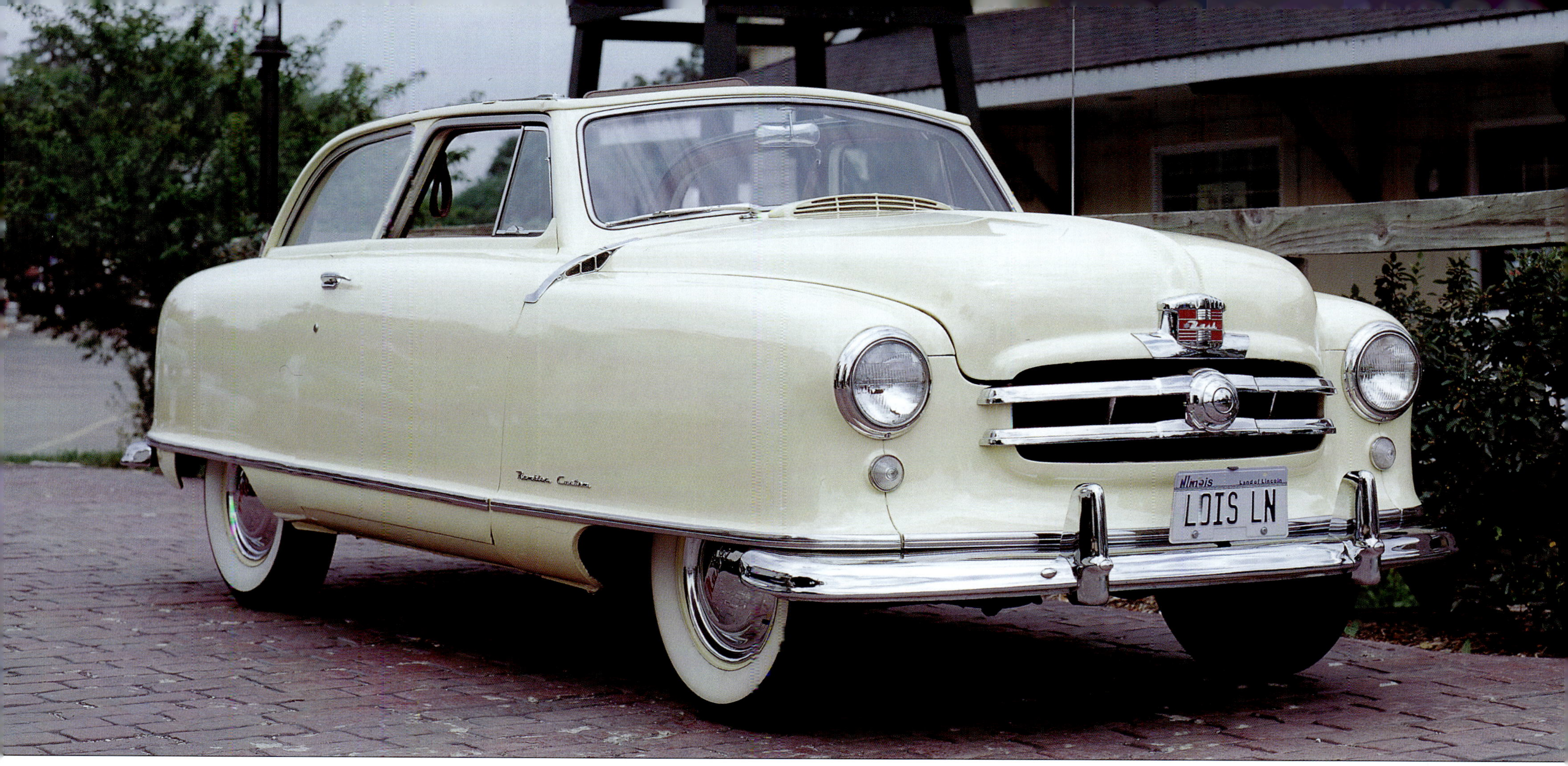
Illinois
Land of Lincoln
LOIS LN

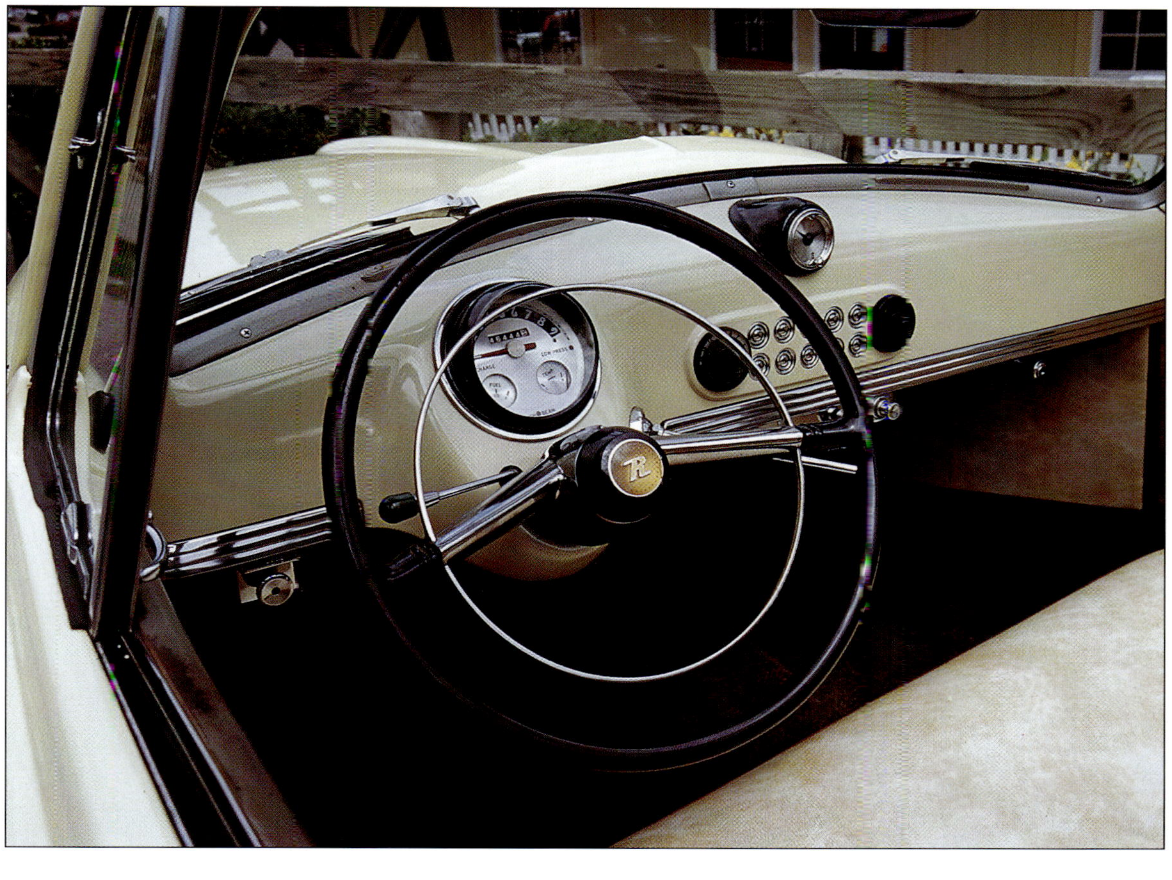

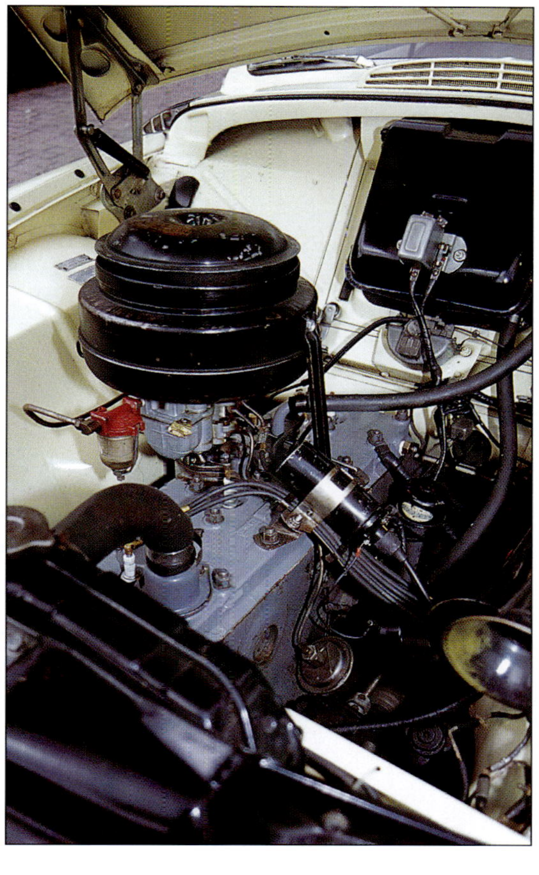

1953 OLDSMOBILE FIESTA

General Motors could afford to do anything in 1953, so offering a bevy of "dream" convertibles for sale was no big deal. Among them was Oldsmobile's fancy, flashy Fiesta.

Detroit wowed 1950s America with all manner of futuristic "dream cars," but only General Motors built some for sale—four in 1953 alone. All were costly limited-edition convertibles, but while Chevrolet's sporting 'Vette and the Cadillac Eldo became long-running fixtures, Buick's Skylark lasted only two years and the Oldsmobile Fiesta ended after a single season and just 458 copies.

"Dream cars" often preview forthcoming design ideas. The Fiesta hinted at '54 Olds styling with "hockey-stick" side trim and wraparound Panoramic windshield. Otherwise it was basically a stock but fully equipped 98 convertible with a tuned 170-horsepower version of Olds's 303-cubic-inch Rocket V-8.

Most Fiestas wore colorful two-toning, and all had self-shift Hydra-Matic, power steering and brakes, and leather upholstery among many amenities. The Fiesta wasn't cheap at $5717, but it didn't need to make money. In those days, GM could afford to do anything it pleased.

46

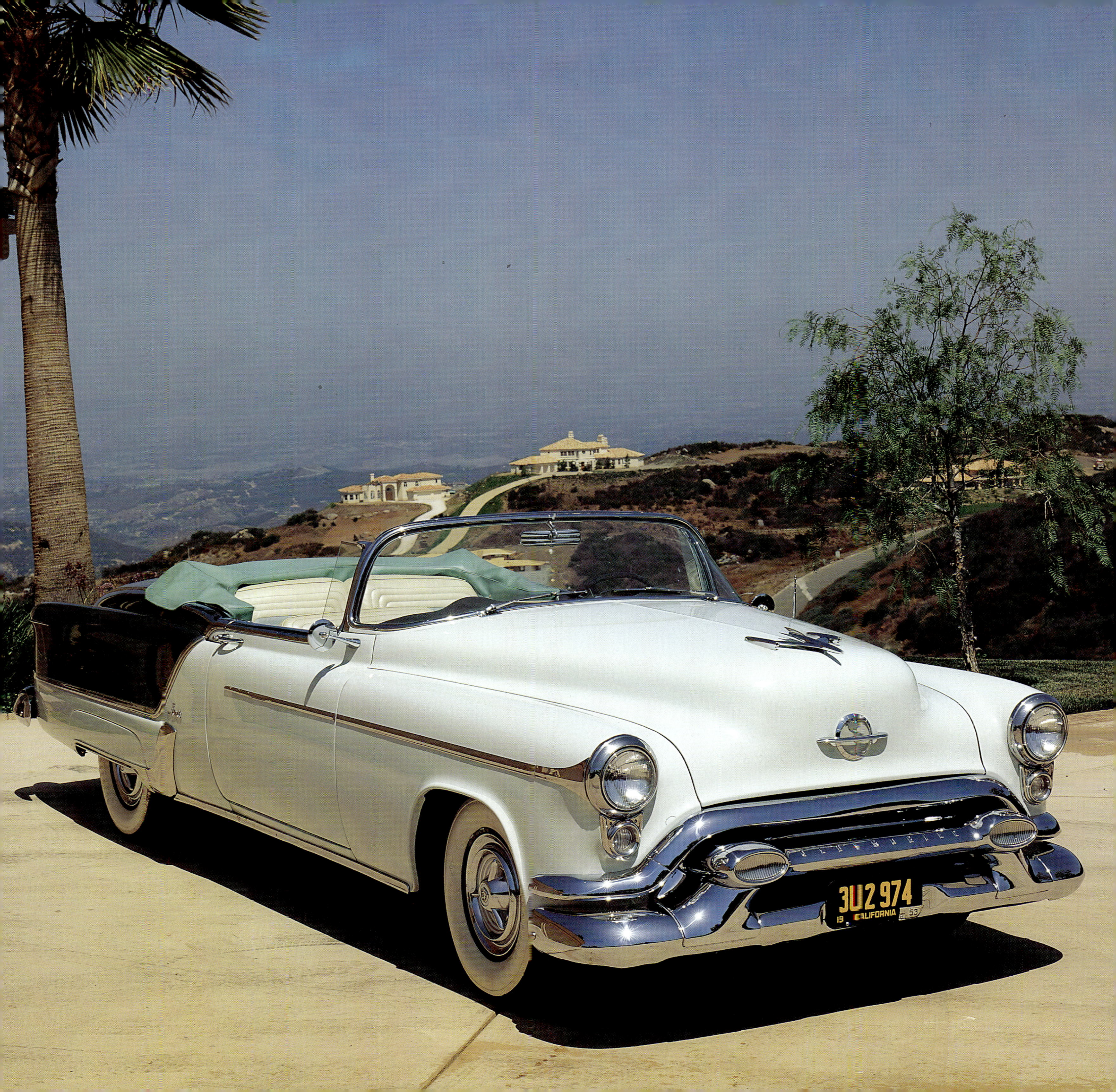
3U2 974
19 CALIFORNIA 53

1954 HUDSON HORNET BROUGHAM

With sales sliding and cash running out, Hudson pinned its hopes on fully restyled "Step-down" models for 1954. The convertible looked great, but it all was too little, too late.

The "Step-down" Hudson was a marvel in debut 1948, but not for long. Hudson's straight-eight engine was way outclassed by newer Big Three V-8s, and although Hudson's six-cylinder Hornet dominated stock-car racing in the early '50s, it was still just a six. Worse, Hudson's unitized "Monobilt" design was costly and difficult to change, and its "torpedo" styling dated quickly. Sales began withering fast, and by 1954, Hudson was in deep trouble. Hoping for salvation, Hudson gave the '54 Step-downs a square-lined makeover. There was still no V-8, but the 308-cubic-inch six in top-line Hornets again delivered 160 healthy horses, 170 with optional racing-inspired "Twin-H-Power" carburetors. Interiors were spruced up too. The Hornet Brougham convertible, still Hudson's only ragtop, was particularly attractive in this new finery, but at $3288 it was overpriced for a six-cylinder car in 1954. So were other Step-downs. As a result, sales skidded again, dropping to 36,436 for the model year. Of these, an estimated 3857 were ragtops.

Compounding these woes was the 1953-54 Jet, an ill-advised compact that cost a bundle and didn't sell. With all this, Hudson had little choice but to join with Nash in 1954 to form American Motors. Three years later, Hudson was gone, a victim of too little change for fast-changing times.

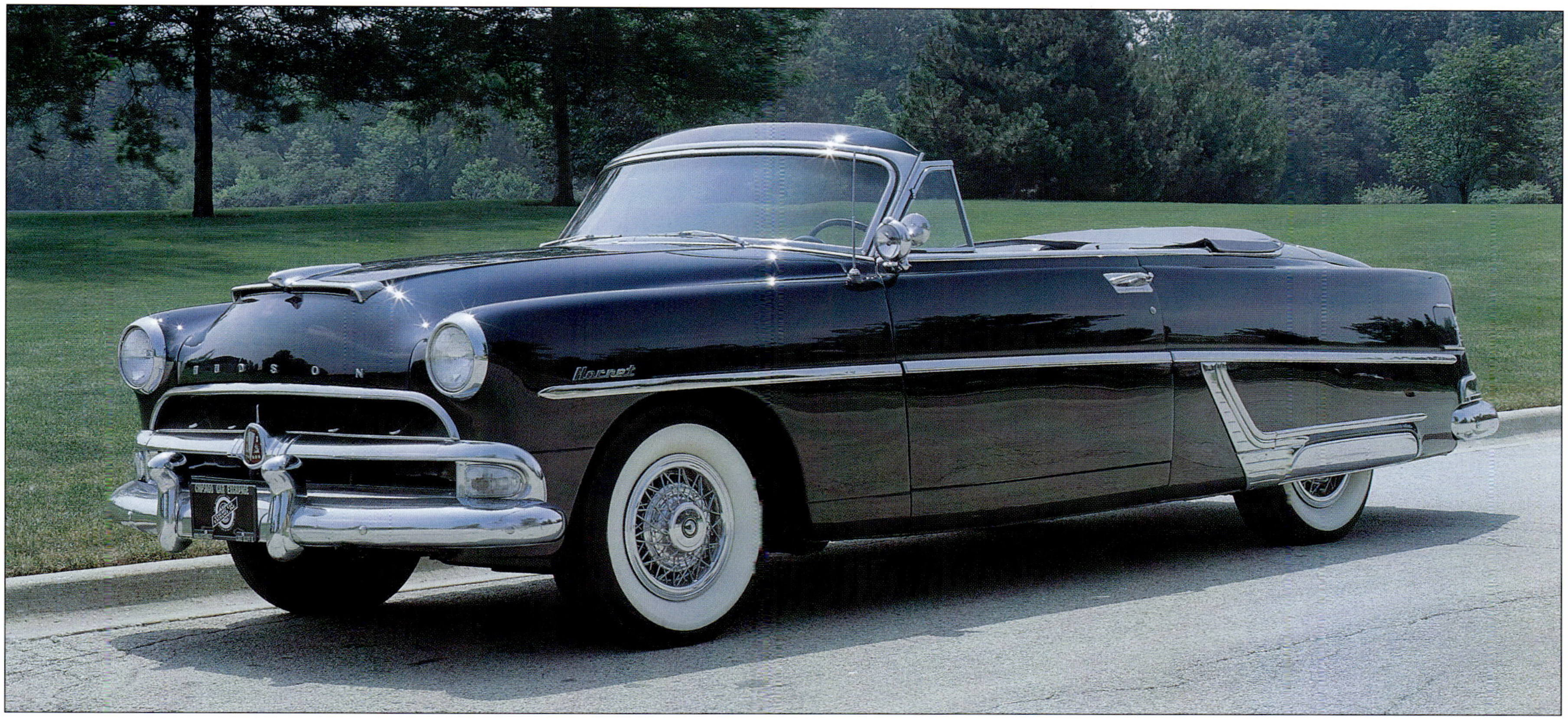
HUDSON
Hornet

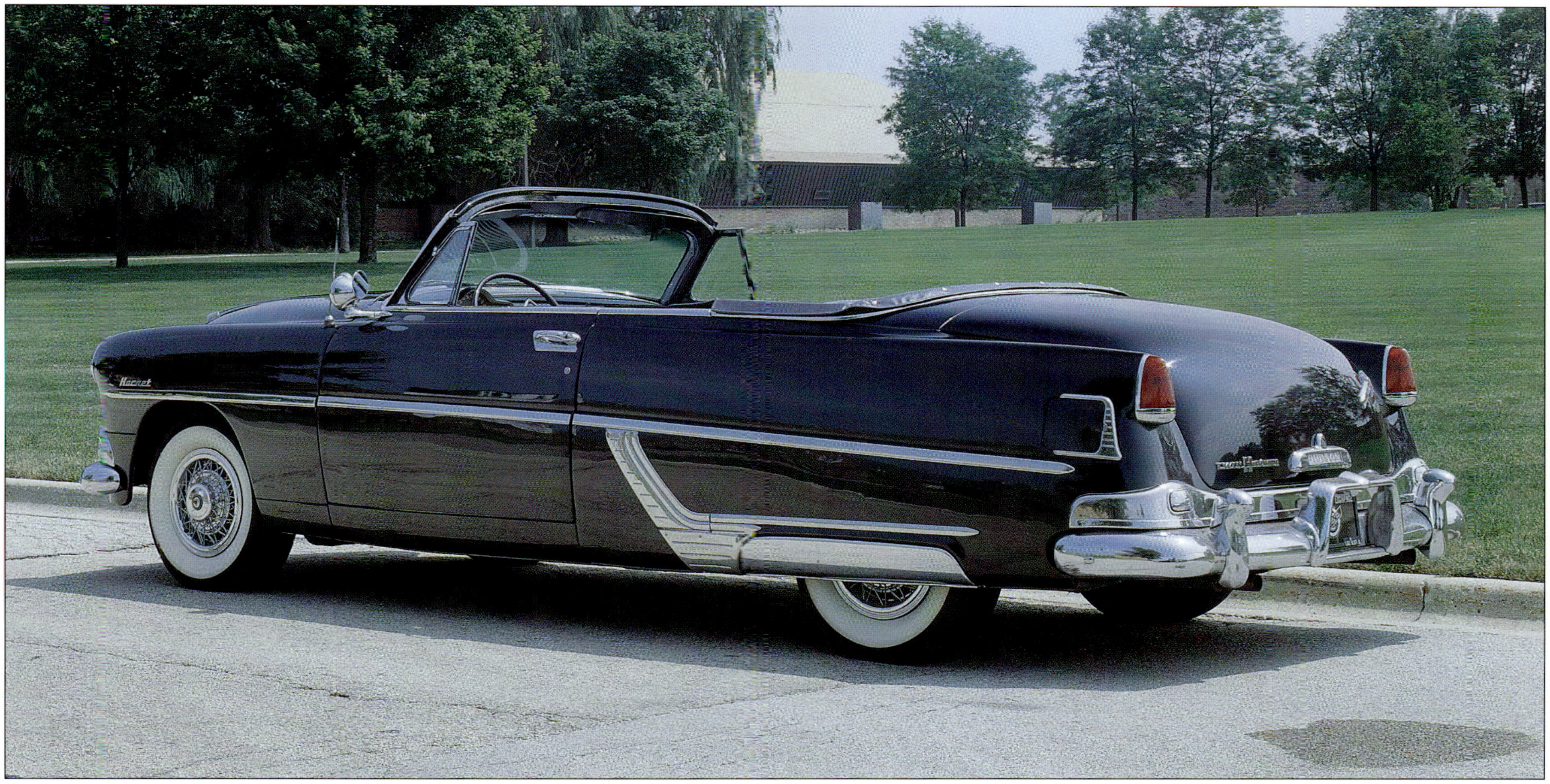
Hornet

1954 PACKARD CARIBBEAN

Though dashing and exclusive, the 1954 Caribbean convertible was merely part of Packard's brave front in the face of steady sales losses. That it cost a king's ransom hardly helped.

Sporty cars didn't attract many sales in the '50s, but they sure attracted buyer attention that helped move less interesting stuff. Even once-mighty Packard got into this act with its 1953 Caribbean. The brainchild of new company president James Nance, this flashy top-line convertible was part of his effort to restore Packard's pure-luxury image and thus boost sales after years of decline from an over-reliance on medium-price cars.

The Caribbean borrowed visual cues from the earlier two-seat Pan American show car, but was a full six-passenger model derived from Packard's standard convertible. That meant the same 122-inch wheelbase as Clippers and lesser Packards, so the Caribbean wasn't as impressive as it could have been, though its 327-cubic-inch straight-eight engine was shared with the longer "senior" models. Designers ladled on fully radiused wheel cutouts, air-scoop hood, jaunty "continental" spare tire, wire wheels, even tiny bright tailfins. Still, the basic design was two years old, while the price was a towering $5210—$1000 more than a ragtop Cadillac 62. That was supposed to give the Caribbean an air of exclusivity, and it did. Only 750 buyers stepped up.

For 1954 the Caribbean added flat-top rear wheel arches (for a longer look) and standard two-tone paint, radio, heater, power seats, and power windows. What's more, its engine was pushed to 359 cid and 212 horsepower—America's most potent postwar straight eight—while price was optimistically pushed to $6100. "There is no more glamorous car than the new Packard Caribbean," brochures exclaimed. "The swank continental look will turn all eyes." But the '54 found only 400 buyers as total Packard sales dropped some two-thirds. And even worse was yet to come.

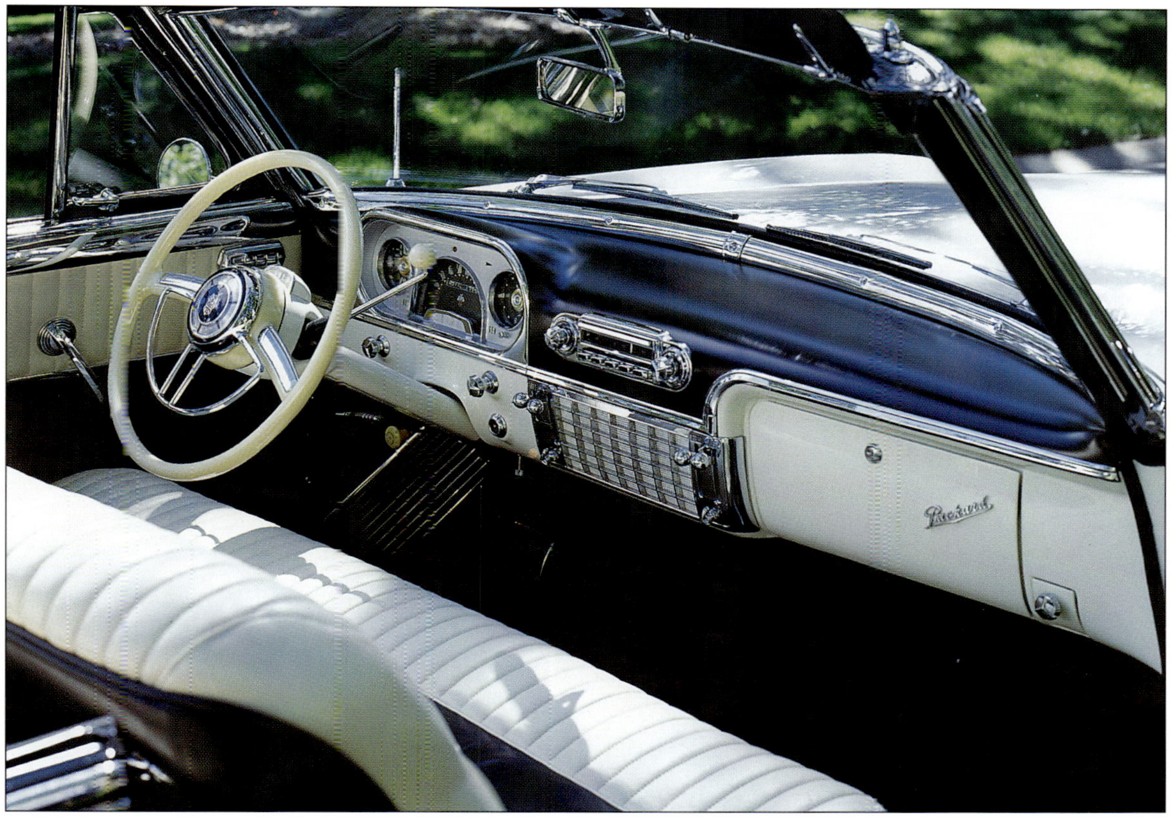

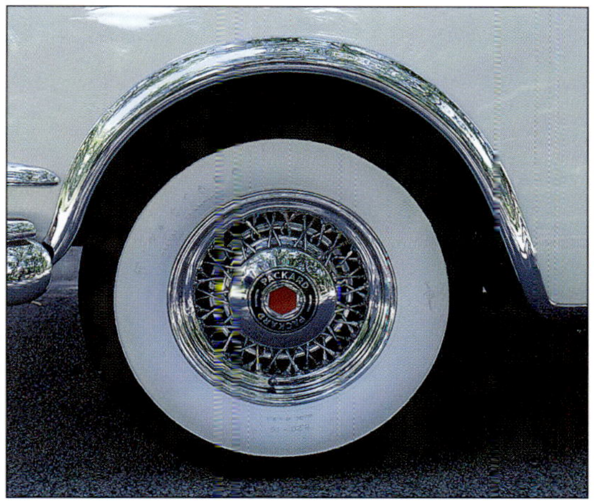

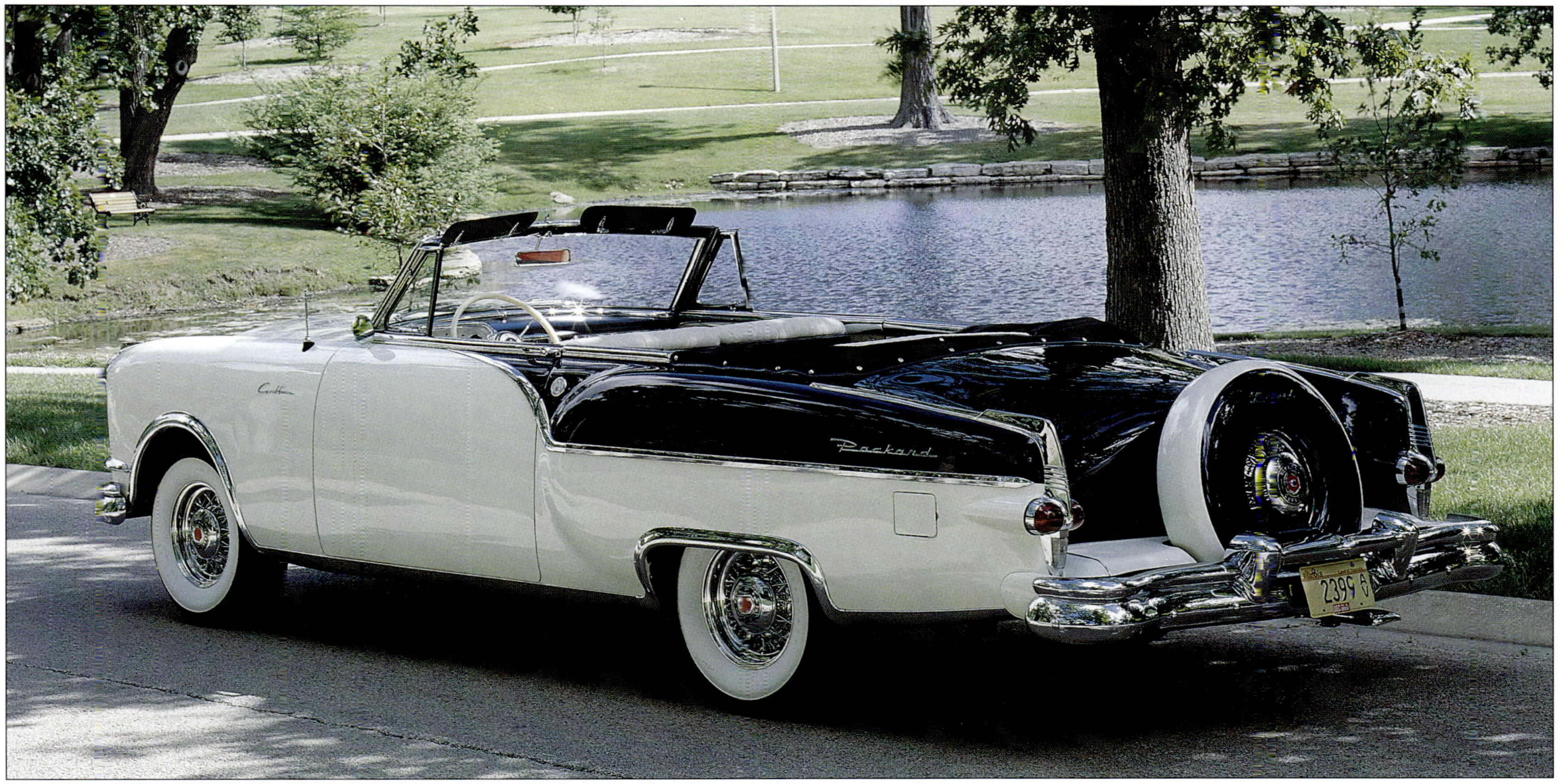
Packard

1955 BUICK CENTURY

Detroit had a banner 1955, and Buick mirrored the heady times by offering no fewer than four convertibles. Performance fans looked no further than the fleet, fast, flip-top Century.

American prosperity peaked in 1955, and Detroit cashed in with record sales for most every nameplate. Buick was no exception, soaring 66 percent to more than 737,000 units, moving it from fourth to third in industry sales.

Flip-top fans had special reason to love Buick in '55, because this was one of the few makes with a convertible in each series. They ranged from a $2590 Special through a $3225 Super and on to a top-shelf $3552 Roadmaster. But the really rapid ragtop was the $2991 Century. Buick had revived its prewar "factory hot rod" for 1954 while giving all models a squarishly handsome new look with show-car-inspired wraparound windshield. The Century returned for '55 with the same adroit facelift accorded other Buicks, but was more potent than ever thanks to a newly fortified 322-cubic-inch Fireball V-8 with 236 horsepower. Also aiding performance was Variable Pitch Dynaflow, a much-improved version of Flint's popular automatic transmission.

Buick's '55 restyle produced a leaner, meaner look, and the Century delivered on its promise. Though magazines didn't test the convertible, *Motor Trend* clocked the light 2-door sedan at just 9.8 seconds to 60 mph and 106.5 mph flat out. Other Buicks weren't far adrift. All were very racy, though cars like these seldom hit the track. Still, the '55s were quick enough to give Buick its only two stock-car racing wins until the 1980s.

Needless to say, the '55 Century was a highly desirable road car. And though not usually the case, its convertible sold fairly well at 5588 units, far fewer than the open Special but somewhat more than the Super and Roadmaster. But then, as we said, 1955 was a *very* good year.

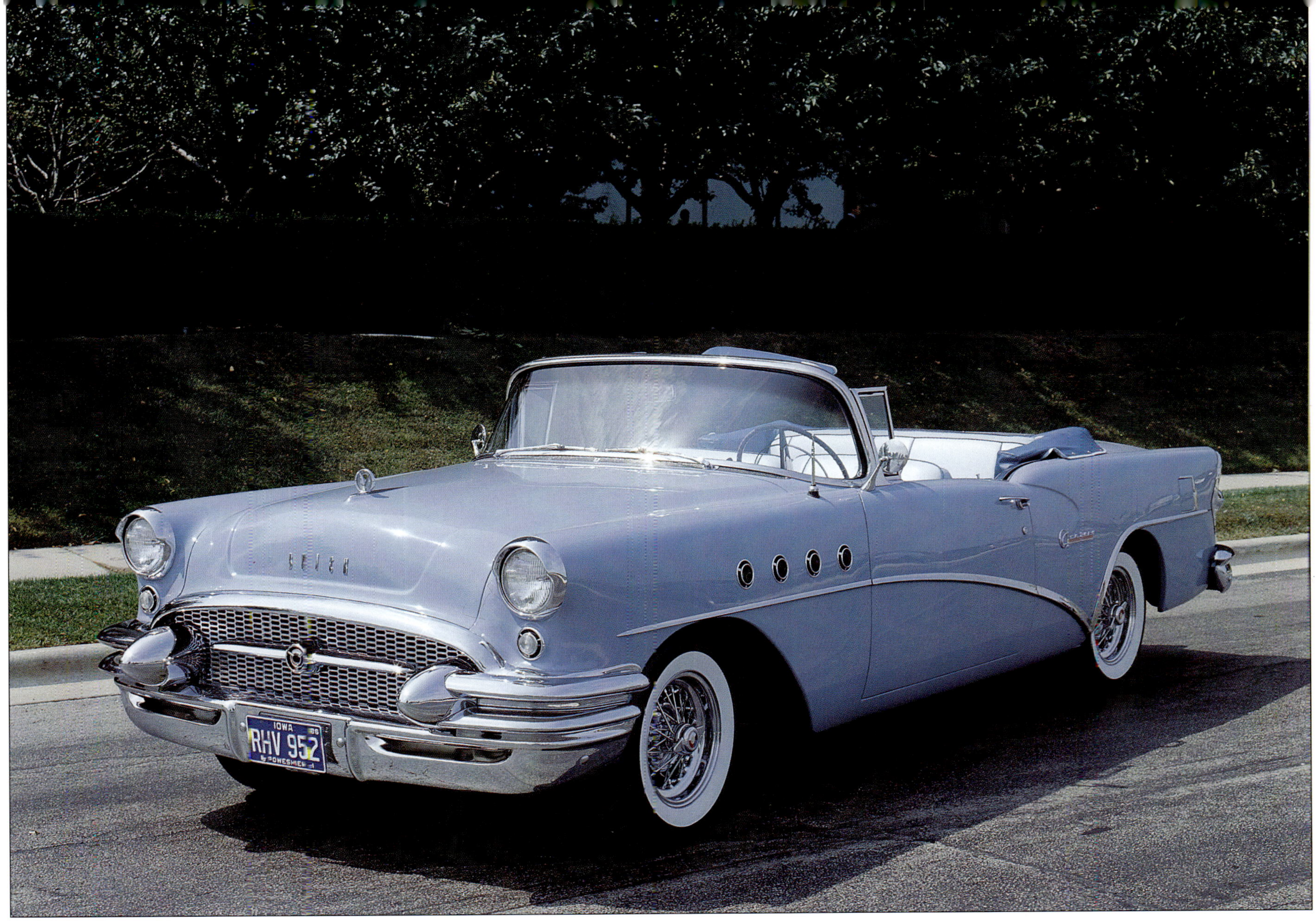
IOWA
RHV 952

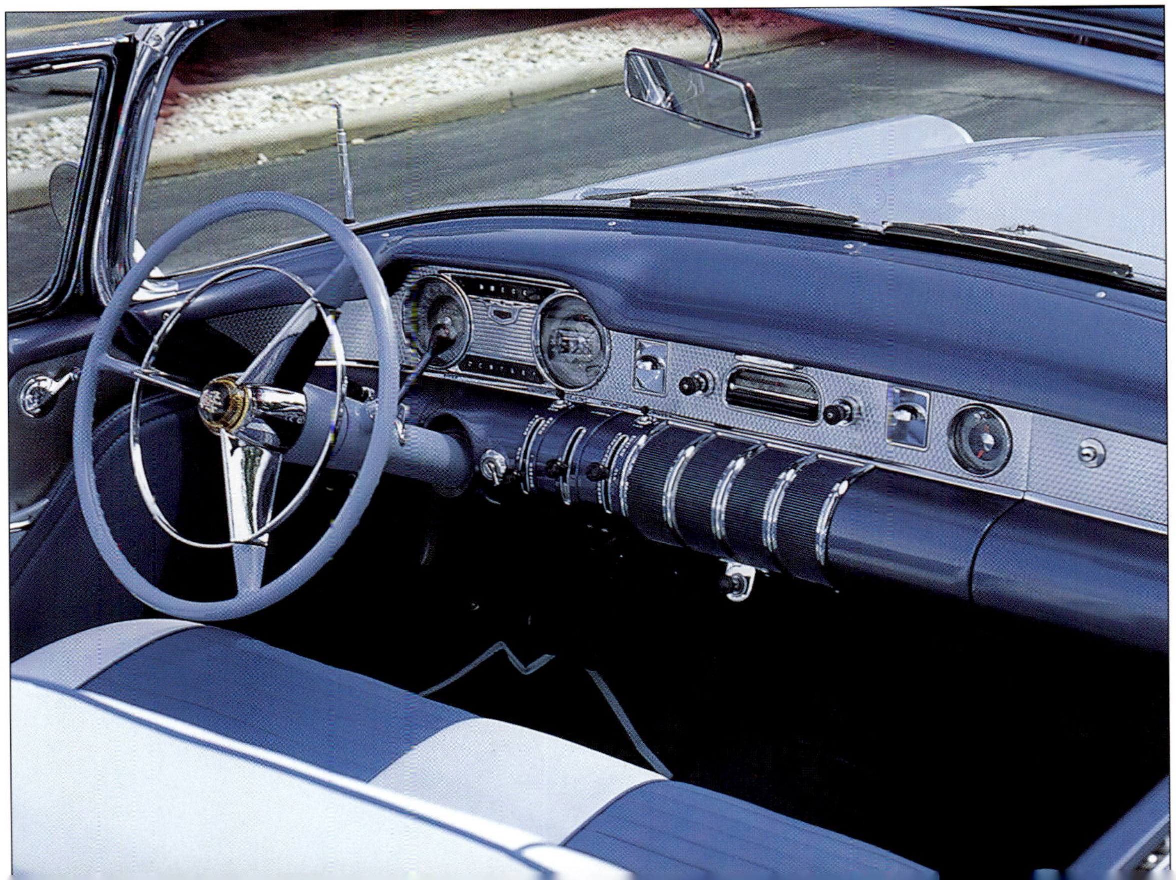

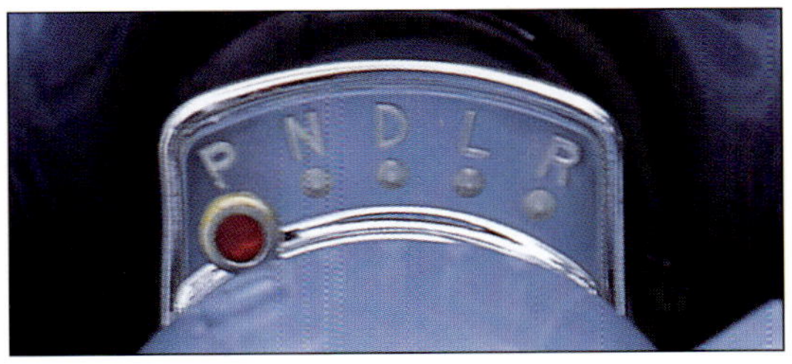
P N D L R

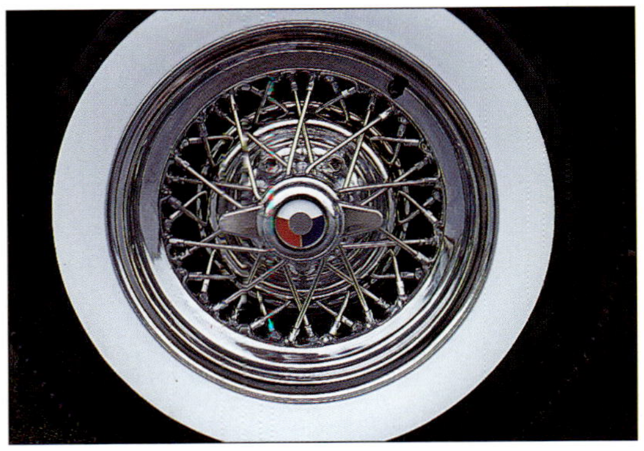

1955 CADILLAC SERIES 62

Cadillac went from strength to strength in the 1950s with luxury cars that delivered exactly what buyers wanted year after year. The '55s were some of its best and the most popular Caddys yet.

Unlike more recent times, it seemed Cadillac could do no wrong in the mid-'50s, each year's cars carefully planned to build on the appeal of previous models. Take 1955. The '54 Caddys had been fully restyled to look more contemporary yet still unmistakably Cadillac. Because size was everything, wheelbases stretched three inches across the board, out to 129 on the volume Series 62. A deft facelift made this package even more attractive for '55, highlighted by a smoother hood, broader grille, and artfully revised exterior trim.

Cadillac's 331-cubic-inch V-8 was still state of the engine art, and retuning added 20 horsepower for '54. Higher compression and improved breathing yielded 30 more for '55—250 in all except for the plush Eldorado convertible, which had moved from 1953 limited edition to regular-model status; it boasted an exclusive 270-bhp V-8.

Besides a consistent product formula, close attention to customer tastes fueled much of Cadillac's success in these years. For example, the division responded to buyer preference in transmissions by standardizing self-shift Hydra-Matic for all its '55s. Cadillac had obviously gauged the market well, as sales of the 62 convertible, for instance, jumped by 1840 units to 8150.

Of course, 1955 was a big Detroit year, and Cadillac managed to retail a record 140,777 cars in all. Happy days? You bet.

54

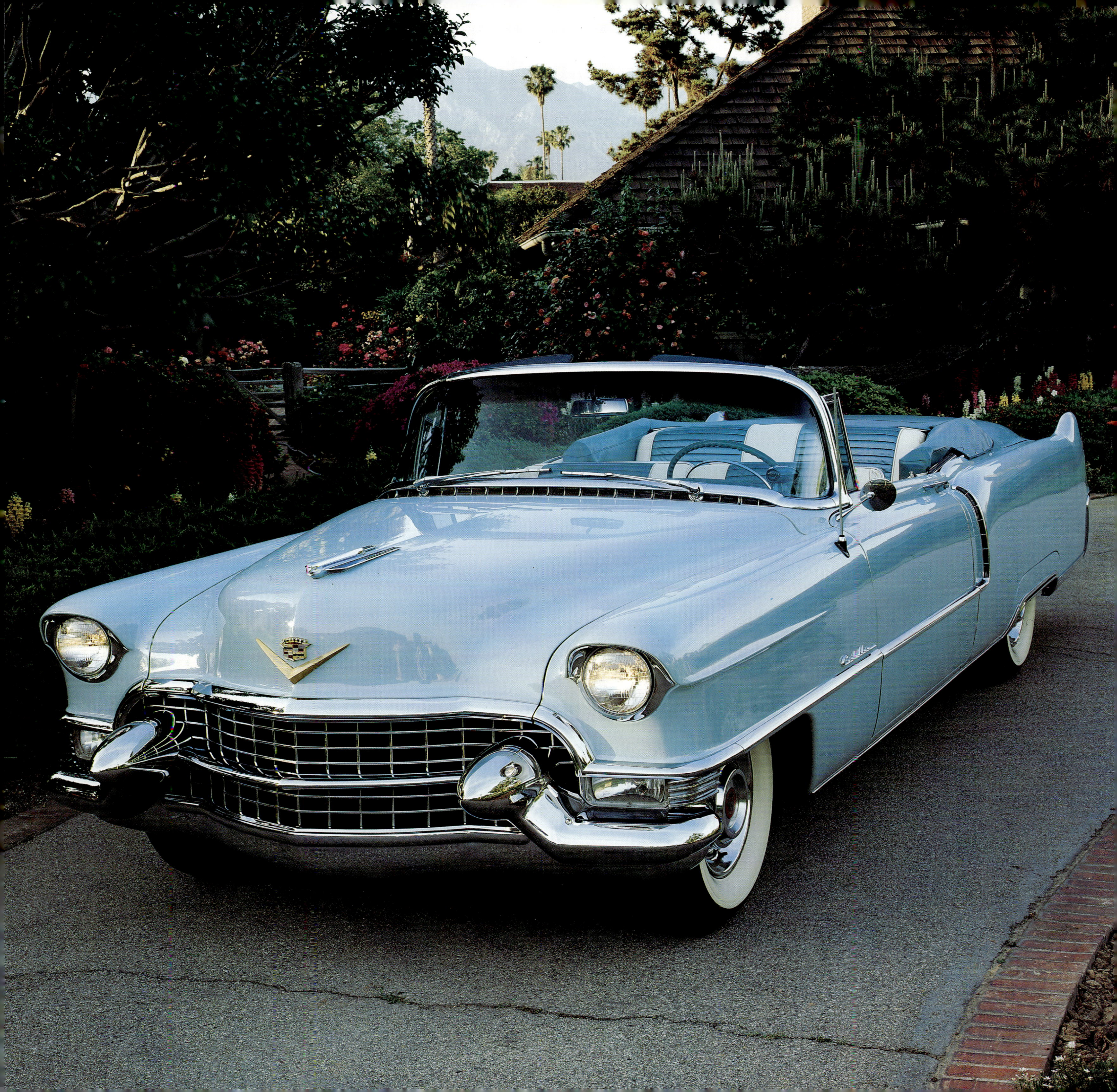

1955 CHEVROLET BEL AIR

"New Look! New Life! New Everything!" That was Chevrolet 1955, a revolution for America's favorite low-priced car. No wonder that year's Bel Air convertible has become such a popular collectible.

Chevrolet was America's most popular car for 1955, which is saying something for a year in which Americans bought cars as never before. But then, the '55 Chevys were something really special.

Start with styling. In a complete change from Chevy's stodgy past, the '55s were thoroughly up-to-date with Sweep Sight wrapped windshields atop "longer-lower-wider" bodies. Even so, wheelbase was unchanged at 115 inches, and the overall design was balanced and tasteful for the day. Vying for glamour with the top-line Bel Air convertible was a nifty new two-door wagon, the Bel Air Nomad, with unique hardtop roofline.

More exciting still was Chevy's first modern V-8, the 265-cubic-inch Turbo Fire that was already writing performance history. Though developed in just 15 weeks, this milestone motor was absolutely right from the start, and its 162-180 horsepower backed up Chevy's boast as 1955's "Hot One." You could still get a reliable 235.5-cid "Stovebolt Six," now with 123 bhp, but the V-8 was what most people wanted. Matching Chevy's newfound performance was an updated chassis with ball-joint front suspension, open "Hotchkiss" drive, and standard tubeless tires.

Chevy built 41,292 ragtop Bel Airs for '55, not nearly enough to go around—then or now. As popular as they were more than 40 years ago, they enjoy even greater popularity today. And that's really saying something.

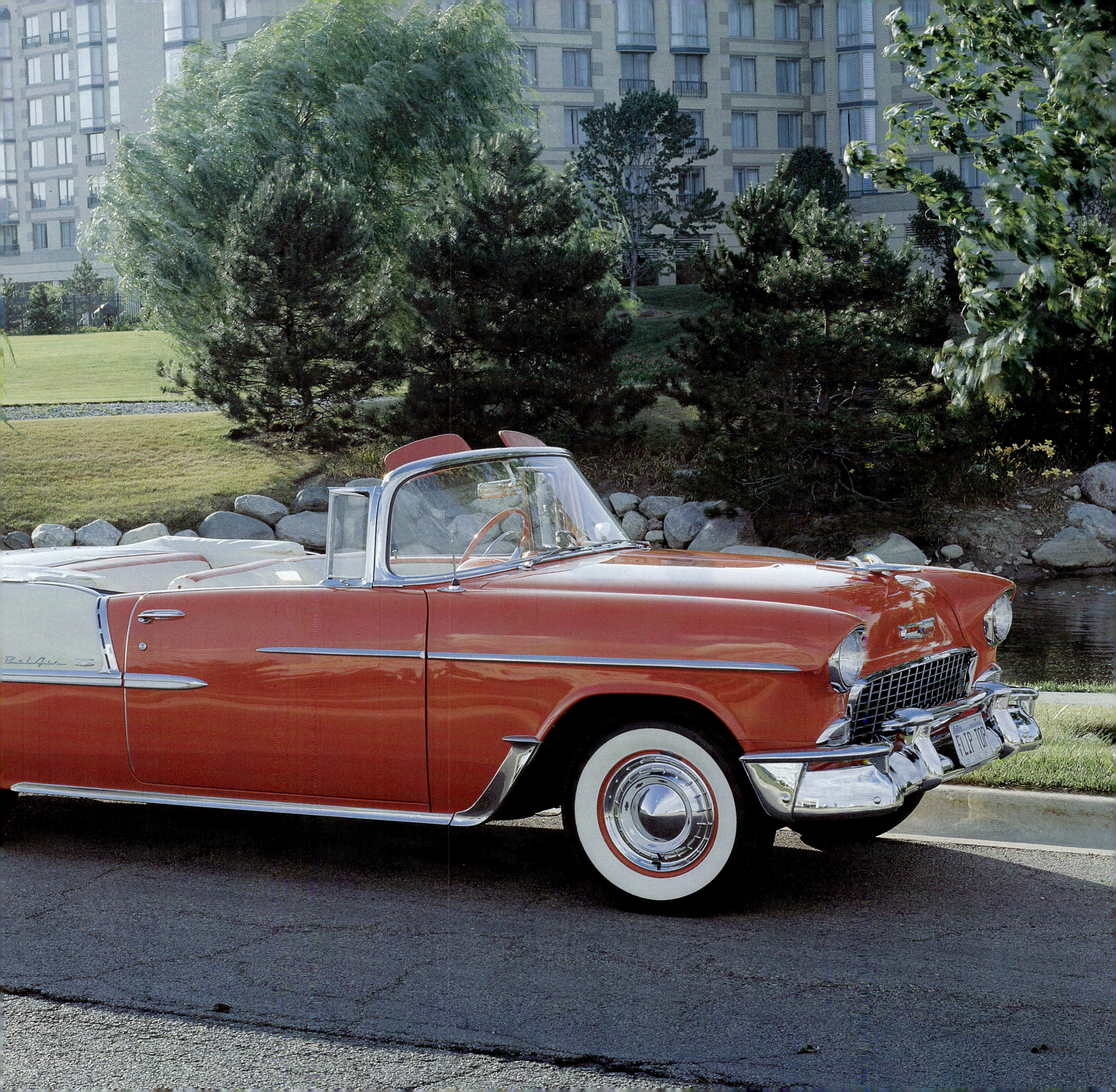
FLIP TOP

1955 MERCURY MONTCLAIR

After years as a "super Ford," Mercury stepped into the sun for '55 with bold new styling all its own, plus bigger engines and a lush new top-line series headlined by—what else?—a convertible.

Mercury was born in 1939 as a "super Ford," a little larger and faster maybe, but still basically a Ford. For 1955, however, Mercury claimed its own upper-class identity with unique styling and a colorful new top-line series called Montclair, home to Mercury's lone convertible. The result was a 27-percent sales gain over '54 to nearly 330,000 cars, a high-water mark that wouldn't be exceeded until the mid-'60s.

Priced at $2712, the ragtop Montclair naturally shared the bold new look of Mercury's Customs and Montereys, with longer and lower bodies, wrapped windshields, and squarer, more imposing lines. A slim beltline contrast-color panel distinguished Montclairs, which also included a unique low-roof four-door sedan and the interesting Sun Valley hardtop with a green-tinted transparent roof insert above the front seat. Introduced as a '54 Monterey, the Sun Valley sold just 1787 copies for '55 versus 10,668 convertibles—proving perhaps that there's no substitute for real top-down motoring.

Also back from '54 was Mercury's first overhead-valve V-8, newly enlarged to 292 cubic inches and good for 198 horsepower with standard dual exhausts in Montclairs, which also came with self-shift Merc-O-Matic transmission. "Uncle" Tom McCahill clocked 0-60 mph at 12.8 seconds with a hardtop, so Mercury was still something of a "hot" car. Yet all '55s rode and handled better, thanks to refinements in the year-old ball-joint front suspension, and larger brakes improved stopping power.

Montclairs were Mercury's best in '55, but they could be even better with options like power windows, four-way power seat, and first-time factory air conditioning. Of course, the convertible hardly needed A/C—just a sunny day and room to roam.

58

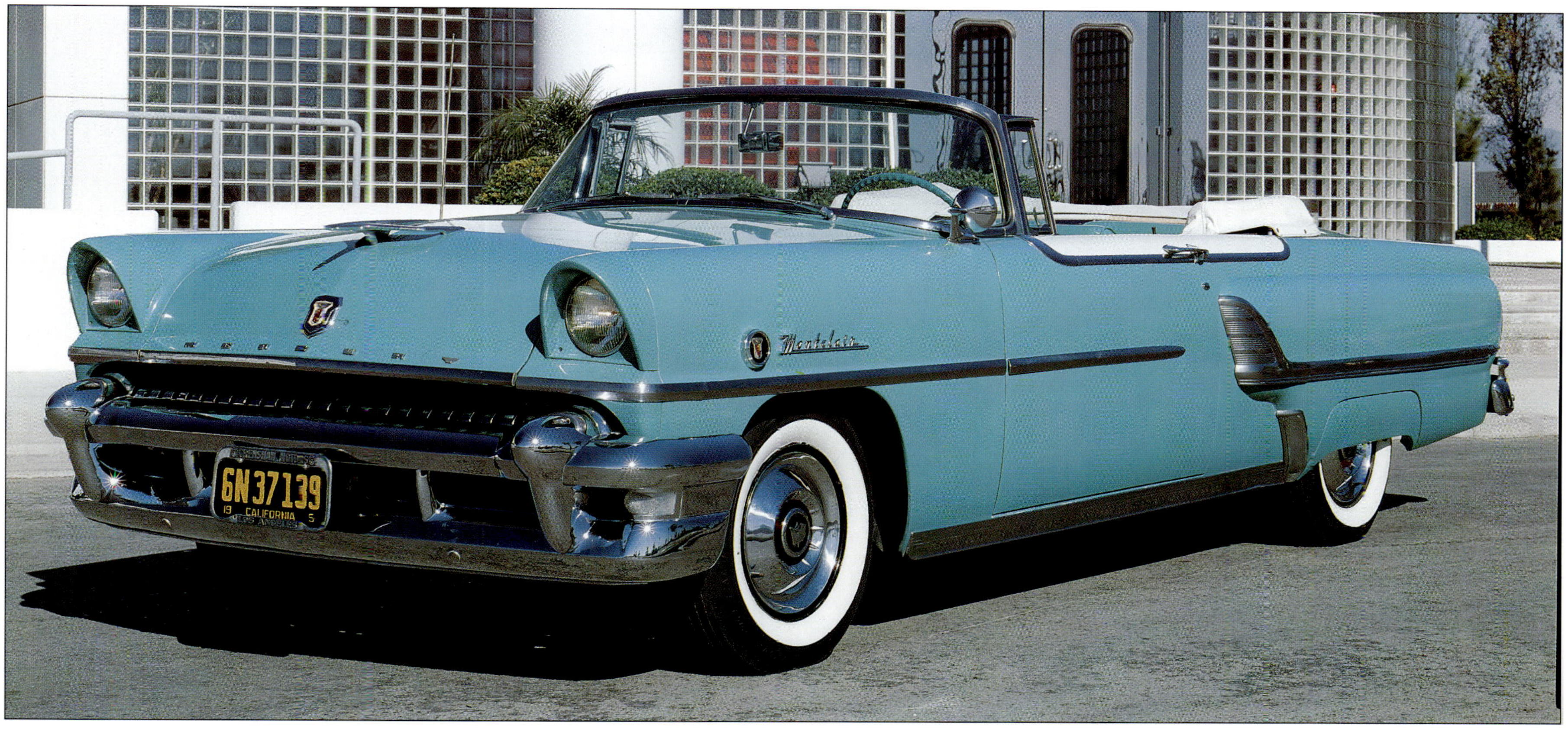
6N37139
CALIFORNIA

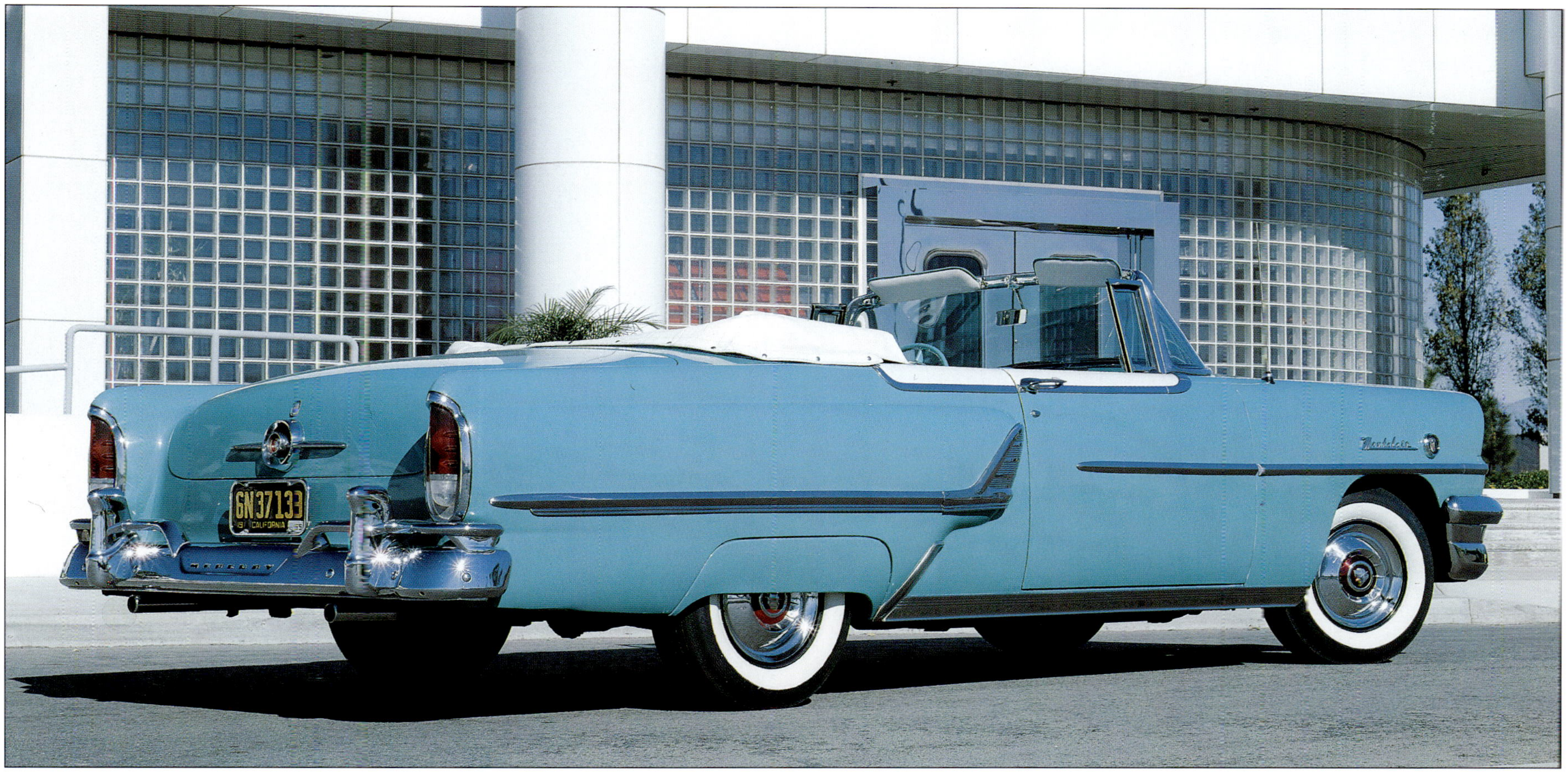
CALIFORNIA

1956 FORD THUNDERBIRD

It wasn't a sports car, but Ford's two-seat Thunderbird was one of the most coveted convertibles of the '50s No wonder it became an "instant classic."

You still see two-seat Thunderbirds on the boulevards of Beverly Hills, which is only fitting. Ford might have been inspired by European sports cars, but the Thunderbird ended up an all-American boulevardier convertible designed for comfort and smooth, powerful straightline performance. That the "Little Birds" were also uncommonly handsome only hastened their climb to "instant classic" status, one reason so many survive today.

A sturdy steel body and amenities like roll-up windows were other appealing T-Bird virtues. As proof, the debut '55 outpolled Chevrolet's fiberglass Corvette by 23 to 1 at 16,155 units. The '56 slipped to 15,631, but that was hardly bad for a specialty car in a "fall-back" sales year.

The '56 T-Bird was much like the '55, but a standard "continental" spare tire opened up needed trunk space, front-fender ventilator doors enhanced cockpit comfort, and the available lift-off hardtop gained distinctive "porthole" windows that helped visibility. Typical of the time, the '56 also offered more power, courtesy of a new 312-cubic-inch V-8 packing 215 horsepower with optional stick-overdrive or 225 with self-shift Fordomatic. The previous year's 292 continued with the standard three-speed manual, but was upped to 202 bhp. Handling took a step backward, as springs and shocks were softened, but buyers loved the resulting smoother ride.

A deft restyle and even more power lifted sales to 21,380 for 1957, but any two-seat T-Bird is a car for the ages. Just ask those happy owners in Beverly Hills.

60

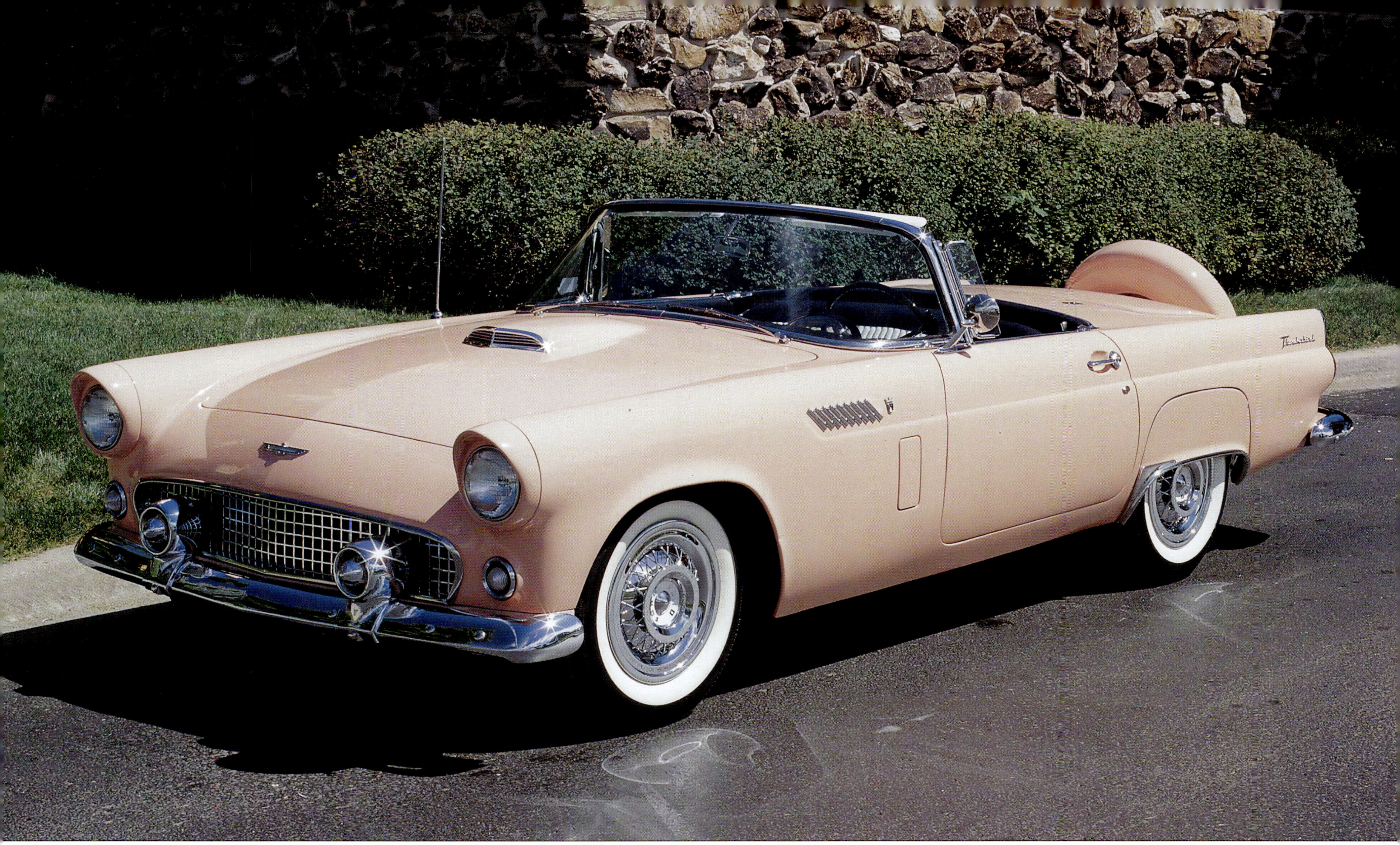

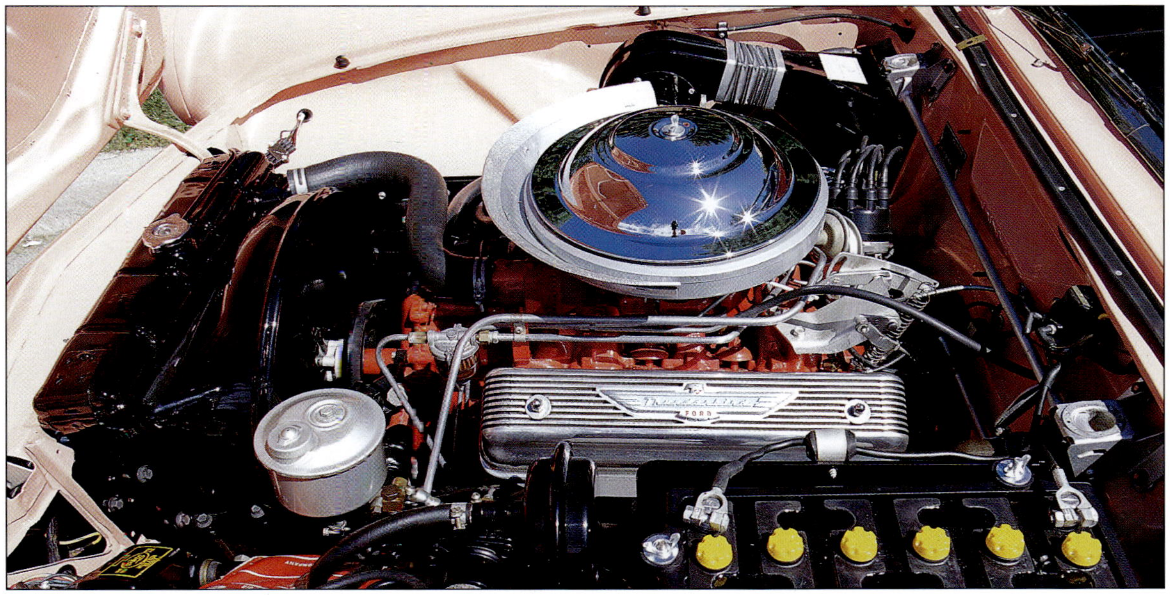

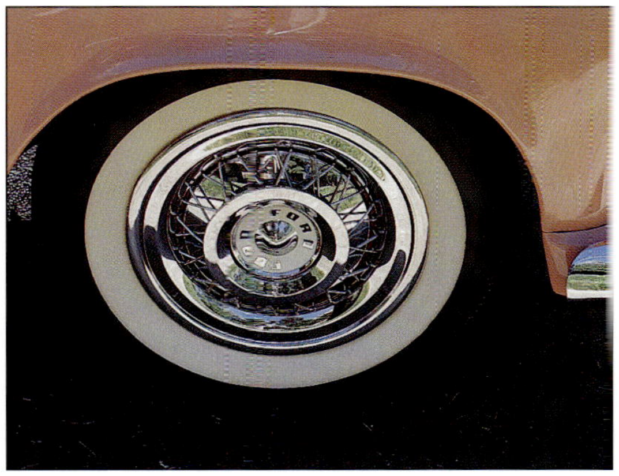

1956 LINCOLN PREMIERE

In 1956 "new" was America's watchword, and more people chose Lincoln than ever before. Seldom had cars changed so much in a single year—and been so appealing, too.

Lincoln was one of the few makes to miss out on Detroit's 1955 sales boom, but it came back strong for '56 with dream-car styling, massive new proportions, and horsepower to match. Ads proclaimed the '56s "Unmistakably Lincoln," but there was nary a trace of the lithe and lively Mexican Road Race-winning models of 1952-55.

Styling borrowed heavily from the 1954 Mercury XM-800 show car and conveyed substance without looking fat or resorting to glitter. Wheelbase grew three inches to 126, overall length added seven inches, and width swelled by three inches. Even so, the '56s didn't weigh much more than corresponding '55s, and with a mighty new 368-cubic-inch big-block V-8 packing 285 horsepower, they were the quickest Lincolns yet. They also cost a whopping $500-$700 more than the '55s, but such was the price of "progress" in those days.

Lincoln continued with two series for '56: Capri and new upmarket Premiere, each with a four-door sedan and hardtop coupe. A convertible was exclusive to Premiere and the priciest '56 Lincoln at $4747. Though just 2447 were built, Ford's luxury nameplate moved just over 50,000 cars in all, versus some 27,000 for '55.

Today these Lincolns are bona fide collector's items, the rare ragtop especially. Considering all they offered, it's a wonder they didn't "go gold" a long time ago.

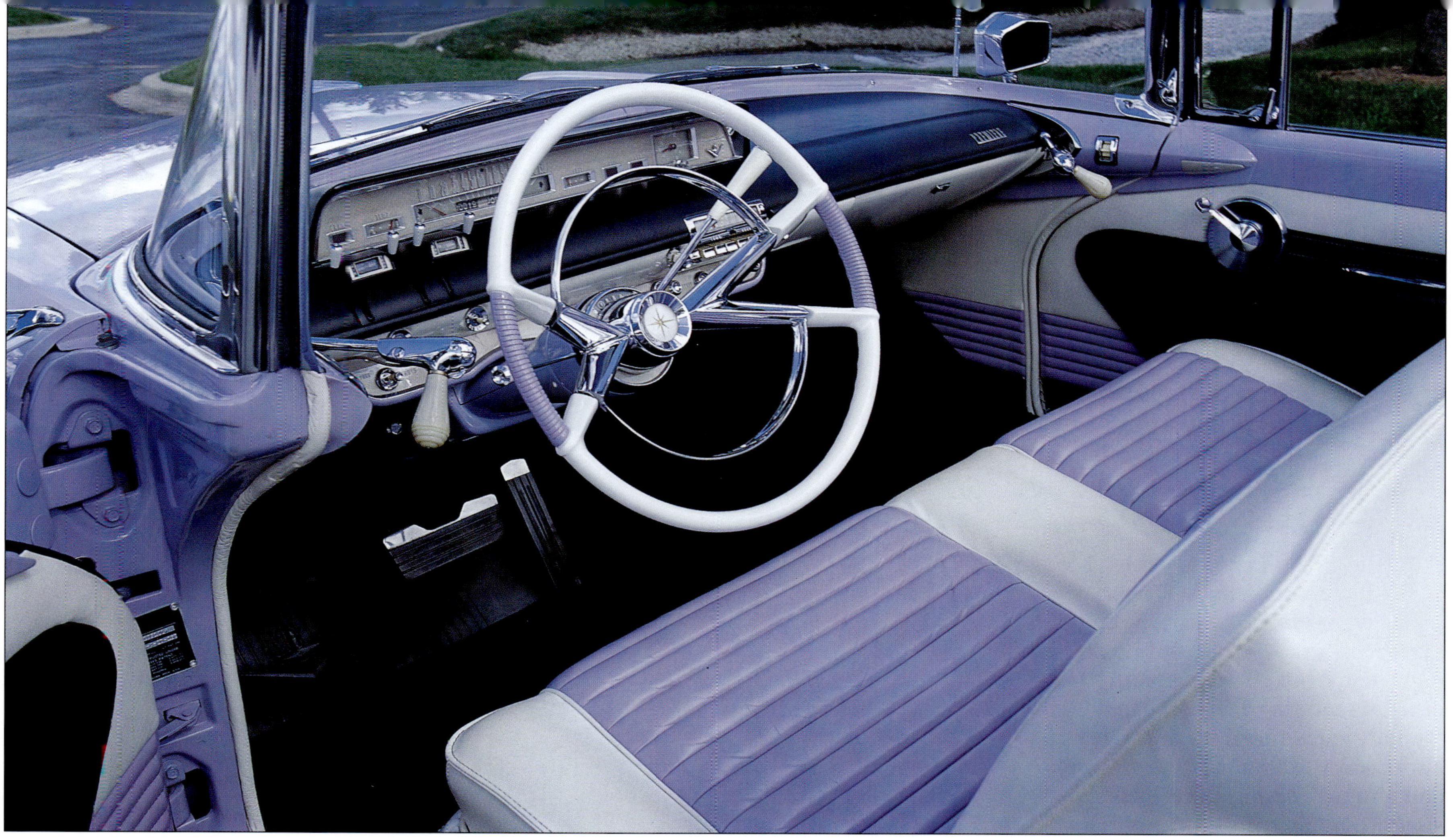

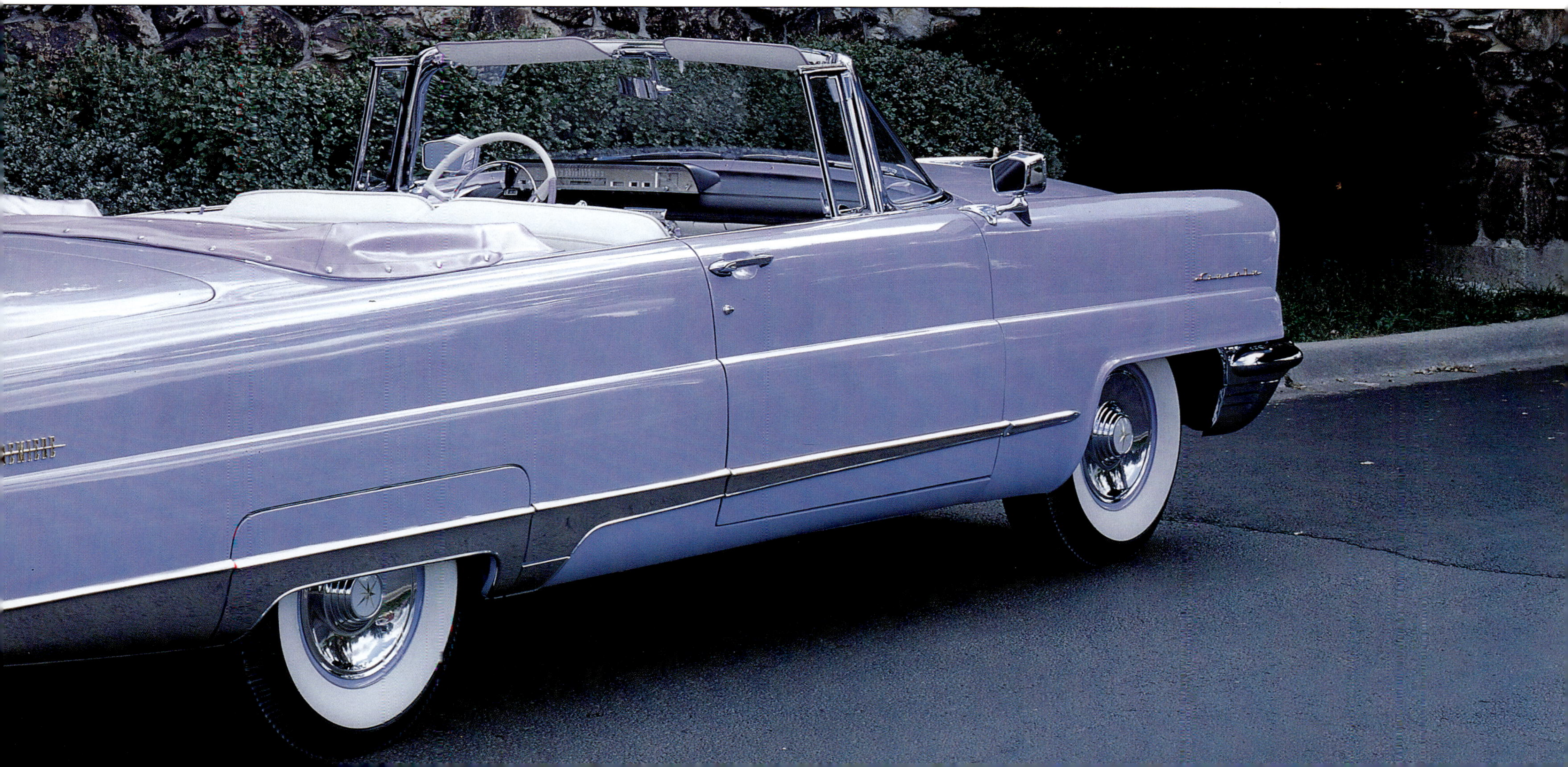

1956 PACKARD CARIBBEAN

The '56 Caribbean was the most potent, most advanced convertible in Packard history. Sadly, it was also the last.

The 1956 Packards evolved from the nearly all-new '55s that were created with scarce funds in a crisis atmosphere. But an amazingly adept restyle successfully modernized vintage-'51 bodies, and Packard introduced its first V-8, an improved Ultramatic transmission, and a new "Torsion Level" suspension providing truly extraordinary ride and handling. Trouble was, new partner Studebaker was fast dragging Packard toward oblivion, so 1956 would be the finale for "real" Packards.

Among them was the last edition of the top-line Caribbean convertible, priced at $5995 and newly partnered by a $5495 hardtop coupe. Both carried a V-8 enlarged to 374 cubic inches and 310 thumping horsepower, plus most every known luxury-class amenity, including new front seat covers that reversed from cloth to leather. But Packard was looking terminal, and no '56 sold well. The ragtop Caribbean managed just 276 copies before a two-year run of half-hearted "Packardbakers" ended the life of a once-great make.

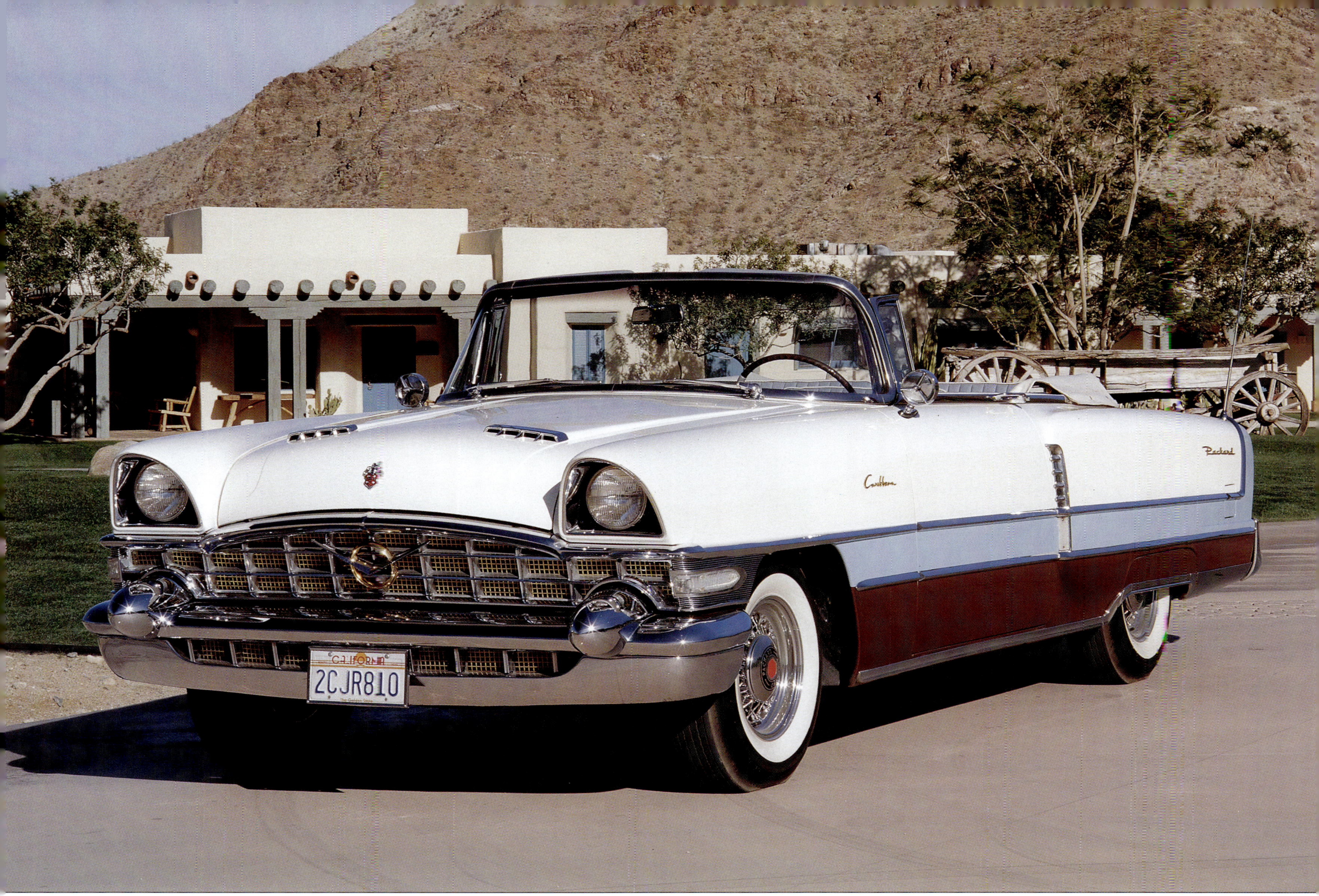
2CJR810

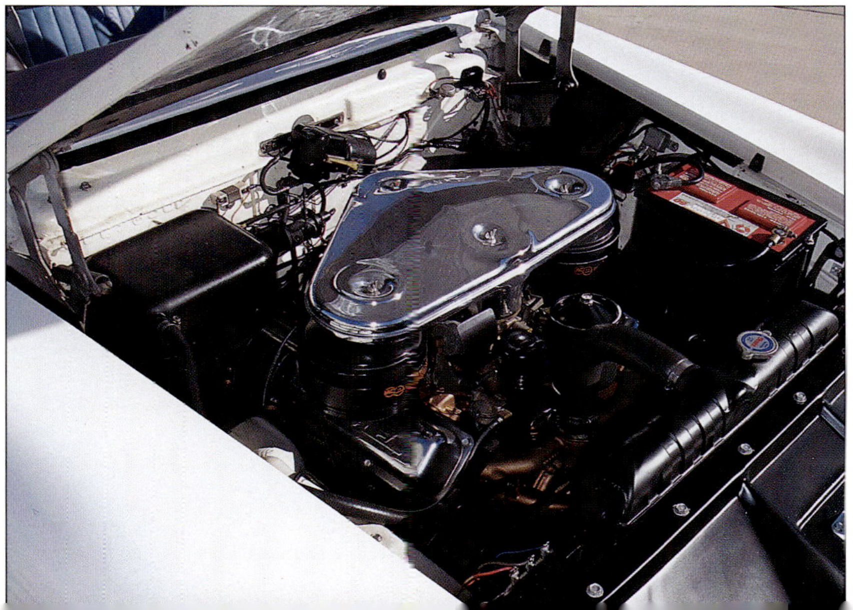

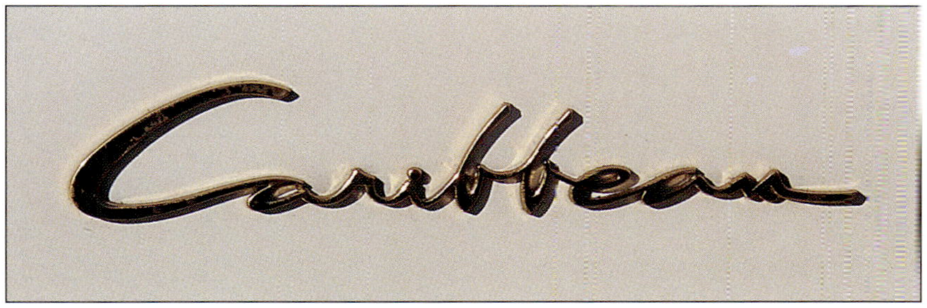
Caribbean

1957 CHEVROLET BEL AIR

The '57 Chevrolet has long been an icon for the age of fins, flash, and horsepower—a King of Cool to rival Elvis. And the coolest of all? Why, the Bel Air convertible, of course.

As an icon of its age, the '57 Chevrolet ranks right alongside Elvis, Marilyn Monroe, and *Leave It to Beaver*—curious for a mass-market car in the last year of a three-year cycle. Nevertheless, these Chevys struck a chord that resonates to this day—even among those born long after the cars were built.

Of course, there were plenty of reasons to like the '57 Chevys. Though styling was only another facelift of '55, it looked great: longer-lower-wider thanks to prominent new tailfins, a switch from 15- to 14-inch wheels, and a big new bumper/grille. Ribbed rear-fender appliqués readily identified top-line Bel Airs, including the $2511 convertible.

Far more exciting, Chevy's 265 V-8 was punched out to 283 cubic inches and offered in no fewer than six versions with 185 to 283 horsepower. The latter came from newly optional Ramjet fuel injection, which made for near racing-level performance right off the showroom floor. Chevrolet advertised it as the first American production car to achieve the magic goal of "one horsepower from every cubic inch of engine displacement," though the Chrysler 300B's optional engine actually beat it by one year. Even a four-barrel 270-bhp model could run 0-60 mph in well under 10 seconds.

But perhaps the main reason for the '57s' enduring mystique is that they were the last of the "Hot Ones," arguably the most attractive and roadable Chevys of the decade. As the song says, you don't know what you've got 'til it's gone.

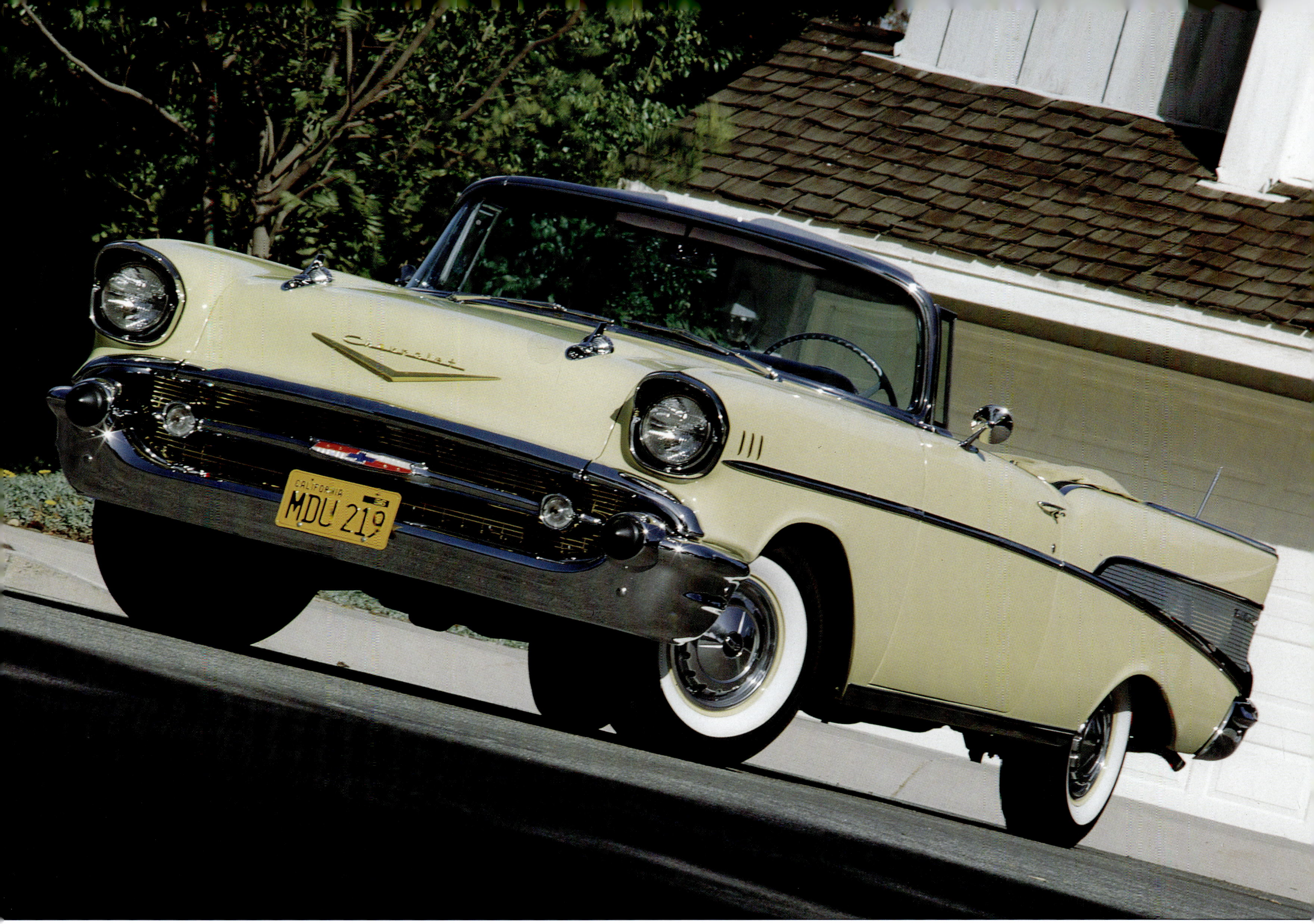
CALIFORNIA
MDU 219

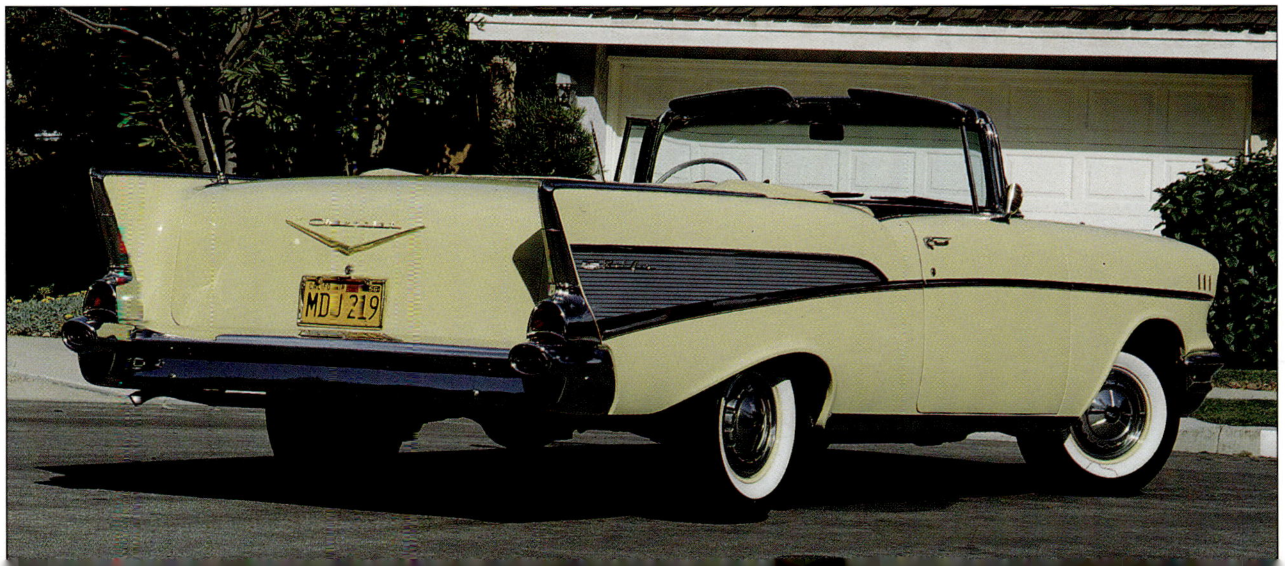

1957 CHRYSLER NEW YORKER

Chrysler Corporation led the styling parade for 1957 with the "Forward Look," dramatically lower cars with soaring fins and dart-like profiles. Among the handsomest of the bunch was the elegant New Yorker convertible.

After completely overhauling its cars for 1955, Chrysler Corporation did it again for '57. From Plymouth to Imperial, every model had "The Forward Look," with dramatically lower bodies, crisp thin-section rooflines, acres more glass, and lean dart-shaped profiles with soaring tailfins. Suddenly, Chrysler was Detroit's new styling leader. In fact, its '57s so impressed General Motors designers that they immediately started over on their '59 models.

The Chrysler-branded '57s were perhaps the handsomest of the bunch, thanks to a simple grille and rear end, plus tastefully restrained ornamentation. The $4638 New Yorker convertible was particularly elegant with the top lowered.

Like sister divisions, Chrysler also set new standards for ride and handling by introducing torsion-bar front suspension for '57. Another benchmark was new three-speed Torque-Flite automatic transmission, a quick, smooth shifter that would prove exceptionally trouble-free, though not its gimmicky pushbutton controls. Further enhancing performance, Chrysler's efficient Hemi V-8 was enlarged for New Yorkers from 354 to 392 cubic inches, good for 325 standard horsepower.

Though Chrysler sales were strong in '57, the droptop New Yorker attracted just 1049 orders. Rarer still was a new high-performance 300 convertible with 375 or 390 bhp; it saw only 454 copies. Today, collectors wish there'd been a lot more of both.

68

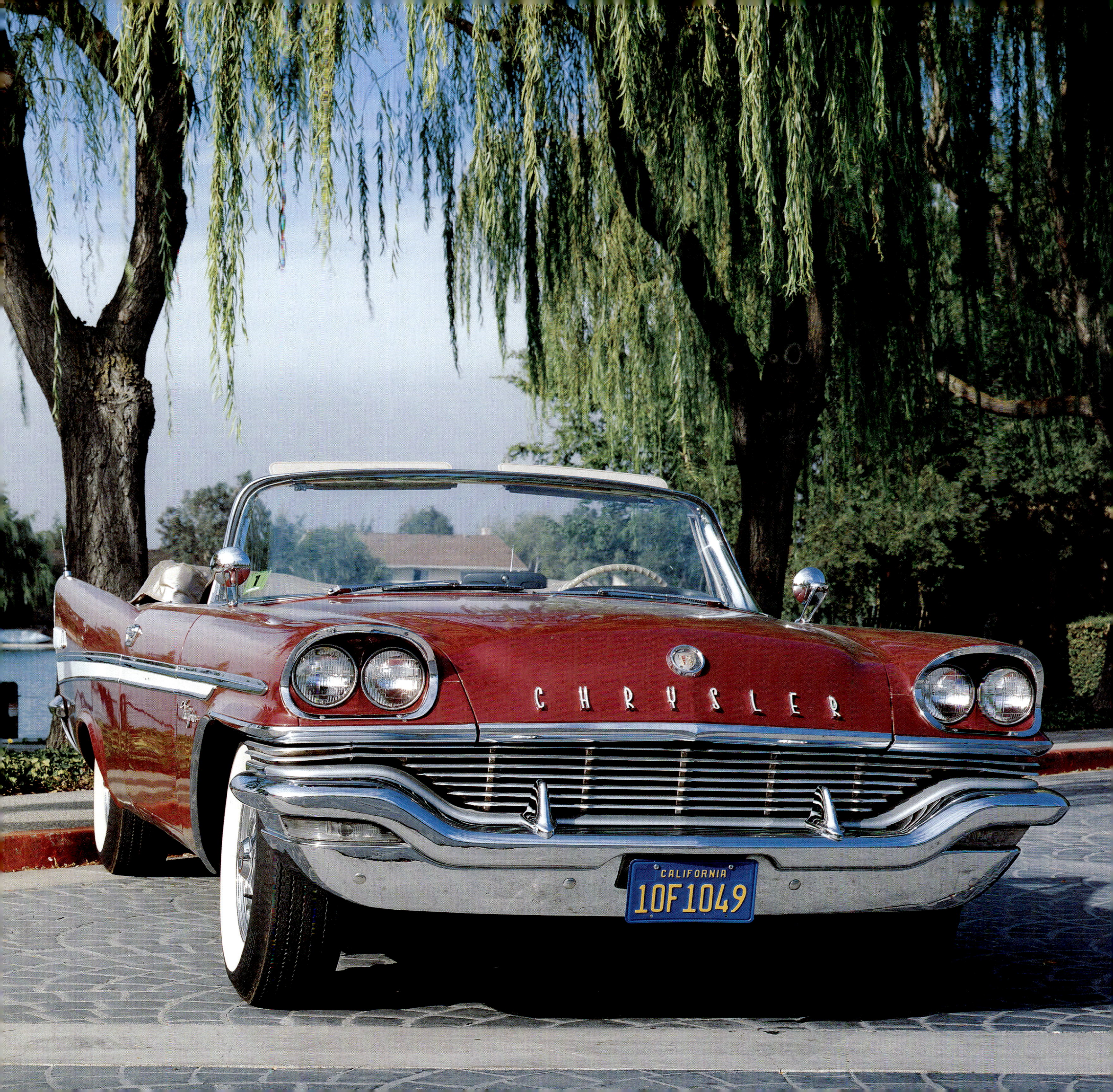
CHRYSLER
CALIFORNIA
10F1049

1957 FORD FAIRLANE 500 SKYLINER

It may not have been a "better idea," but the '57 Ford Skyliner was a symbcl for the age of gadgetry: America's only "hardtop convertible" that actually did convert.

Ford offered two convertibles for 1957: the usual cloth-roof Sunliner and the first "hardtop convertible" that really did convert. What's more, all '57 Fords were all new—dramatically longer, lower, and wider, with "dream car" styling that looked like something from another brand. With all this, Ford exceeded its 1955 sales record while outproducing rival Chevrolet for the first time in decades.

That new "retractable hardtop" was called Skyliner, a name borrowed from Ford's 1954-56 plexi-roof hardtop. Offered like the Sunliner in a new top-line Fairline 500 series, it was the sort of technical wonder Americans expected as the "space age" beckoned. At the touch of a button, a bevy of motors, relays, and wires raised a rear-hinged panel on an elongated deck, slid the top into a deep well, then closed the deck over it. Though quite complex and far from foolproof, this system was more reliable than was once reported, and the top's stately passage up or down was a surefire crowd-pleaser.

Luggage space was limited to a small box in the "trunk," and the added hardware made the Skyliner pricey for a Ford at $2942—$437 more than the Sunliner. Even so, the '57 Skyliner sold reasonably well at 20,766, though that was well down on the conventional convertible's 77,726.

Sales then tapered off, so the Skyliner was dropped after 1959 as a costly indulgence by money-conscious Ford execs. Today, though, a "retrac" still pulls crowds like nothing else.

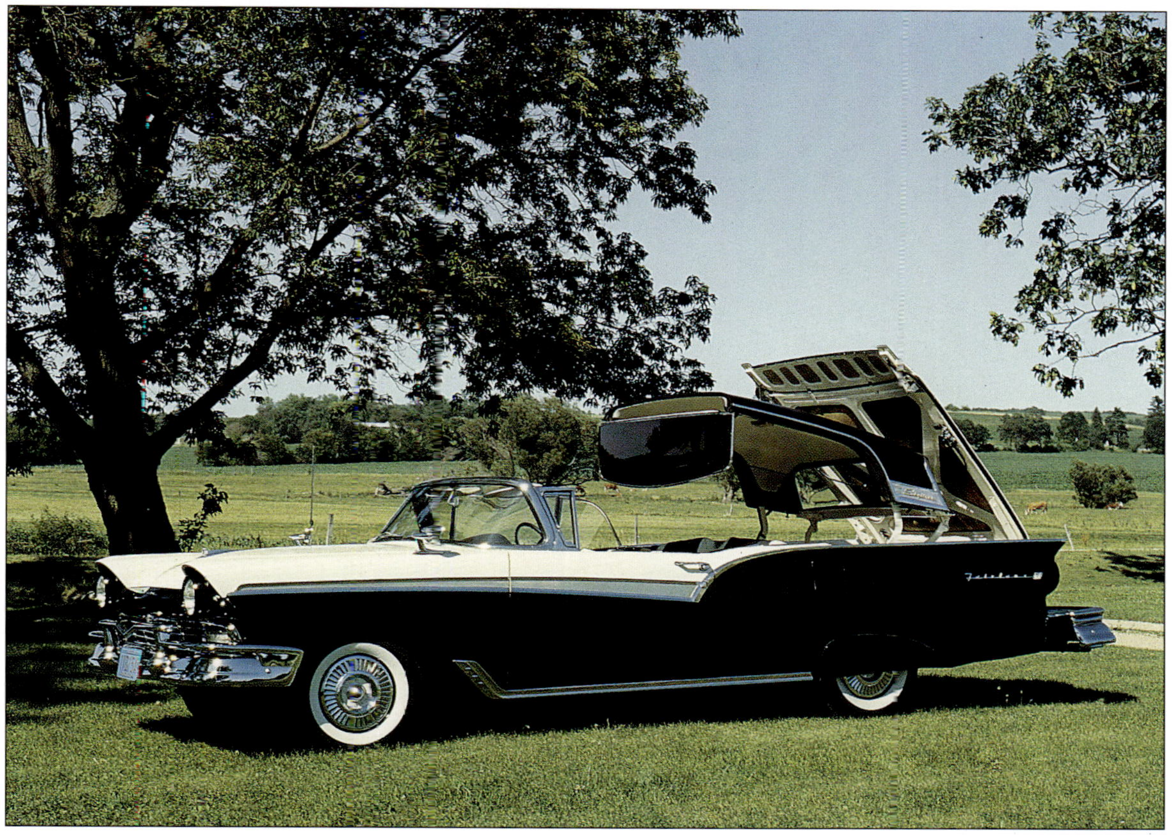

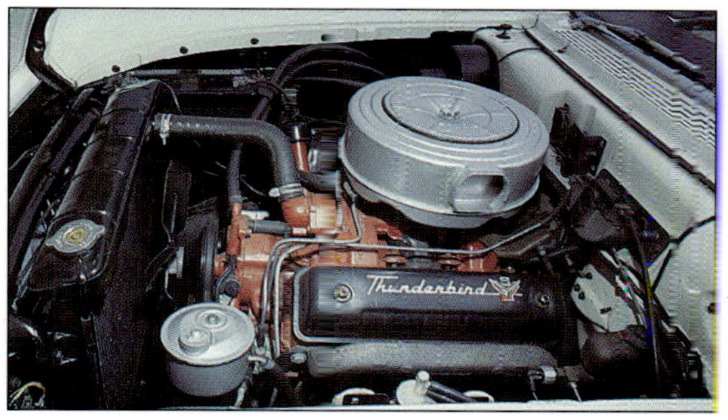
Thunderbird

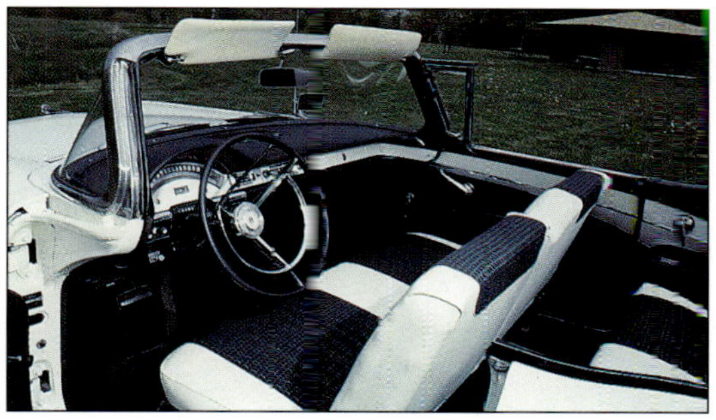

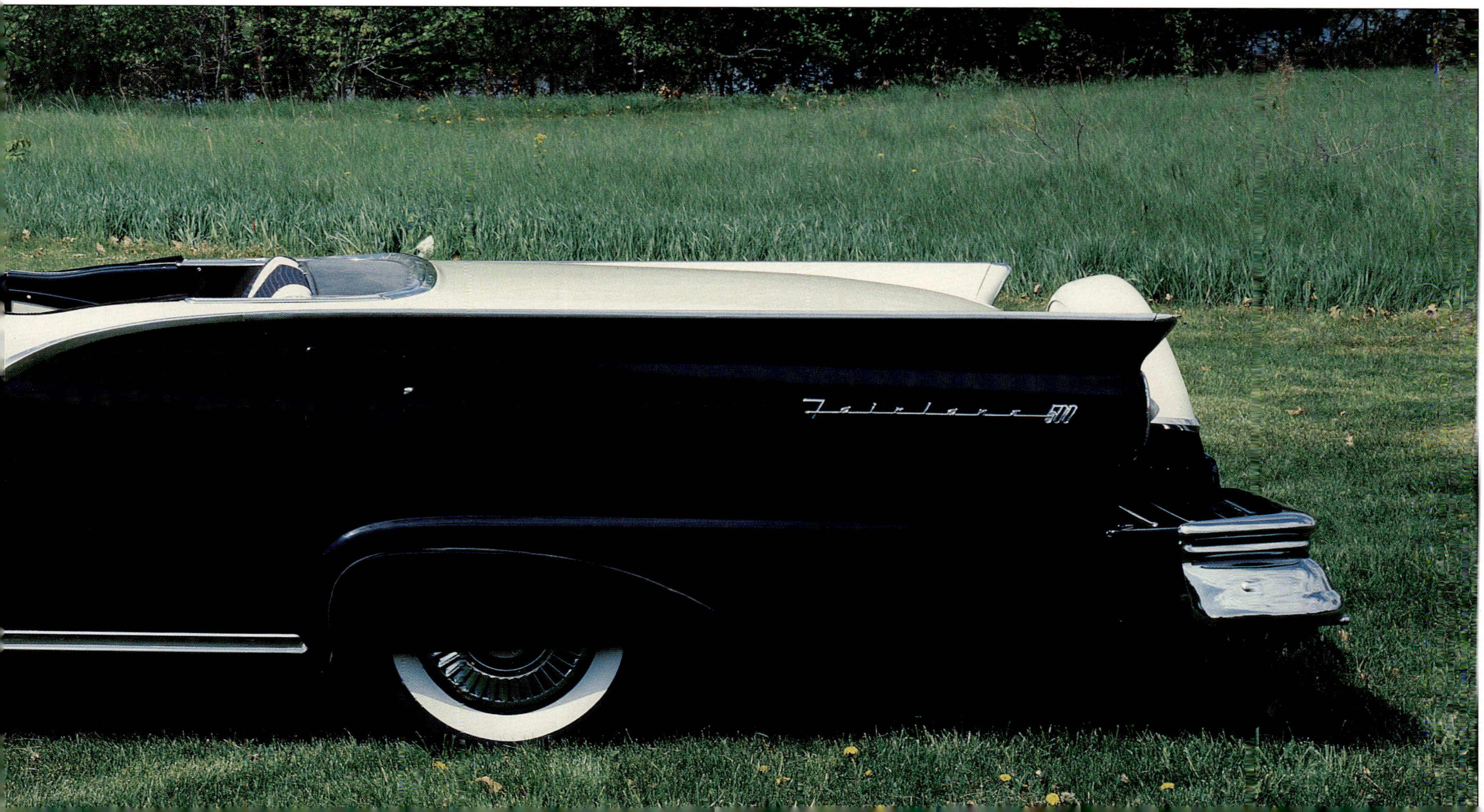
Fairlane 500

1957 LINCOLN PREMIERE

Lincoln's successful '56 formula wasn't vastly changed for '57, except for rear fenders that sprouted some of the loftiest fins in Detroit. But even bigger ones had been planned.

Fins flew higher than ever in 1957, and Lincoln had some of the tallest in Detroit—a literal big change from the low, handsomely sculpted rear fenders of 1956. The appendages might have been even higher, but cooler heads fortunately prevailed in the design studio.

Otherwise, Lincoln's successful '56 formula was little changed for '57. The only other visual difference was "QuadraLites," conventional 7-inch headlamps above 5-inch "road" lamps. Under the hood, Lincoln's 368-cubic-inch V-8 gained higher compression and 15 horsepower for an even 300.

The Premiere convertible again headed the line, but joined other models in being quite a bit more expensive—$5381. Only 3676 were built. Even then it wasn't the rarest '57 Lincoln, but as a ragtop, of course, it was surely the most desirable.

72

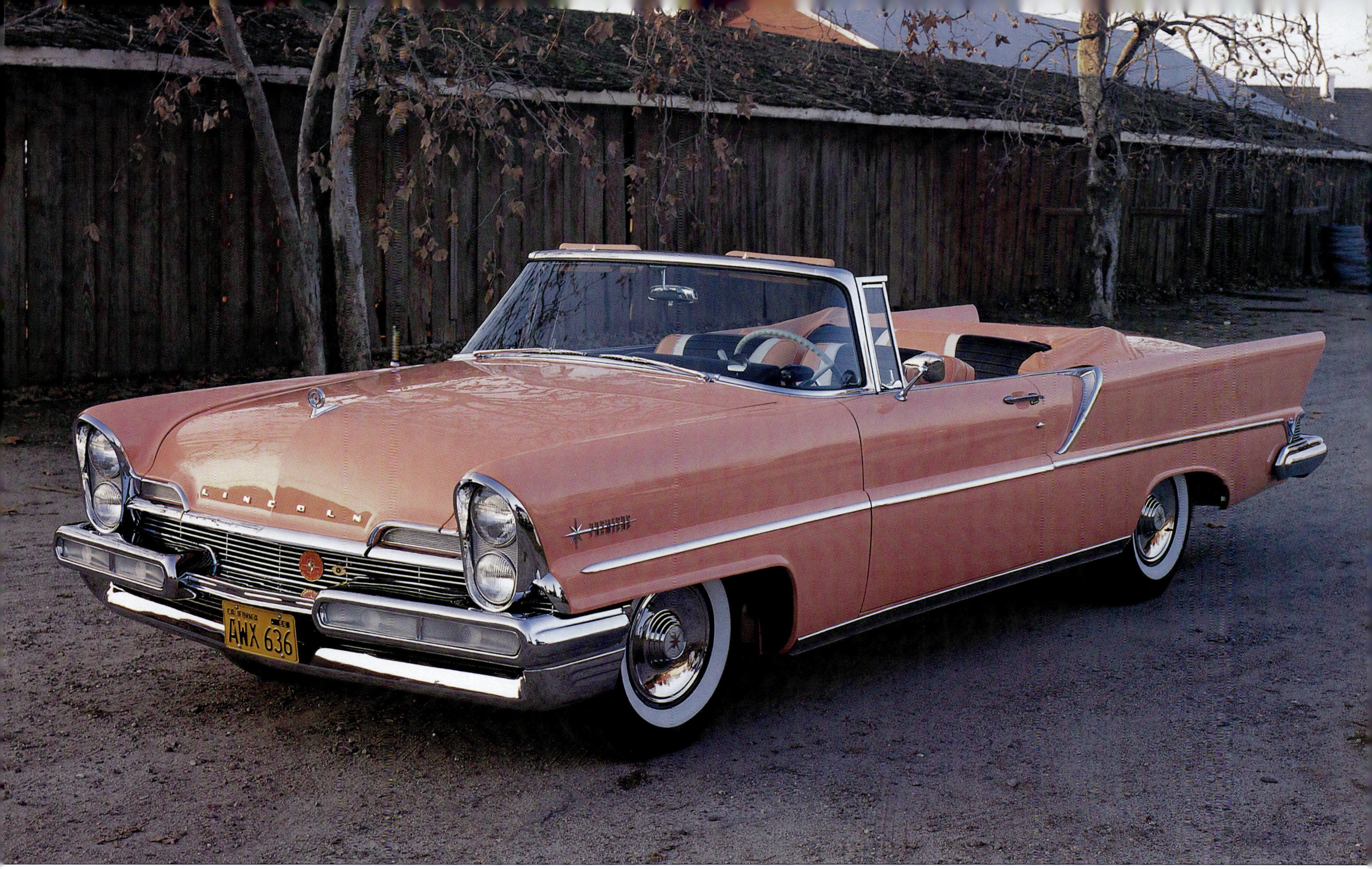
LINCOLN
AWX 636

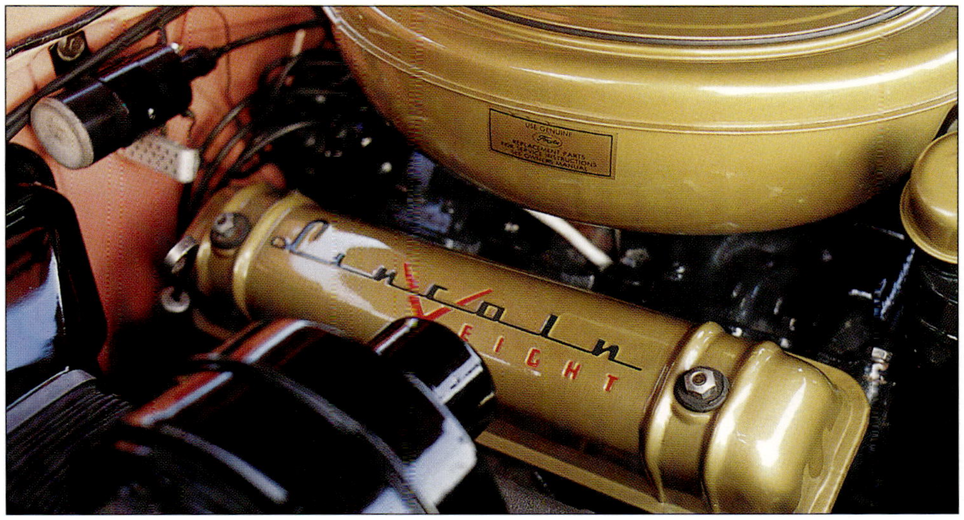
Lincoln
EIGHT

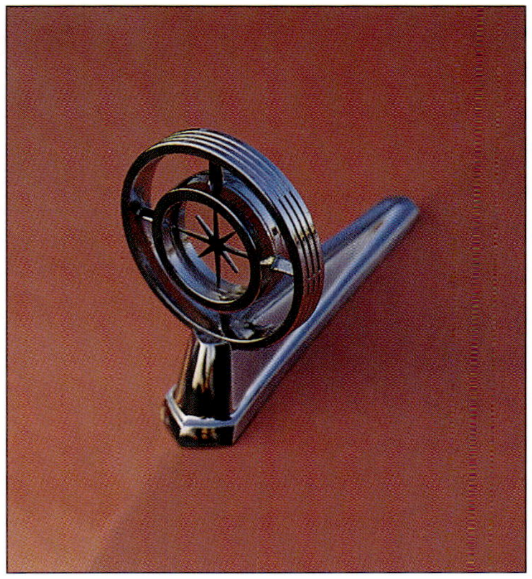

1957 OLDSMOBILE SUPER 88

Olds didn't race much by 1957, but it could still be one hot car thanks to the new J-2 performance option packing a heady 300 horsepower. In a Super 88 convertible it made for a very racy ride.

Oldsmobiles weren't raced much by 1957 and didn't need to be, having become consistently good-selling medium-priced cars known for innovation. Even so, one Lee Petty and his son Richard drove Olds convertibles on the sands of Daytona and hardtops at other stock-car venues. And if a little heavy in street form, a '57 Olds could still be quite rapid with a new performance option called J-2.

Available for any model at just $83, the J-2 included a trio of two-barrel carburetors, plus higher compression and low-restriction air cleaner to take the 371-cubic-inch "Rocket" V-8 from 277 stock horsepower to 300—good for 0-60 mph in under 8 seconds. There was also a racing setup with radical camshaft and heavy-duty internals, but at $385, it was seldom ordered.

The J-2 added spice to an Olds lineup that didn't look new but was. Basic appearance and even wheelbases stayed the course of 1954-56, but bodies were two inches lower and longer, so styling was a bit more rakish. Olds turned 60 in '57 and celebrated by adding models, including a convertible to the base Golden Rocket 88 series to join a Super 88 and Starfire 98. The last sold best despite costing the most ($4217), attracting 8278 orders. Next came the Super ($3447) with 7128 sales, followed by the 88 ($3182) with 6423.

Any '57 Olds made a fine road car, though switching from 15- to 14-inch tires—an industry trend that year—was more for appearance than handling. Yet even a ragtop looked good only until a '57 Chrysler pulled alongside. Olds styling had become dated, and it would only get worse before it got better.

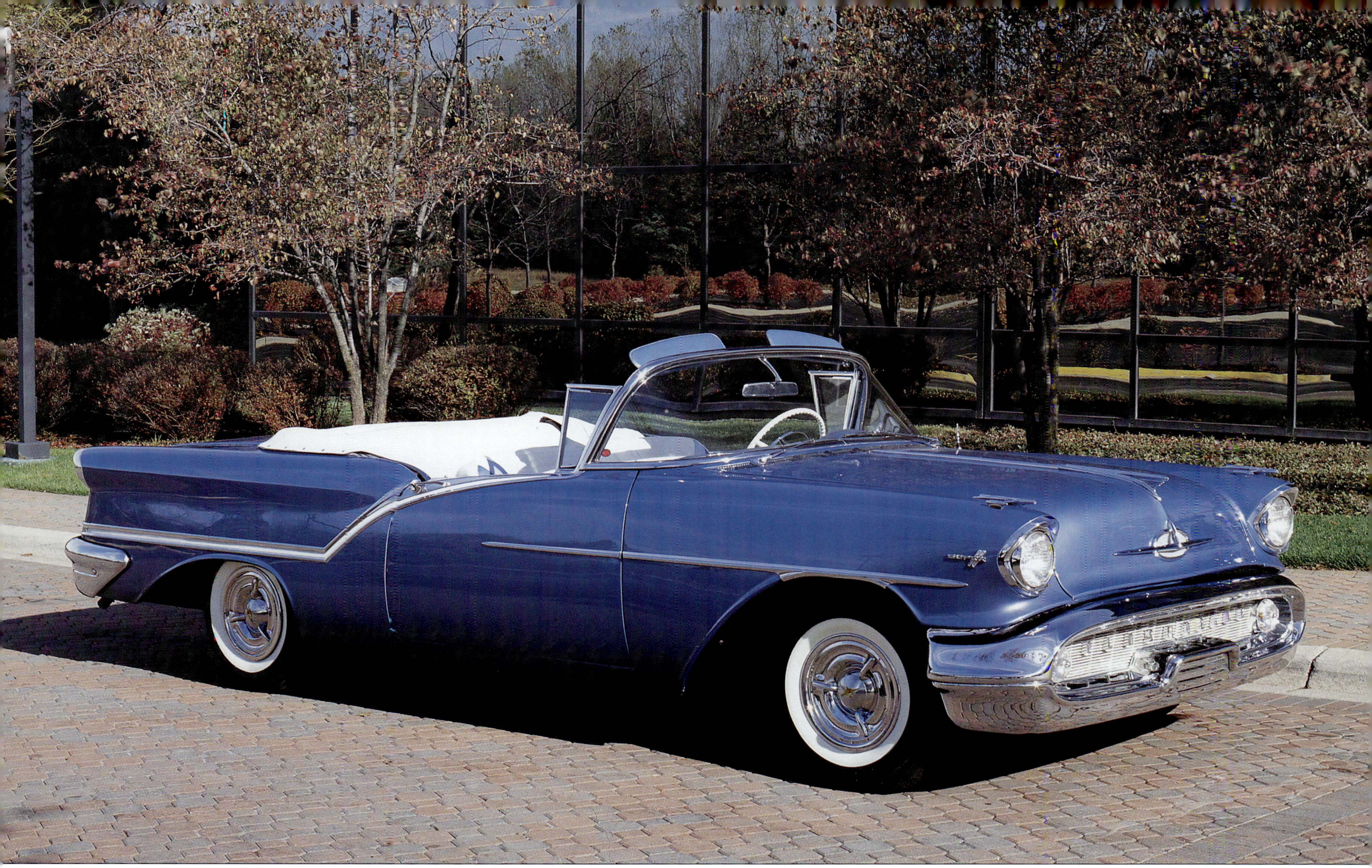

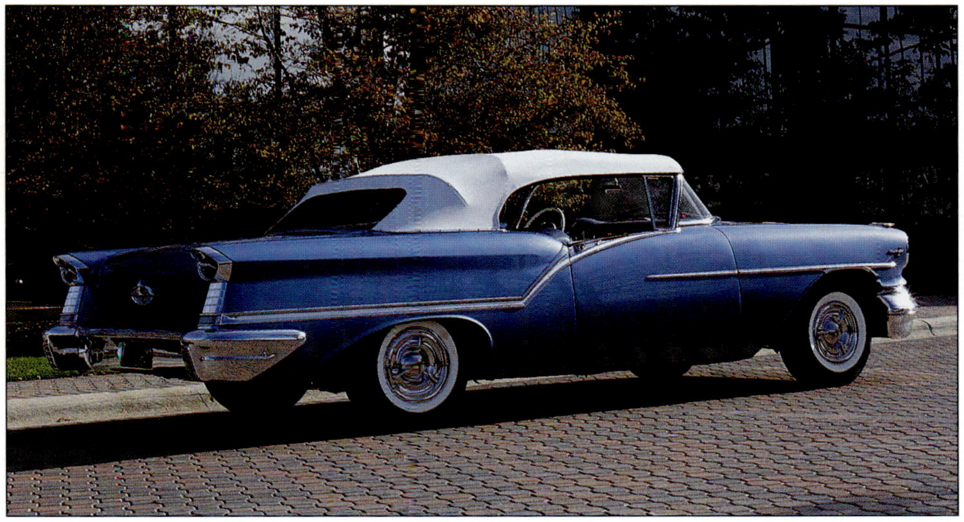

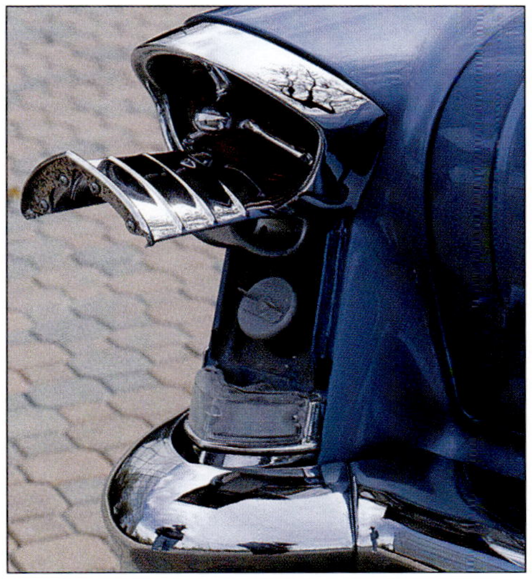

1958 CONTINENTAL MARK III

The first Continental convertible in 10 years arrived for 1958 as one of the largest postwar American cars ever built. Massive but clean, it sold surprisingly well for a flagship fliptop.

Bigger was usually better in the Eisenhower era, but that started to change in 1958, when a deep recession caused lots of car buyers to "think small." Still, there's nothing ironic in that year's Lincolns and Continentals, the largest, heaviest postwar Detroiters yet. They were simply out of phase with the times, conceived in boom-market 1955 amid predictions that people would always want the biggest cars they could get.

Riding grand 131-inch wheelbases, these Lincolns were boxy but clean and imposingly massive, though slanted quad headlamps were dubious. Continental was renamed Mark III, but though still a separate make, it was now a more luxurious Lincoln, unlike the unique, timelessly styled 1956-57 Mark II hardtop coupe. At least the Mark III offered more models priced up to $4000 lower. These included two hardtops and a sedan, plus the first open Continental in 10 years.

Despite the recession and a stiff $6283 price, the convertible sold respectably at 3048 copies; only the hardtop sedan did better. Like standard '58 Lincolns, Mark IIIs featured a big new 430 V-8 with 375 horsepower, plus unit construction—the biggest "unibody" cars yet—and surprisingly decent handling. A distinctive reverse-slant rear window with drop-down glass distinguished all Marks—even the convertible. It made for a very complex top mechanism, but then this *was* the '50s.

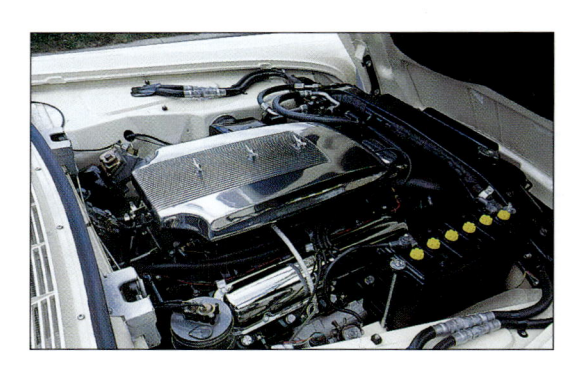

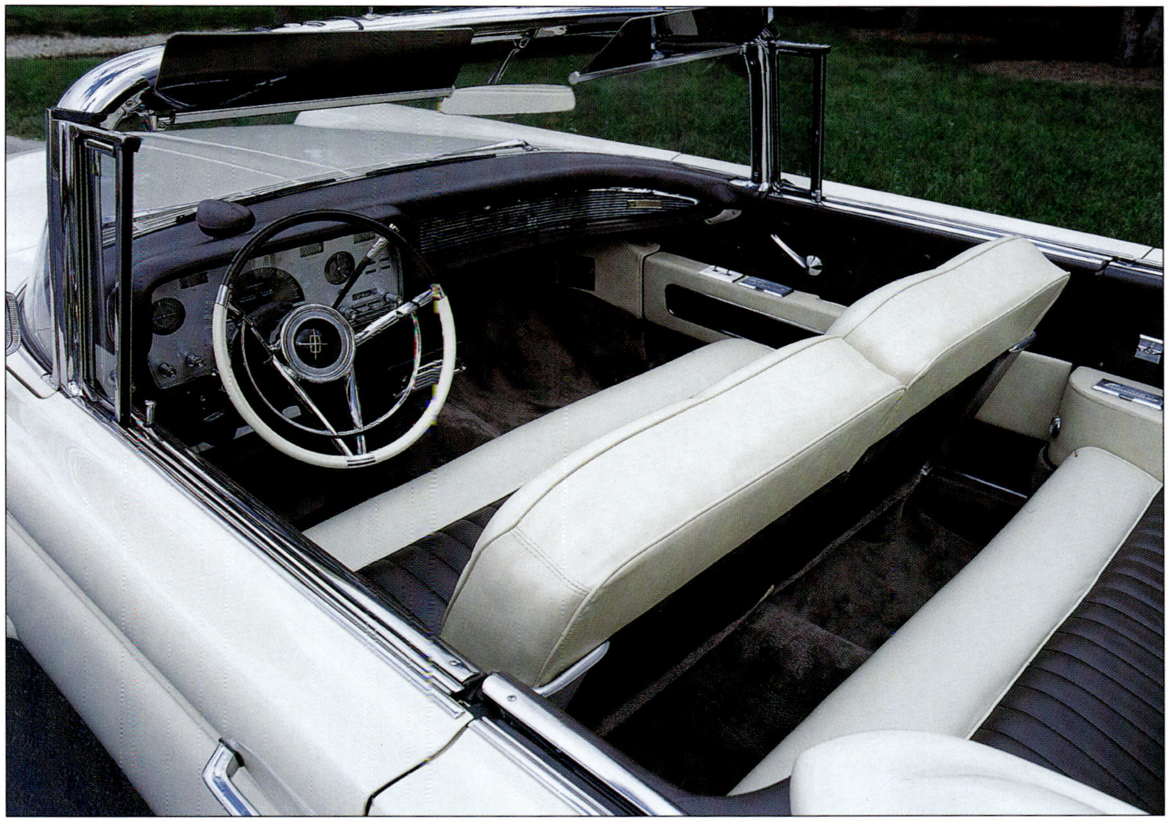

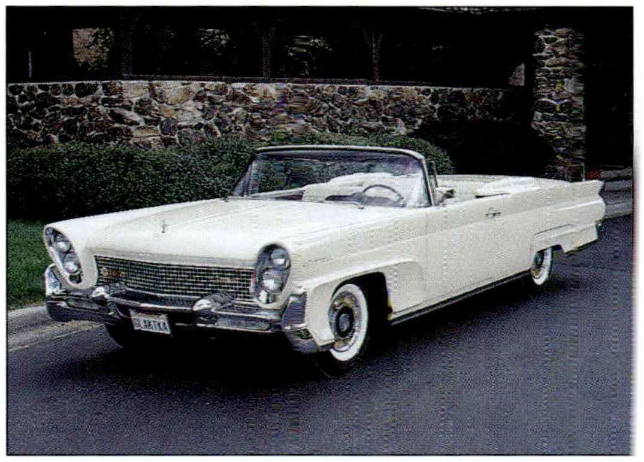

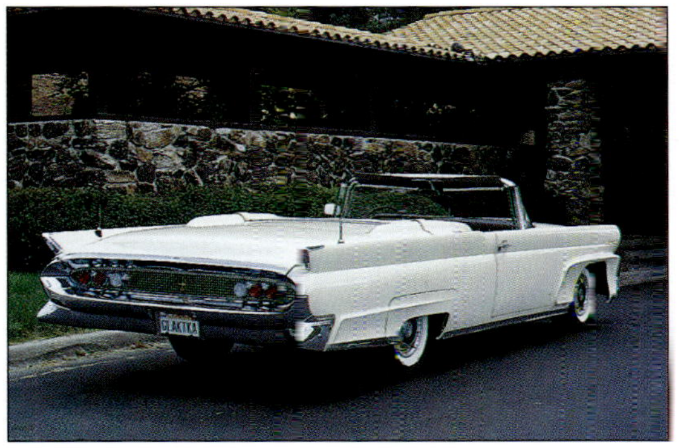

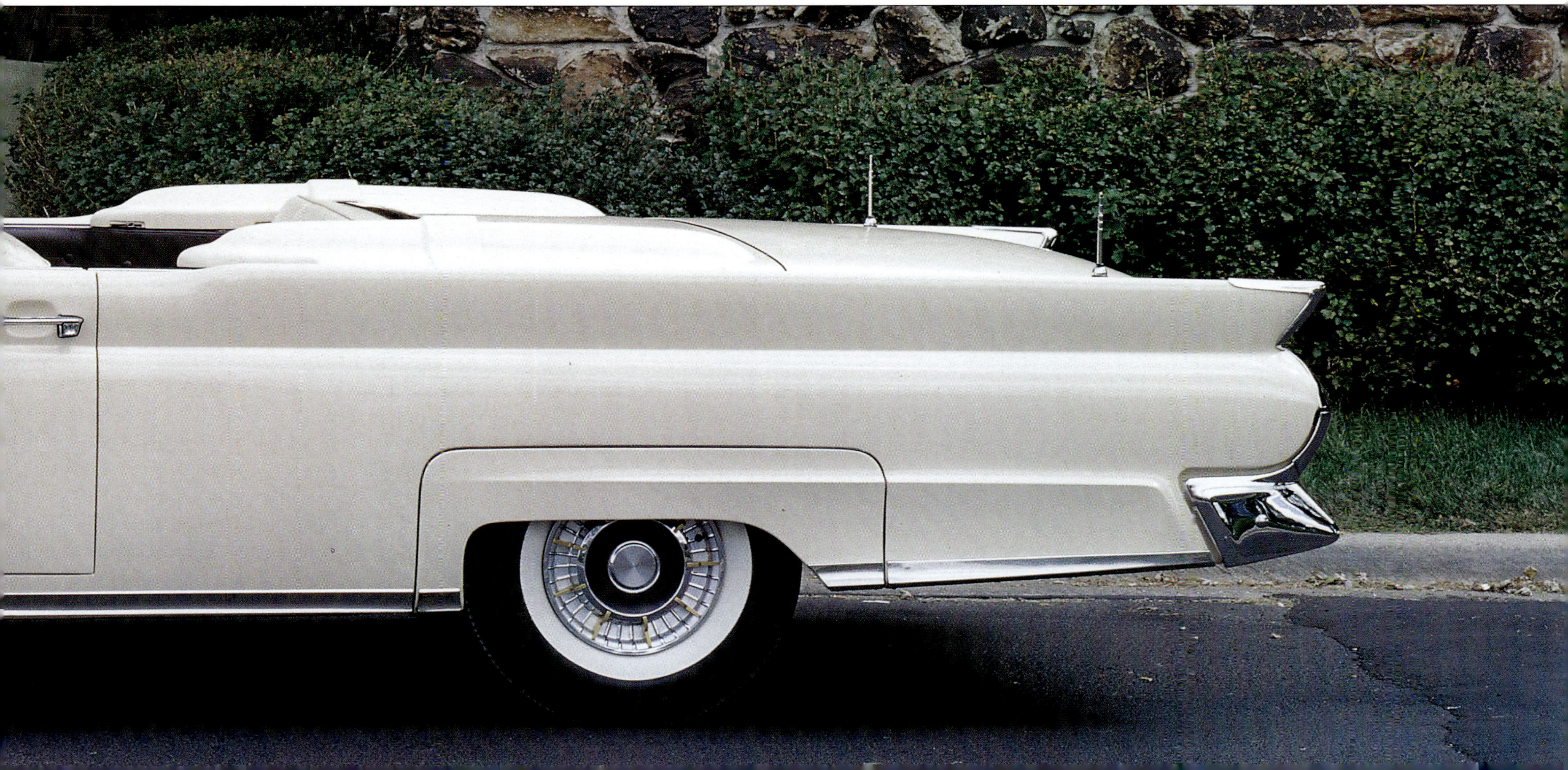

1958 EDSEL CITATION

Edsel was part of Ford Motor Company's plan to beat General Motors at its own game. Instead, it became the biggest flop in automotive history, a classic case of the wrong car at the wrong time.

It wasn't the first "wrong car at the wrong time," but the Edsel was the biggest flop of them all. Indeed, the very name has become synonymous with failure.

Edsel was conceived in boom-market 1955 to bridge the large price gap between Ford and Mercury, part of Ford Motor Company's grand strategy for competing with General Motors toe-to-toe. But with the usual lead times, Edsel didn't appear until 1958, by which time the medium-price market was tanking. Worse, these "new" cars weren't that different from what wasn't selling already.

A '58 Edsel was either upmarket Ford (Ranger, Pacer, and station wagon) or slightly downmarket Mercury (Corsair and Citation). Styling was Edsel's own and not bad for '58, but a daring "horse collar" vertical grille prompted snickers, shock, or both. There were expected gimmicks like a revolving-drum speedometer and "Teletouch Drive" automatic transmission with push-buttons in the steering-wheel hub. Otherwise, the '58 Edsels were familiar FoMoCo fare.

Convertibles were restricted to Ford-based Pacer and Mercury-based Citation models, the latter the costliest '58 Edsel at $3801. The Citation used a 410-cubic-inch version of Ford's then-new big-block V-8 with a healthy 345 horsepower; the Pacer a 303-bhp 361. All Edsels had plenty of go, but not the handling and braking to match. Add in frequently "casual" workmanship, and it's little wonder that only a little over 63,000 were sold. Ford had hoped for 100,000-plus. Among them were 1876 open Pacers and just 930 ragtop Citations.

With that, only Ford-based cars returned for '59, but sales kept sliding. For Edsel it was already too late.

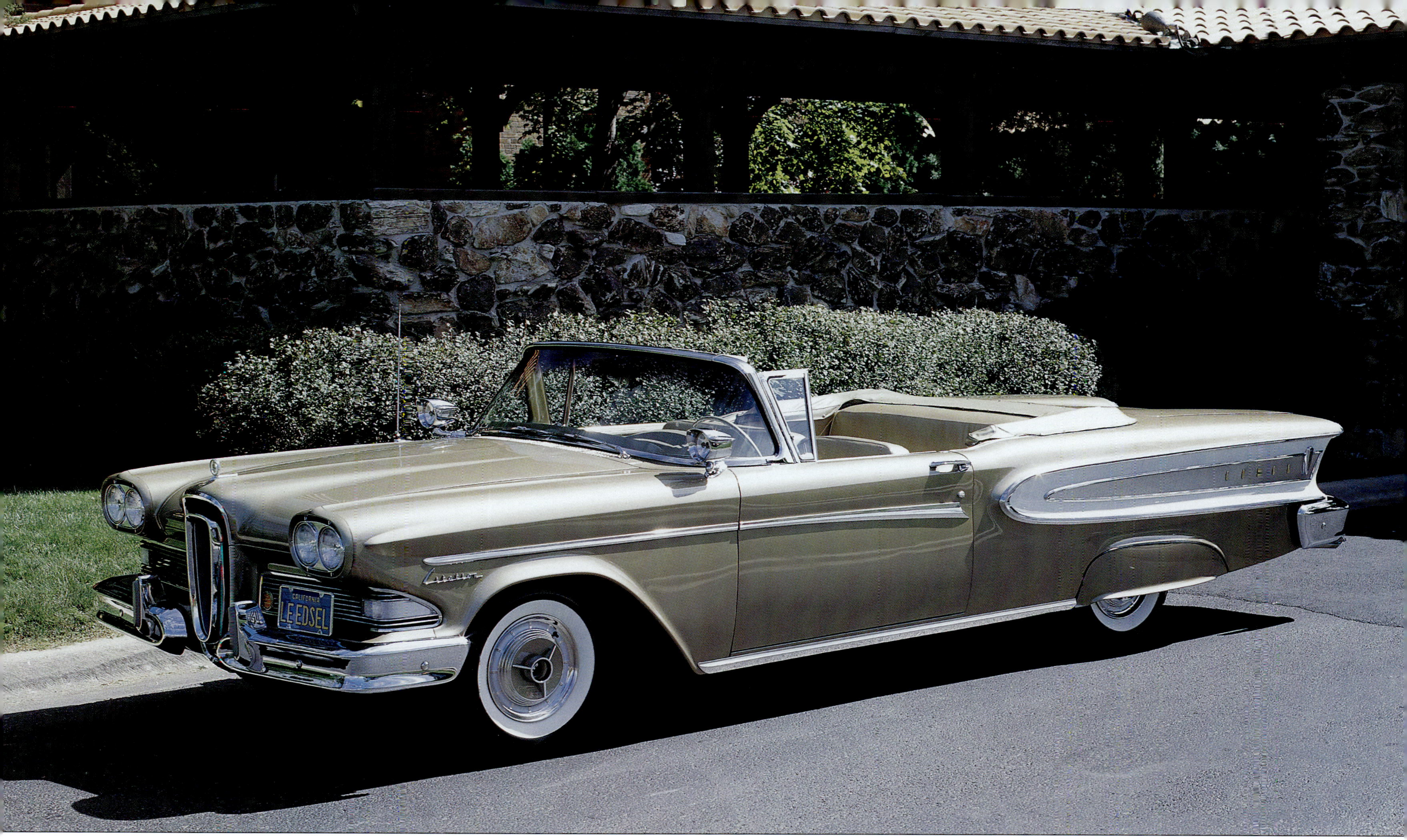
CALIFORNIA
LE EDSEL

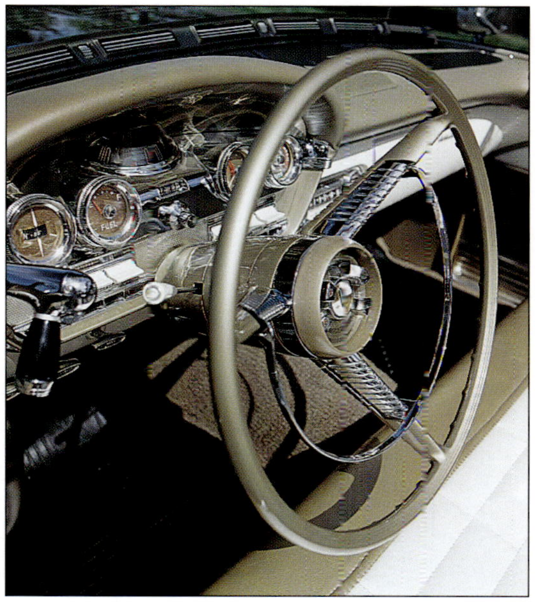

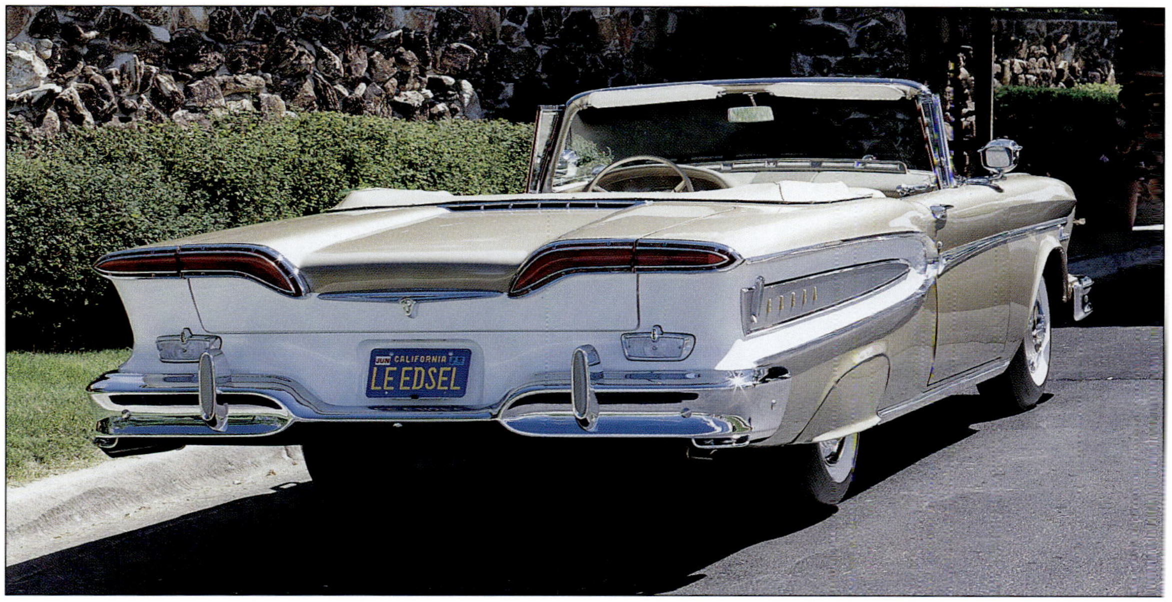
CALIFORNIA
LE EDSEL

1959 CADILLAC SERIES 62

The height of excess or just *Happy Days* exuberance? The 1959 Cadillacs were both, and their towering tailfins have since become an indelible '50s icon.

Depending on your taste—and maybe age—Cadillac's soaring 1959 tailfins are either the literal height of period excess or a campy icon for *Happy Days* exuberance. The result of a crash General Motors redesign effort prompted by Chrysler Corporation's '57 "Forward Look," the '59 Cadillac was almost as radical as that year's "bat-wing" Chevrolet, though the towering fins and bomb-shape taillamps were nicely balanced by lower-slung bodies with tapered lines. There were also worthwhile technical improvements, headlined by a larger 390-cubic-inch V-8 (up from 365) with 325 standard horsepower and a rousing 345 in Eldorados.

The Eldo convertible remained queen of the line at $7401, but the less glittery $5455 Series 62 version was no less arresting. It was certainly more numerous, with a record 11,130 built versus just 1320 ragtop Eldos. Today, all '59 Cadillacs are firmly enshrined as emblems of their era, thanks to those fins—and the fact that Cadillacs would never look so wild again.

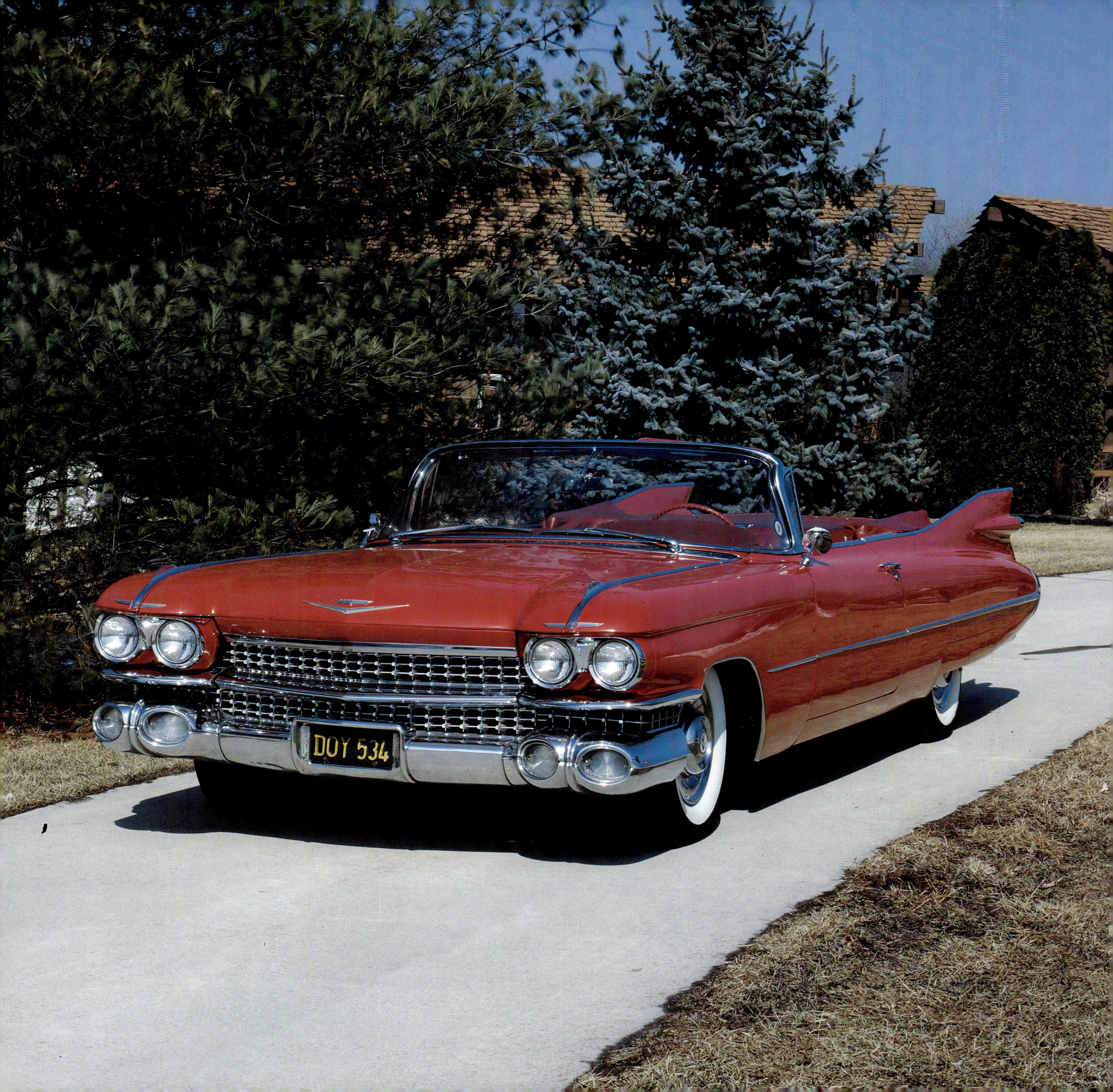
DOY 534

1959 DODGE CUSTOM ROYAL

The '59 Dodges scored a healthy sales gain over the recession-plagued '58s, but the flock still had its rare birds—like a top-line convertible with a new top-line power option.

The Dodge pictured here is a rare bird. For one thing, it's one of only 984 fliptop Custom Royals built for 1959 (base-priced at $3422). For another, it has that year's new Super D-500 option, a 383-cubic-inch V-8 with twin four-barrel carburetors and a blistering 345 horsepower. The point? The Super D-500 was available on any Dodge but wasn't often ordered, so how many other top-line ragtops could have had it too?

That 383 was a new size for Dodge as well as '59 Chryslers and DeSotos, the first of what would be a long line. But you didn't need the Super D-500 to enjoy a Custom Royal ragtop, as its standard engine was a Super Ram Fire 361 with a healthy 305 bhp. In between was a single four-barrel 383 D-500 option with 320 bhp.

All these engines were efficient "wedgeheads" that worked best with responsive TorqueFlite automatic transmission. Rivaling its trademark pushbutton controls for futuristic gimmickry was another new '59 feature: swivel front seats. Our featured Custom Royal has these too, though other Chrysler makes also offered them. The idea was to ease entry/exit in ever-lower cars. This option was fairly popular, but it didn't last beyond 1960.

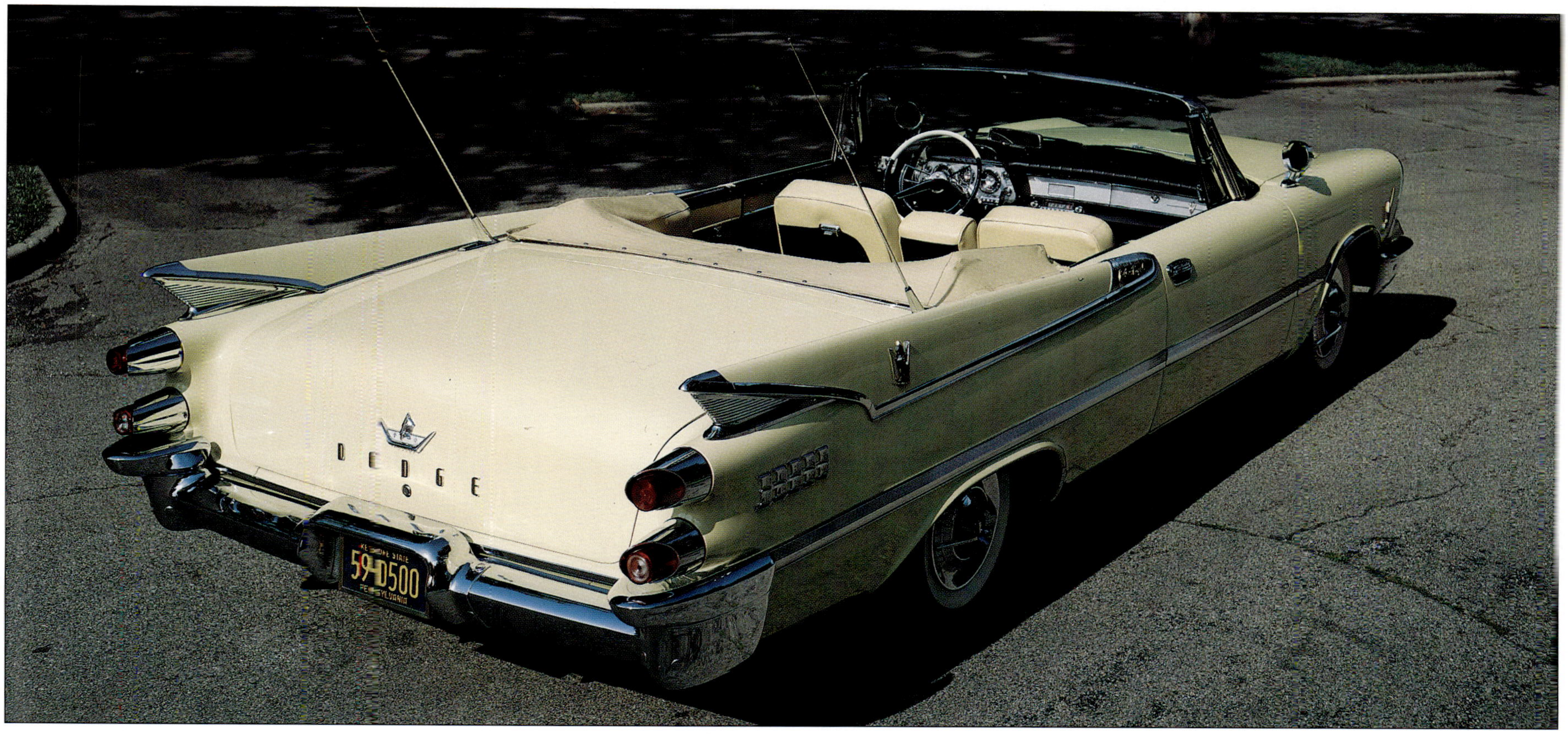
DODGE
59 D500

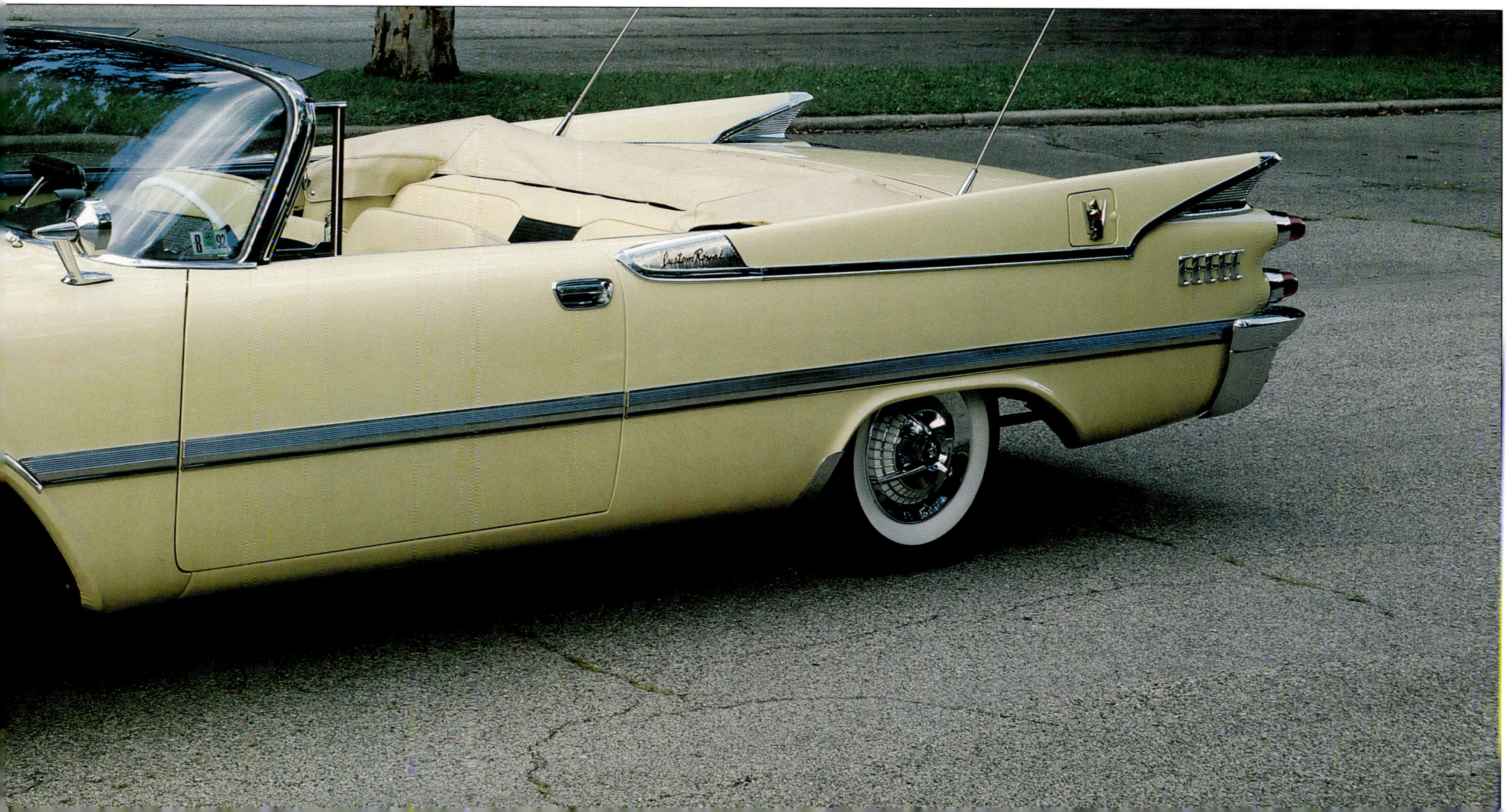

1959 FORD THUNDERBIRD

T-Bird loyalists bemoaned the passing of the "Little Bird," but with a bigger body, rear seats, luxury appointments, and the addition of a hardtop the new "Square Bird" helped Ford triple Thunderbird sales.

Nineteen fifty-eight marked the beginning of a new era for Thunderbird. The 1955-57 two-seat Thunderbirds were originally designed as Ford's answer to the Corvette. While handily outselling the Corvette, the famed "Little Bird" failed to make money for Ford.

Determined to make the next-generation Thunderbird profitable, Ford aimed for the broadest audience possible. By 1959 the addition of two rear seats, longer and dramatically lowered bodywork, and a hardtop model paid off. Ford sold more than 76,000 "Square Birds" that year, 19,000 of which were convertibles—nearly as many convertibles as the Little Bird's best year.

But the open-air Square Bird almost never was. Because of the limited funding available for the 1958 Thunderbird redesign, a decision was made early in the process to eliminate the convertible body from the line. Design work had begun on a hardtop with power-retractable roof panels as an alternative to a true convertible. Engineering issues halted development of the retractable roof, and the convertible was resurrected.

Though low and sleek, base Thunderbirds were not stellar performers, even by the standards of the day. Early tests with the standard 300-horsepower, 312-cubic-inch V-8-equipped Square Bird resulted in 0-60 mph times of 13.5 seconds. But by 1959 an optional 350-horsepwer, 430-cubic-inch V-8 would propel the T-Bird to 60 in a livelier 9.9 seconds.

Though Thunderbird began life as a convertible, by 1958 the roofless T-Birds would account for less than a quarter of production. Later generations would see a continuing decline in convertible T-Birds until the coupe took over completely for 1967. Today however, it is the convertible Square Birds that are prized by collectors.

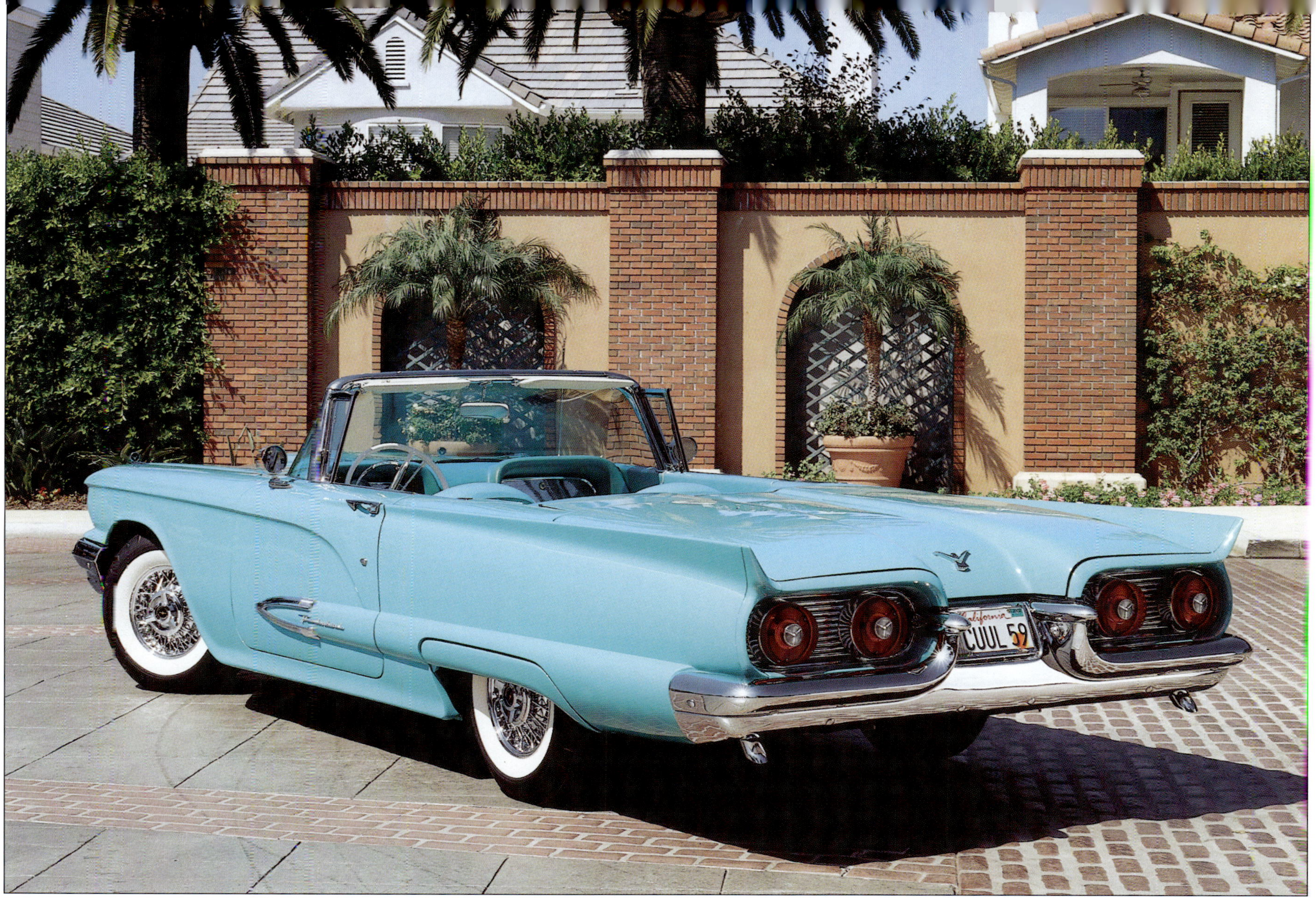
CUUL 59

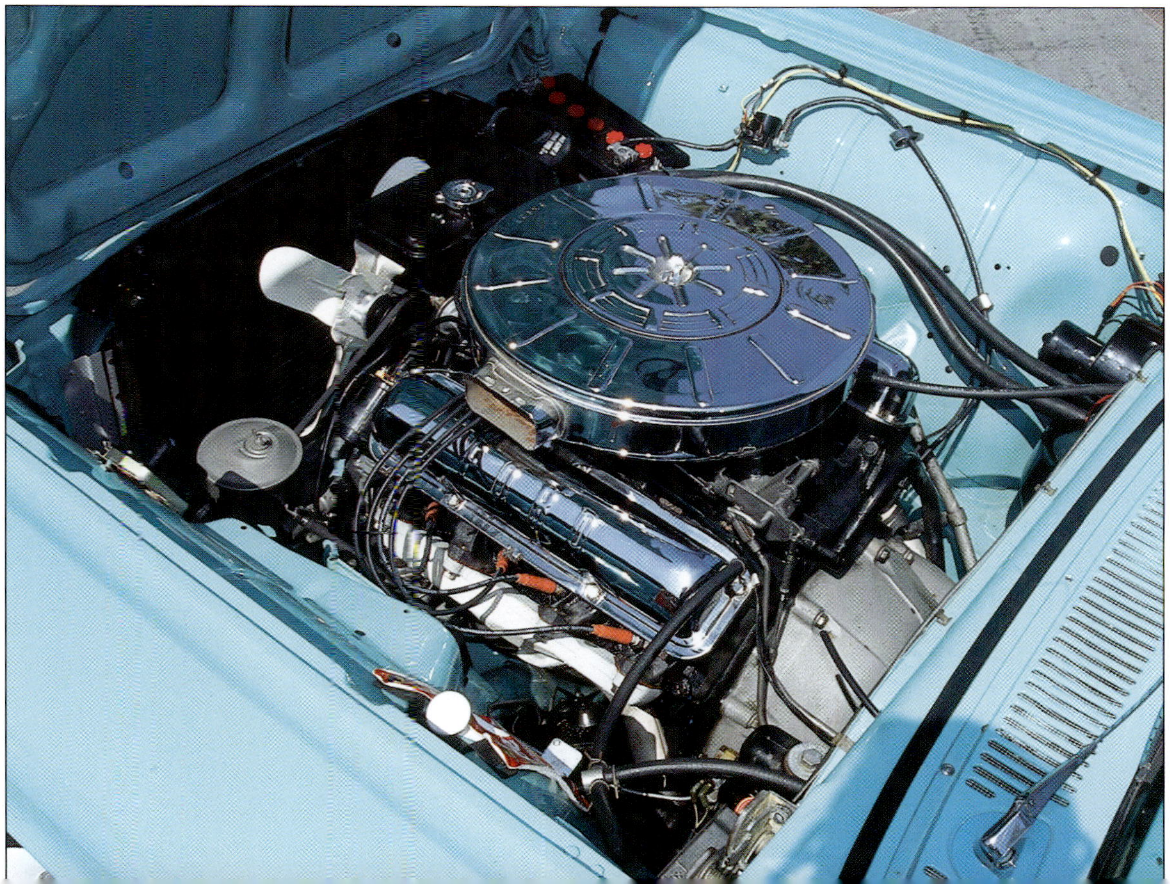

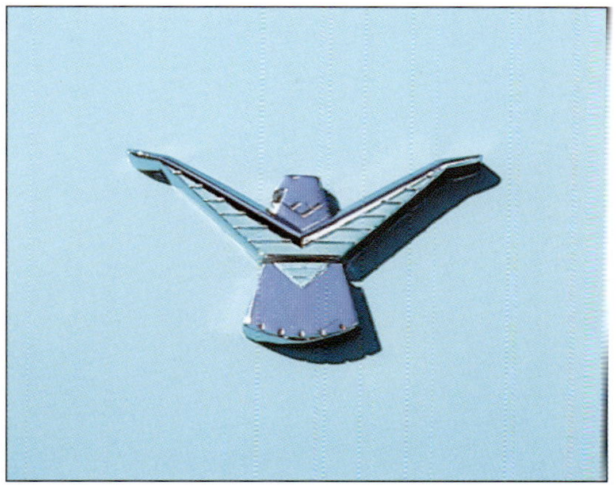

1959 PONTIAC BONNEVILLE

Pontiac completed its turn from "grandma's car" to hot, handsome performer with its 1959 models. As the first "Wide-Track" Pontiacs with 389 V-8 power, they were a solid sales hit.

Pontiacs became "Wide-Tracks" for 1959—big but uncommonly handsome all-new cars that could fly like scalded bats and cornered better than anything else in the medium-price field. It was the start of what would be a dramatic upturn for a traditionally dowdy brand, which moved from sixth to fifth in the sales race.

Leading this charge was the glamorous '59 Bonneville convertible. Though not a limited edition like the 1957 original, it was still a formidable performer with a newly enlarged 389 V-8 making 260 standard horsepower with stickshift or 300 with optional Hydra-Matic. Not enough? Order Tri-Power, with triple two-barrel carbs and up to 345 bhp.

At $3478, the ragtop Bonneville sold a healthy 11,426 units. All came with Pontiac's top-grade "Morrokide" vinyl upholstery. Even "bucket" front seats were available. Pontiac was starting to go sporty in no uncertain terms.

86

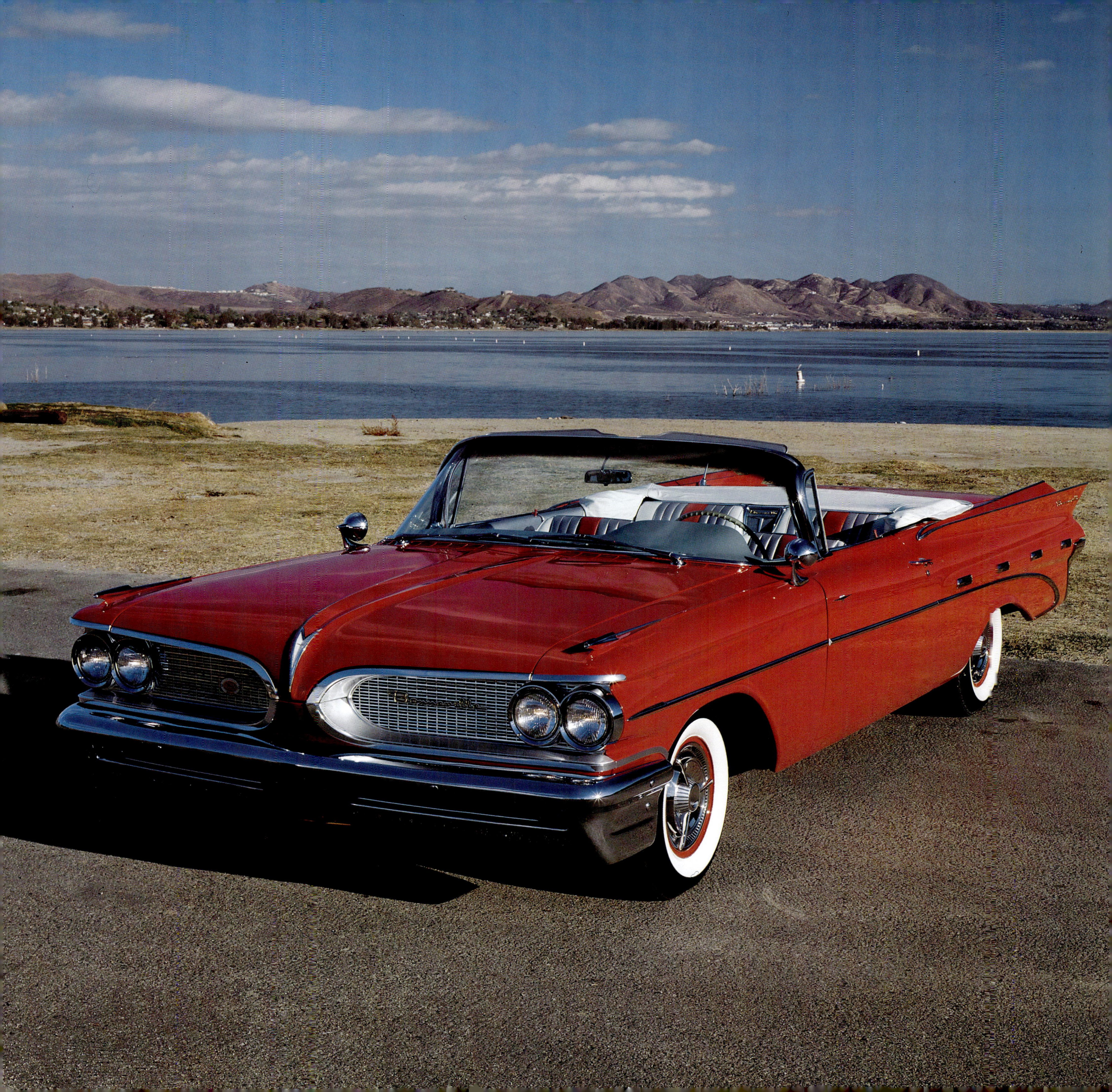

1960 DODGE POLARA

Dodge scored record sales for 1960 with new lower-priced, full-size Darts. Senior Dodges weren't as popular, but George Jetson would have loved the top-line Polara convertible.

After a modest 1959 recovery, Dodge sales boomed by 135 percent to nearly 368,000 for 1960. The main reason was that year's new Dart, a three-series line of lower-priced "standard" models featuring six and V-8 power, Dodge's first "unibody," somewhat extravagant styling, and attractive prices in the $2300-$3000 range.

Covering the $3000-$3600 spread were similarly conceived "senior" Dodges: new Matadors and Polaras on a four-inch-longer wheelbase (122 inches). Styling here was even more flamboyant, with taller tailfins, thrusting pod taillamps, and an oddly shaped face. The top-line Polara included a $3416 convertible offered with 383 V-8s delivering up to 330 horsepower—that from the hot dual-quad D-500 option with new "ram induction" manifolding. Futuristic gimmicks like swivel seats also returned.

Exact numbers aren't recorded, but Dodge likely built few 1960 Polara convertibles and only a handful with the D-500 package. That makes the red beauty here another rare Ram ragtop from the *Jetsons* period of Chrysler Corporation design.

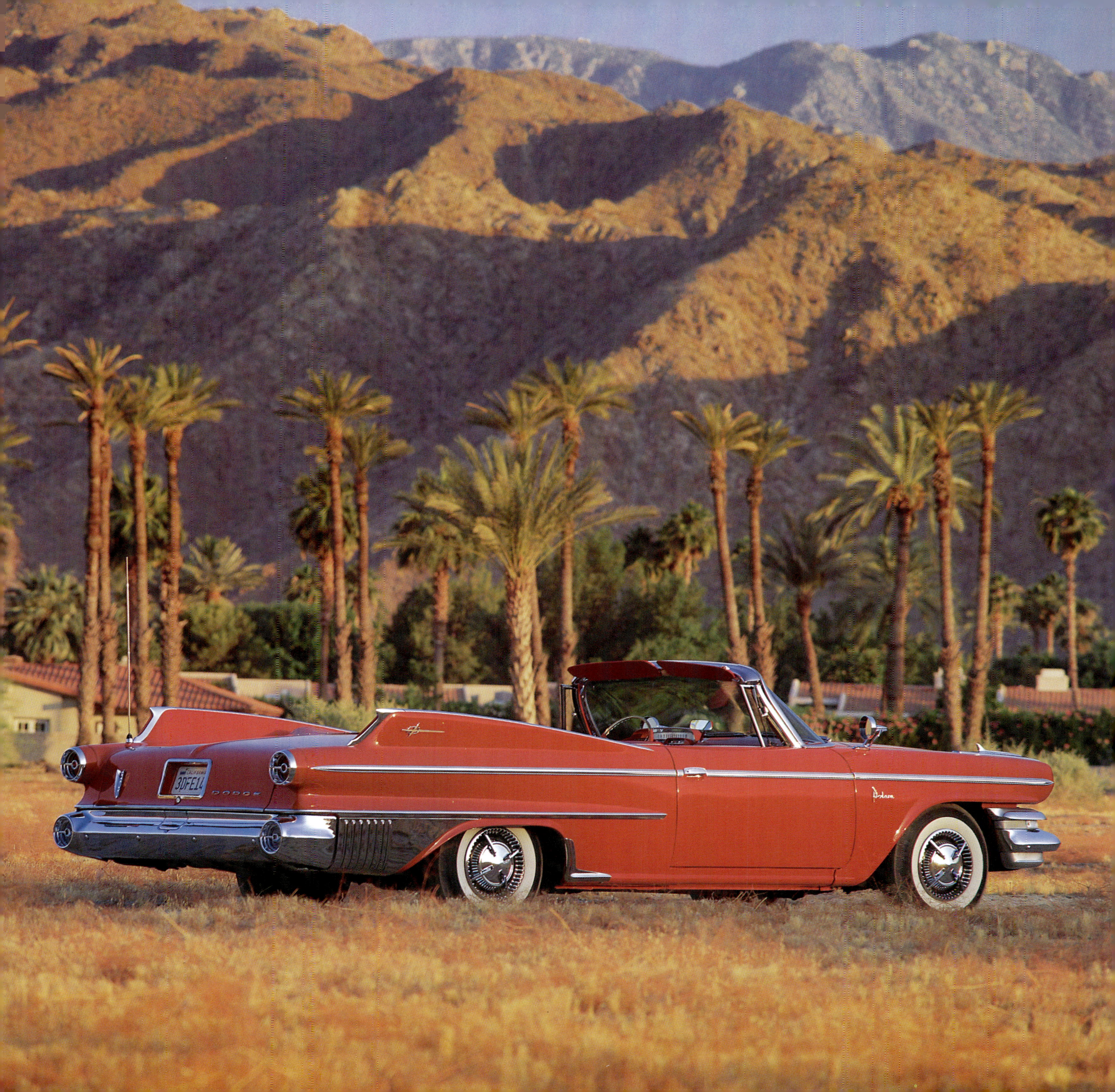
3DFE14
DODGE

1960 EDSEL RANGER

Edsel breathed its last with a token 1960 model run that included just 76 convertibles. Ironically, the redesigned '60s were the most salable Edsels yet, but they simply had no future.

Ford Motor Company needn't have bothered with 1960 Edsels. Only 2809 were built by mid-November 1959, when Ford decided to end the Edsel experiment after two supremely disappointing years. Among those cars were just 76 Ranger convertibles.

Rangers and Villager wagons made up Edsel's reduced 1960 lineup. Edsel's '59 convertible had been an upper-crust Corsair priced at $3072. The 1960 Ranger ragtop started at $3000, but its standard 292-cubic-inch V-8 had only 185 horsepower versus its predecessor's 225-bhp 332. A 300-bhp 352 V-8 was optional across the board for 1960. So was a humble 223 six.

All this applied to Ford, too, because the last Edsels were basically warmed-over '60 Fords. That meant mostly new cars that were longer, lower, much wider, and arguably better-looking than the boxy '59s. Trouble was, these Edsels were low-priced cars, not high-profit "executive" wheels; as such, they were superfluous to Ford's future. Edsel was thus quietly terminated, but it would not be forgotten.

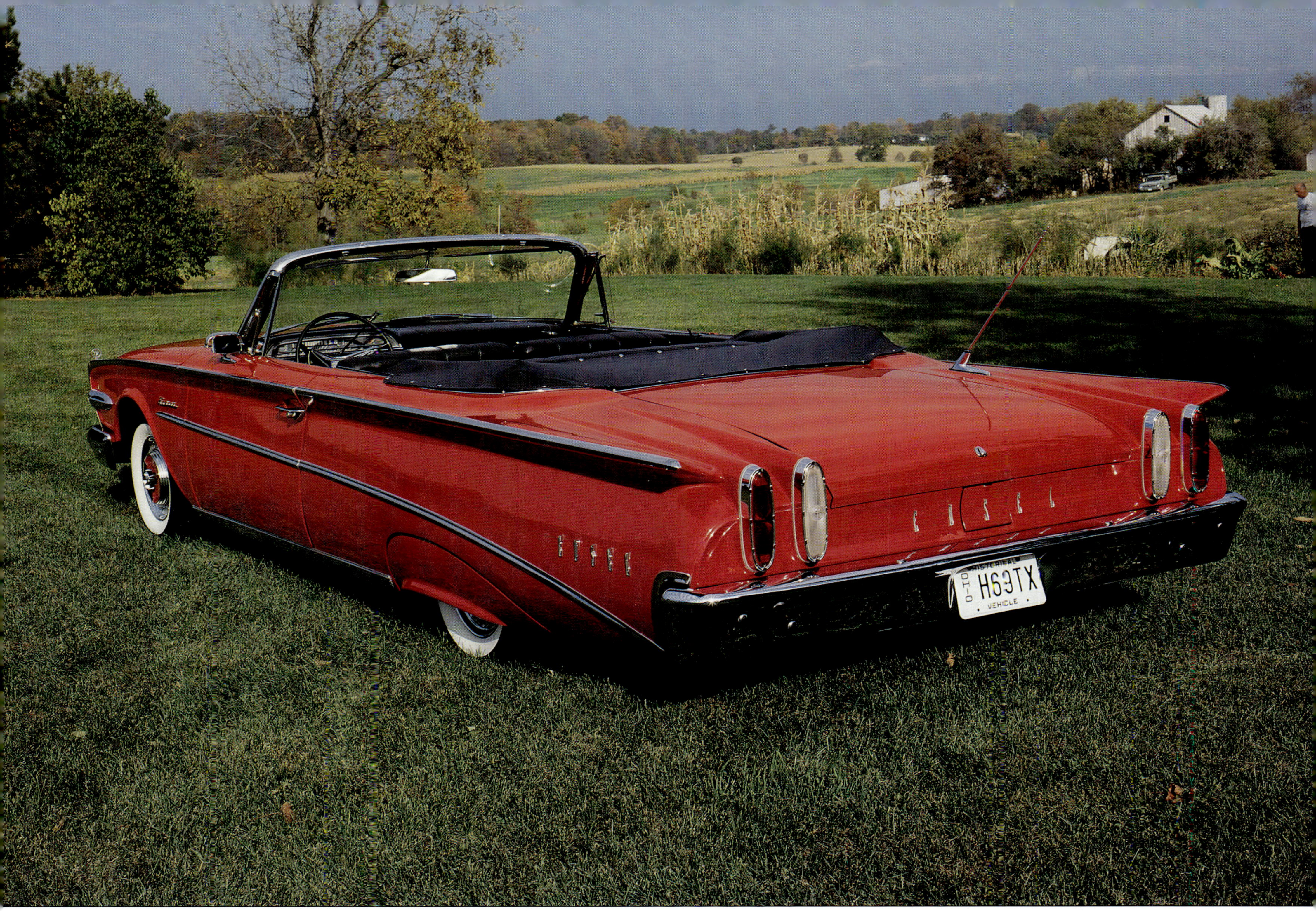
H63TX

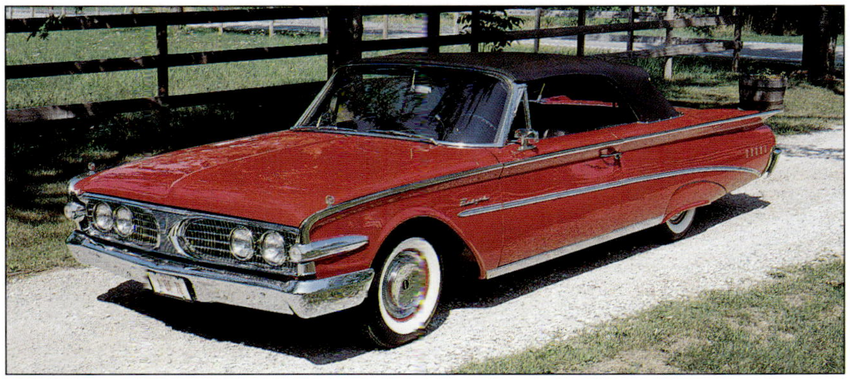

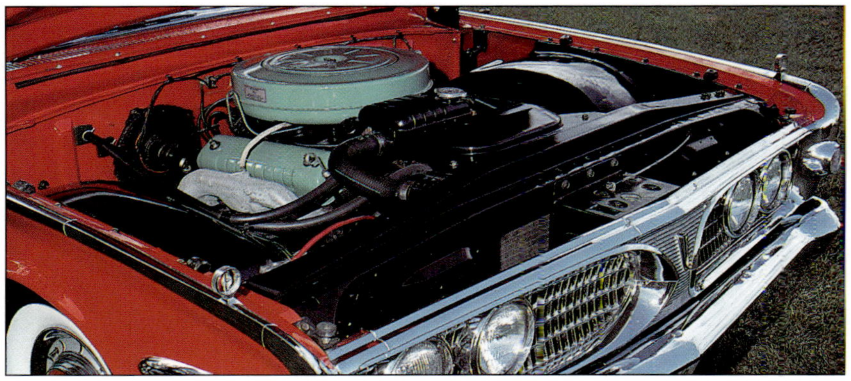

1961 FORD GALAXIE SUNLINER

Clean, simple, and free of clutter, Ford's big ones were among the most pleasing of 1961 cars. They took a while to be fully appreciated, however—even the sun-loving ragtop.

Ford Division greeted the '60s with three separate car lines: a bigger new standard Ford, the popular four-seat personal-luxury Thunderbird, and an enormously popular new compact, the Falcon. Though Falcon was little changed for '61, the T-Bird was all-new, with a sleek "rocketship" profile. Big Fords moved the other way, adopting clean, simple styling on carryover bodies that were actually a bit shorter and lighter than the 1960s. There was also a pleasing absence of frivolous '50s-style gimmicks.

This relative lack of flash may explain why collectors took so long to "discover" the big '61 Fords, but we can be glad they have. Otherwise, we'd be deprived of the sleek Sunliner convertible shown here.

Still part of the top-line Galaxie series, the '61 Sunliner started at $2849. As in earlier years it had a standard V-8, now a 175-horsepower 292. Options included the veteran 352 with 220 bhp (shown here), plus a new 390 big-block with 300 bhp. Ford also sold a few triple two-barrel 390s with 375 or an amazing 401 bhp to leadfoots with big wallets and racing licenses. A dealer-installed four-on-the-floor manual transmission was new, too, but most big Fords had either two-speed Fordomatic or three-speed Cruise-O-Matic self-shifters.

Though total Ford sales fell slightly for '61, the Sunliner virtually repeated its 1960 performance, attracting 44,614 orders. We'd love to own one right now.

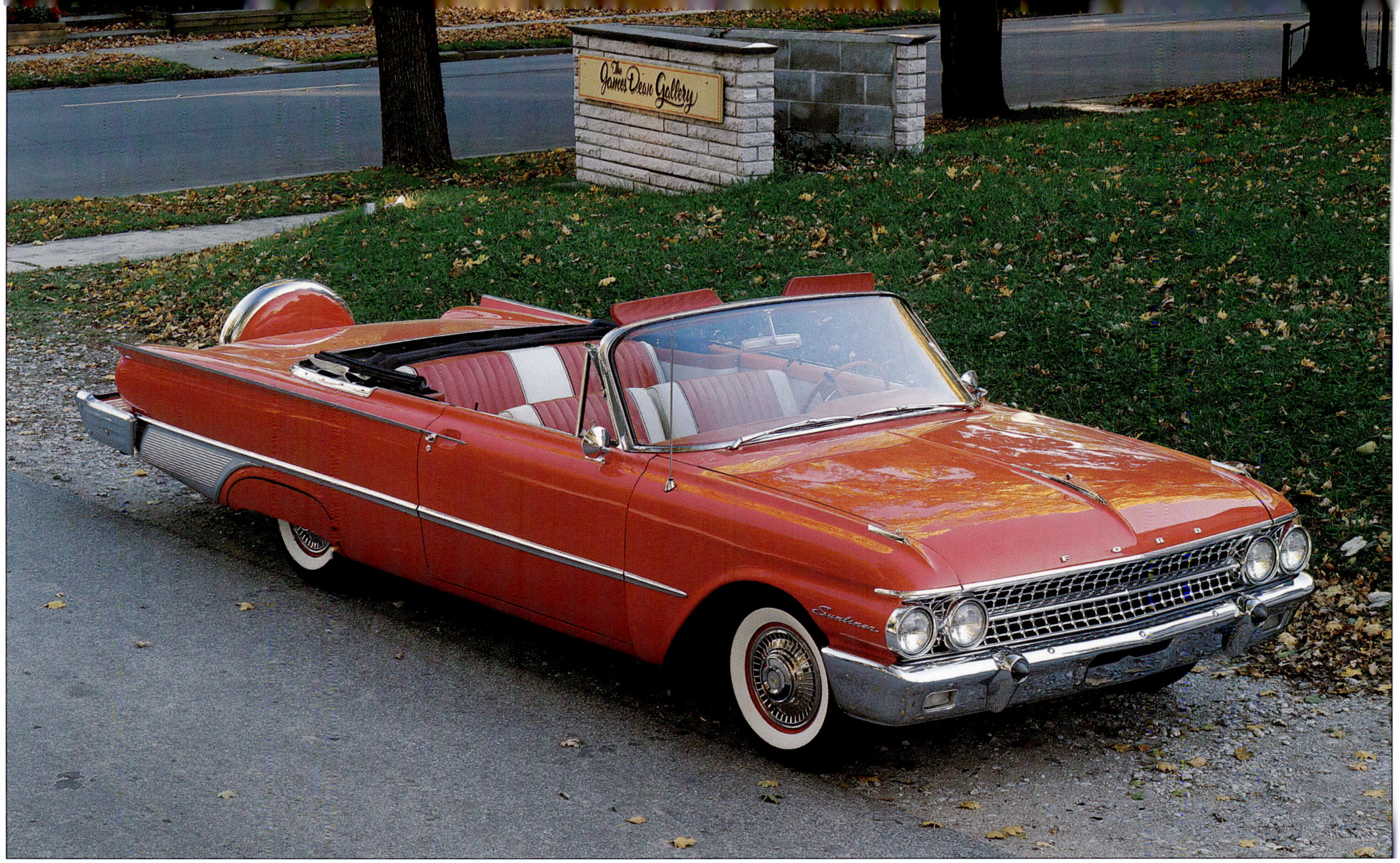
The James Dean Gallery

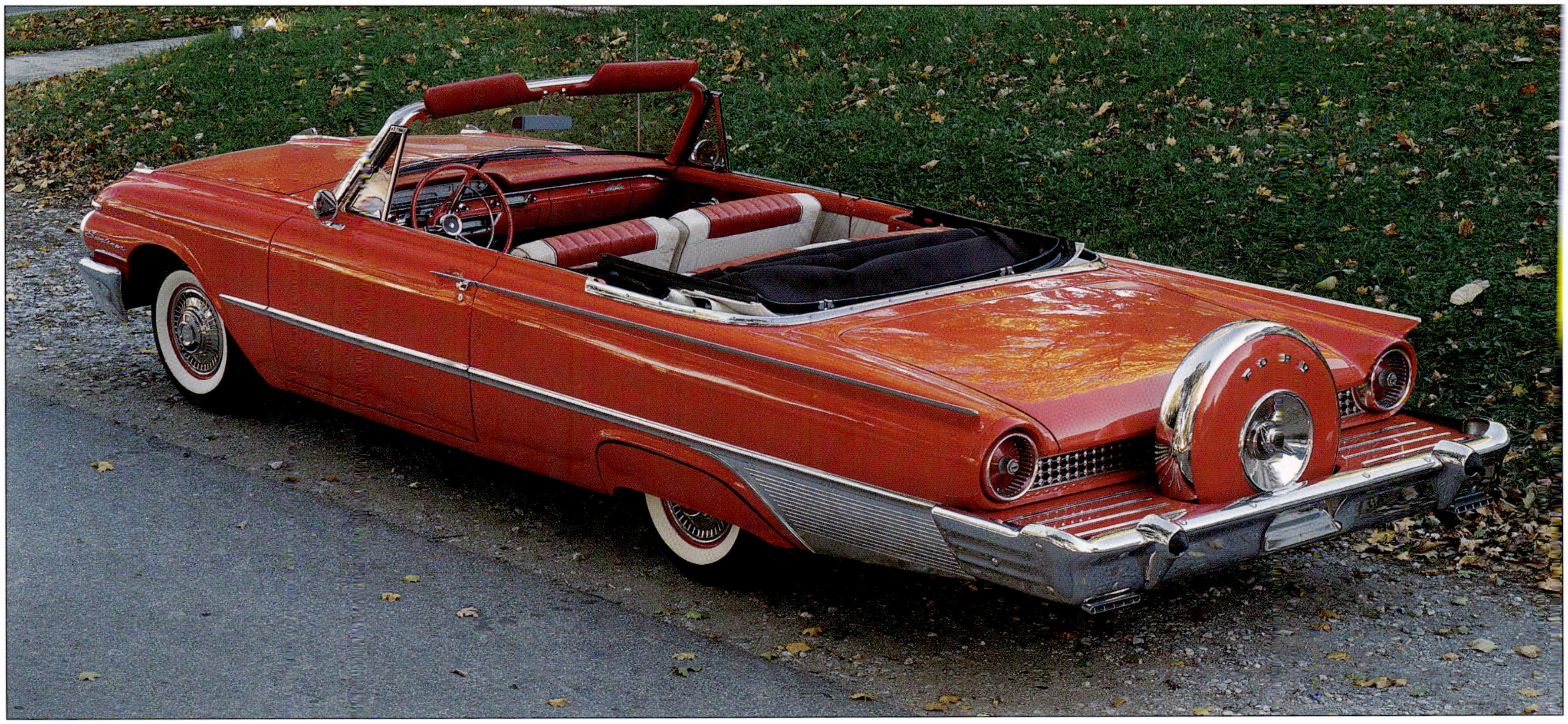

1962 DODGE POLARA 500

Dodge thought smaller big cars would be hot in 1962. Most buyers thought otherwise, but the lighter, sportier new Darts and Polara 500s were hot on the street and unbeatable on the dragstrip.

American car buyers were rushing to compacts by 1962, so Dodge seemed to have good reason for drastically shrinking its standard cars that year. Trouble was, size still mattered to big-car customers, so Dodge's "New Lean Breed" was a tough sell. Oddball styling didn't help. As a result, Dodge dropped 30,000 sales on top of 1961's 25-percent decline. Things would have been worse had true big Dodges not been hastily reinstated during the year.

Among the downsized '62 Dodges that did sell were 12,268 top-line Polara 500s: hardtop coupe, hardtop sedan, and convertible with standard bucket seats and a 305-horsepower 361 V-8. A 310-bhp version was available, along with 330- and 335-bhp 383s and—the real excitement—a big new 413 Ramcharger with up to 415 bhp. Though few Polaras got that thumping "wedgehead," it made the light Dart two-door a dragstrip terror, and Dodge soon ruled in quarter-mile contests. At least it was consolation for the dreary sales performance.

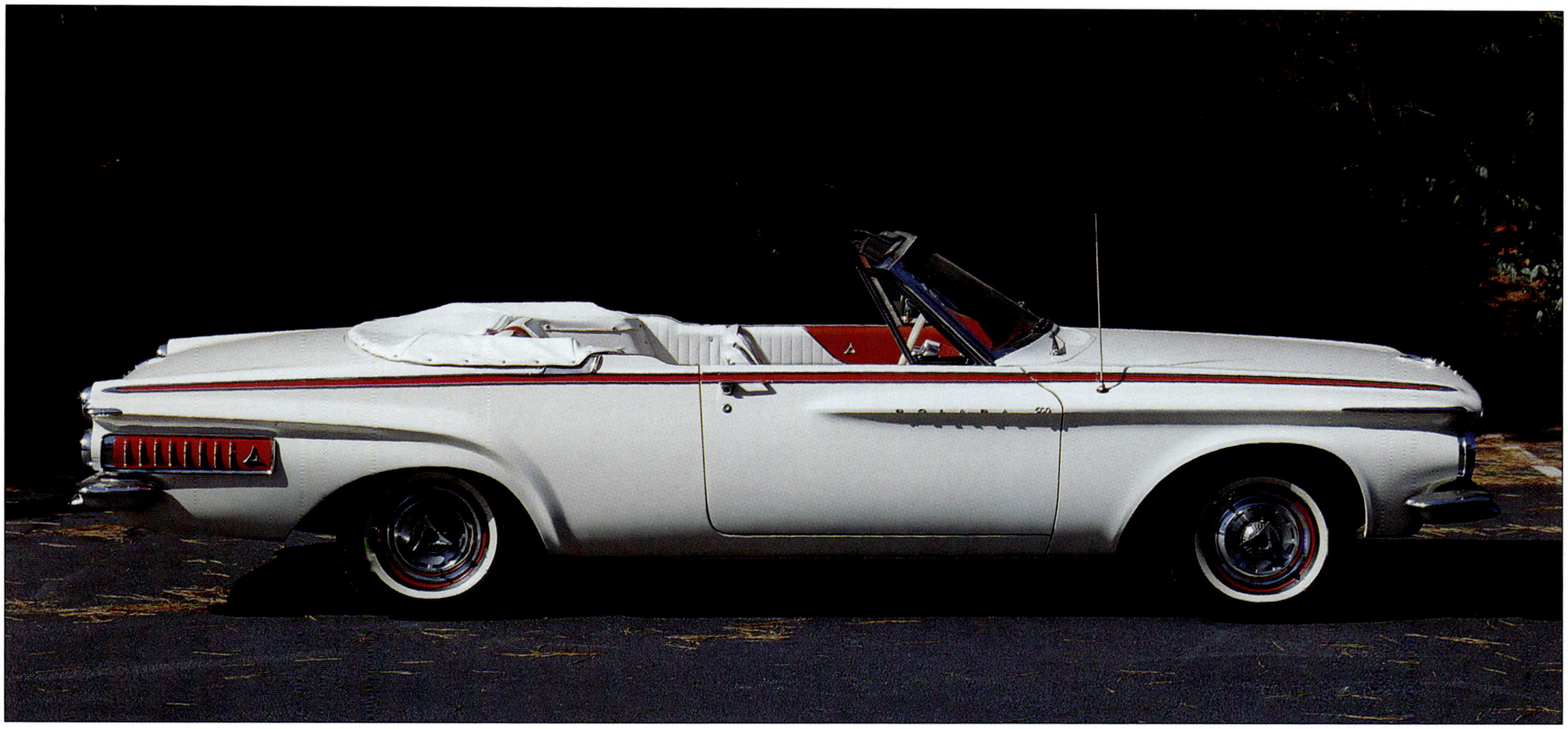

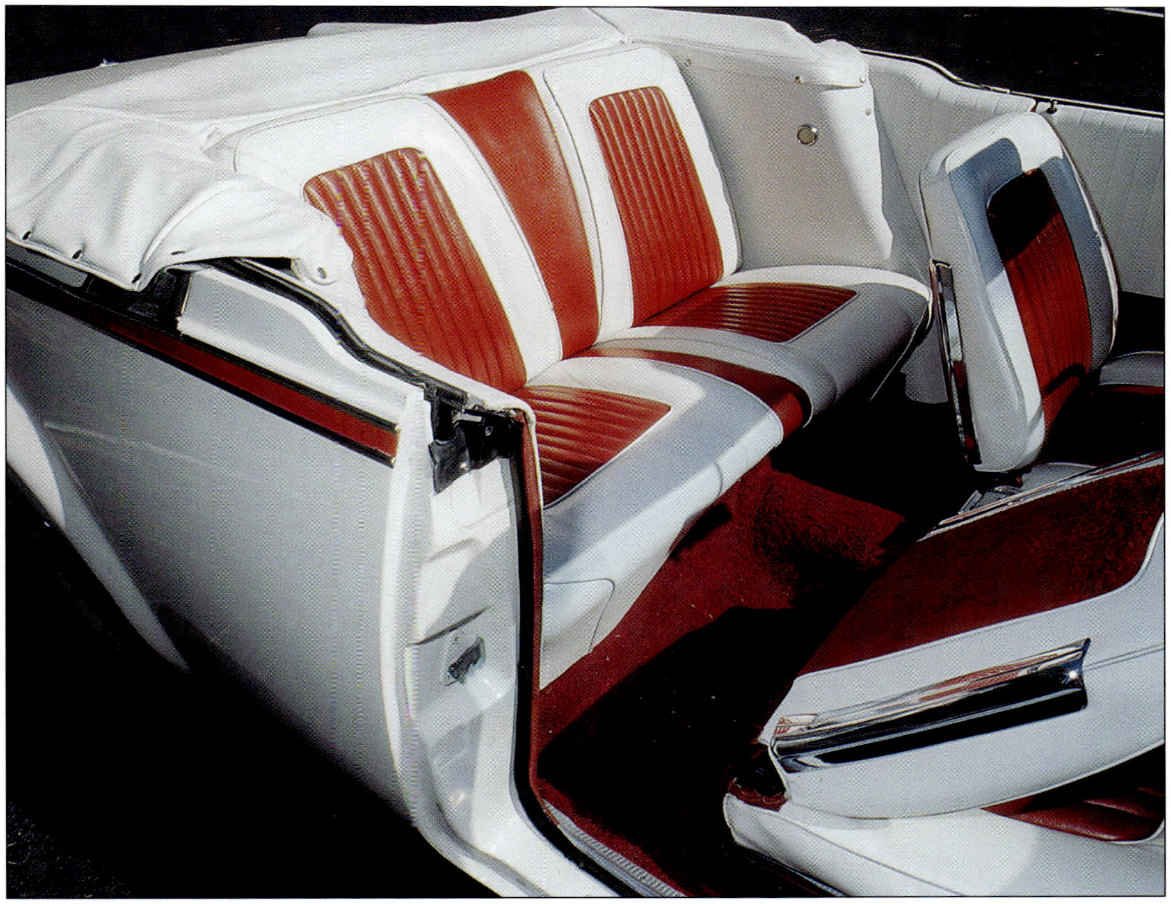

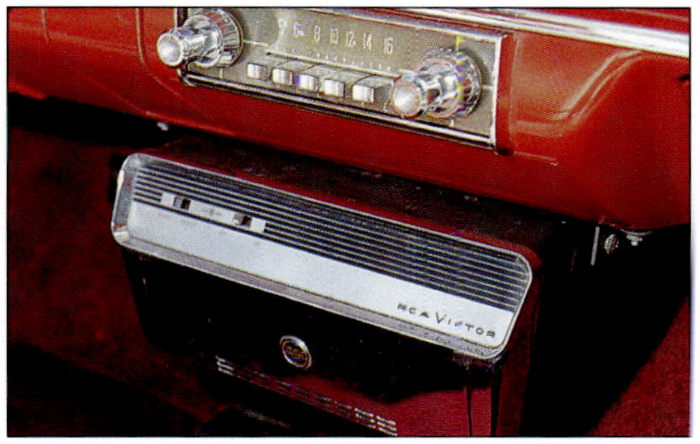
RCA Victor

1963 CHEVROLET IMPALA SS

With crisp new "Jet Smooth" styling and the most powerful V-8s in Chevy history, the big 1963 Impala SS was hard to beat. Still is, in fact—especially the hot-looking droptop.

Detroit's Big Three swore off racing in 1957, largely under pressure from the "safety lobby," yet within a few years they were back at it, sneaking special parts and low-key technical support to all manner of drivers and mechanics—unofficially, of course. Chevrolet was more active than most makes, and in 1961 it came out of the closet with a new SS package that added bucket seats, shift console, and other racy touches to the lush Impala convertible and hardtop coupe. At the same time, Chevy introduced its biggest V-8 yet, a 409 with 360 horsepower. The result was a legendary performer that cast a glow over the entire Chevy line.

The SS proved popular and immediately became an Impala sub-series. Enhancing its appeal for 1963 was Chevrolet's new "Jet Smooth" big-car styling, a crisp, broad-shouldered look that helped SS sales soar beyond 153,000. The SS convertible started at $3186 with an available 250-horsepower 327 V-8. Optional small-blocks offered up to 340 horses, and the "real fine" 409 big-block packed 340 to 425 depending on your courage and budget. Manual four-on-the-floor was available too, but a '63 SS in any form was a great way to go. Still is.

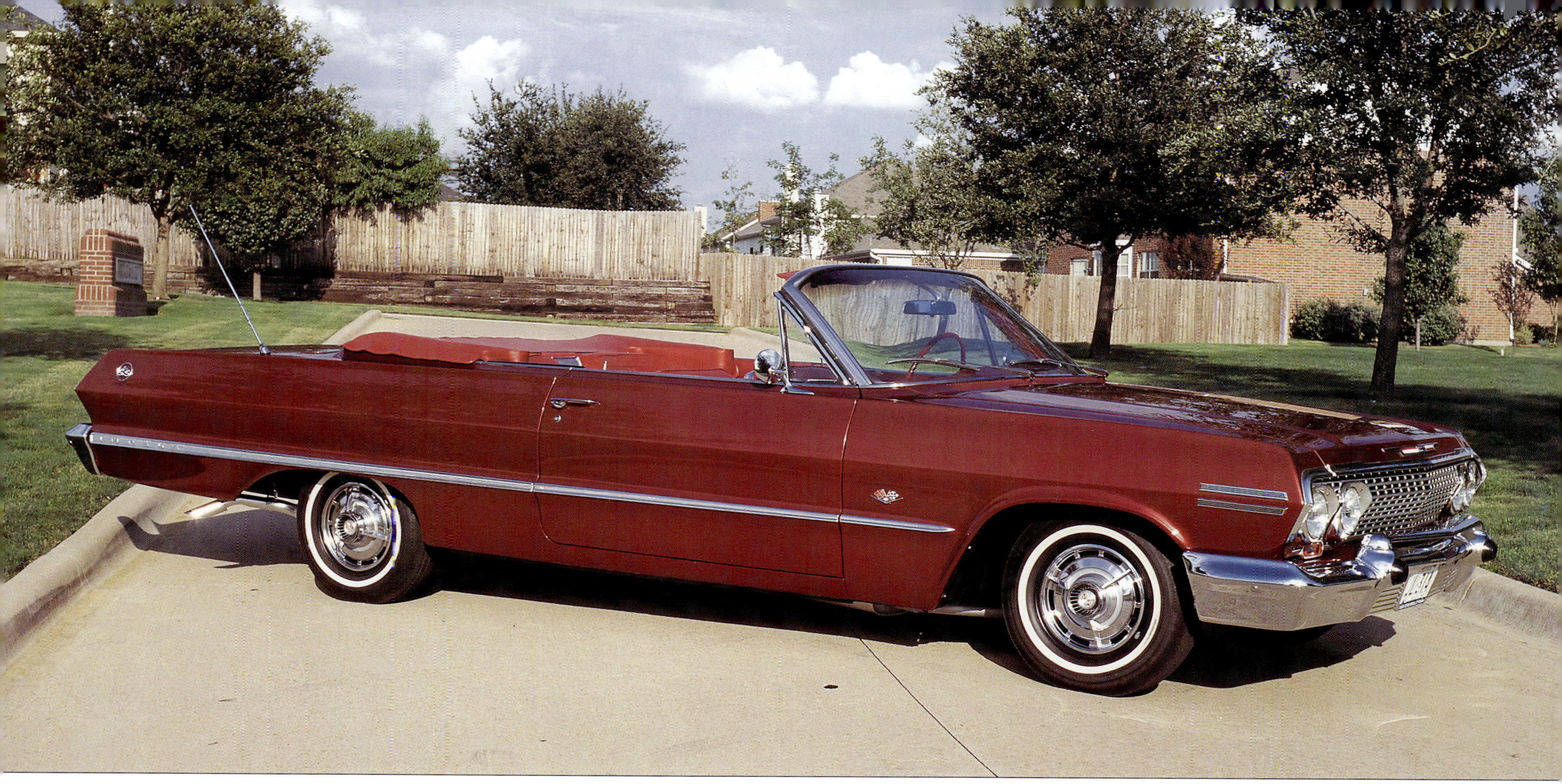

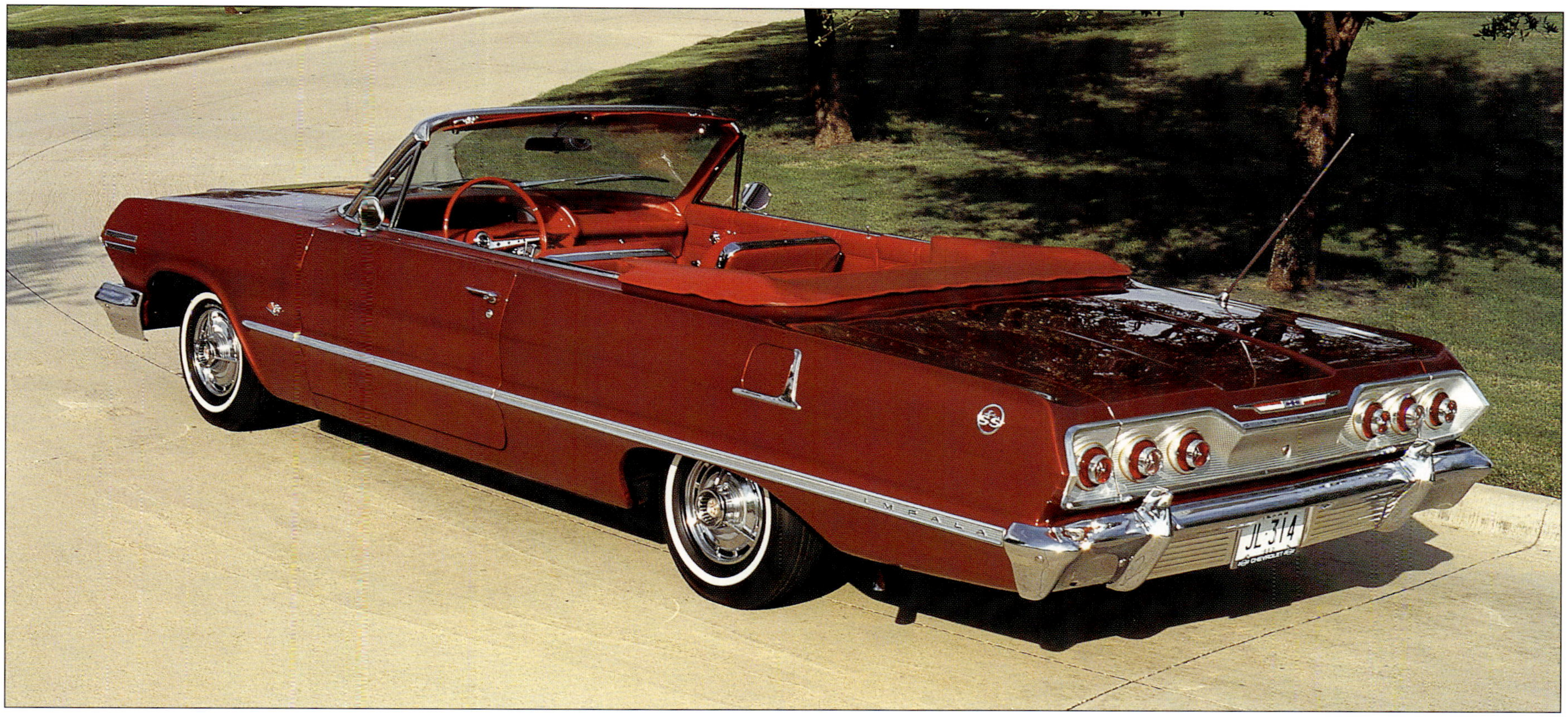
JL·314
CHEVROLET

1963 FORD FALCON FUTURA

In just three years Ford's Falcon was transformed from an economy car into a sporty compact offering bucket seats, V-8 power, even convertibles. Impossible? Not in the go-go '60s.

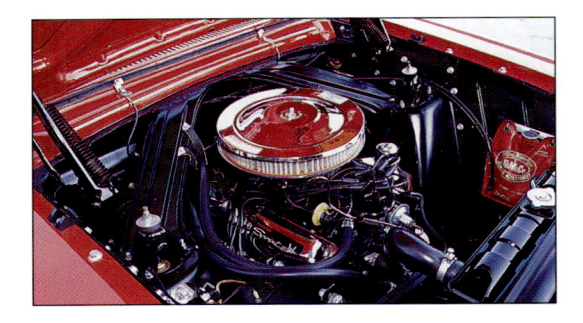

The Ford Falcon was the runaway hit among the Big Three's new 1960 compacts: cheap to buy, cheap to run, utterly conventional. But though Falcon made big money as a "consumer" car, Chevrolet's radical Corvair Monza quickly uncovered an even bigger market for sporty compacts with bucket seats, floorshift, and sprightly acceleration.

Ford, as it happened, was thinking sporty, too, so the Falcon was dressed up when Monza sales quickly took off. The first result was the 1961-62 Futura, a two-door sedan with a mini-Thunderbird buckets-and-console interior. Pushing harder for '63 was a separate Futura series with new convertible and hardtop coupe body styles. Both of these came two ways: six-cylinder standard and, at mid-season, V-8 Sprint. The Sprint package added $130 to the regular ragtop's $2470 base price, but was worth every penny. The reason was Ford's year-old 260-cubic-inch Challenger V-8, a revvy, modern design with 164 horsepower versus 101 for the mainstay 170-cid six. Even better, the V-8 could team with Falcon's first four-on-the-floor manual.

Sprints also came with good-looking wire wheel covers, tachometer, and bright engine rocker covers. A mid-year introduction limited convertibles to just 4602 (versus 31,192 standard Futuras), but the Sprint was a potent image boost for Falcon, especially as the basic 1960 styling was still intact. Adding even more luster were the Sprint hardtops that competed with distinction in European rallies during 1964-65.

But the Sprint wouldn't last beyond 1964. The reason was that Ford introduced an even sportier compact that year: the wildly successful Mustang.

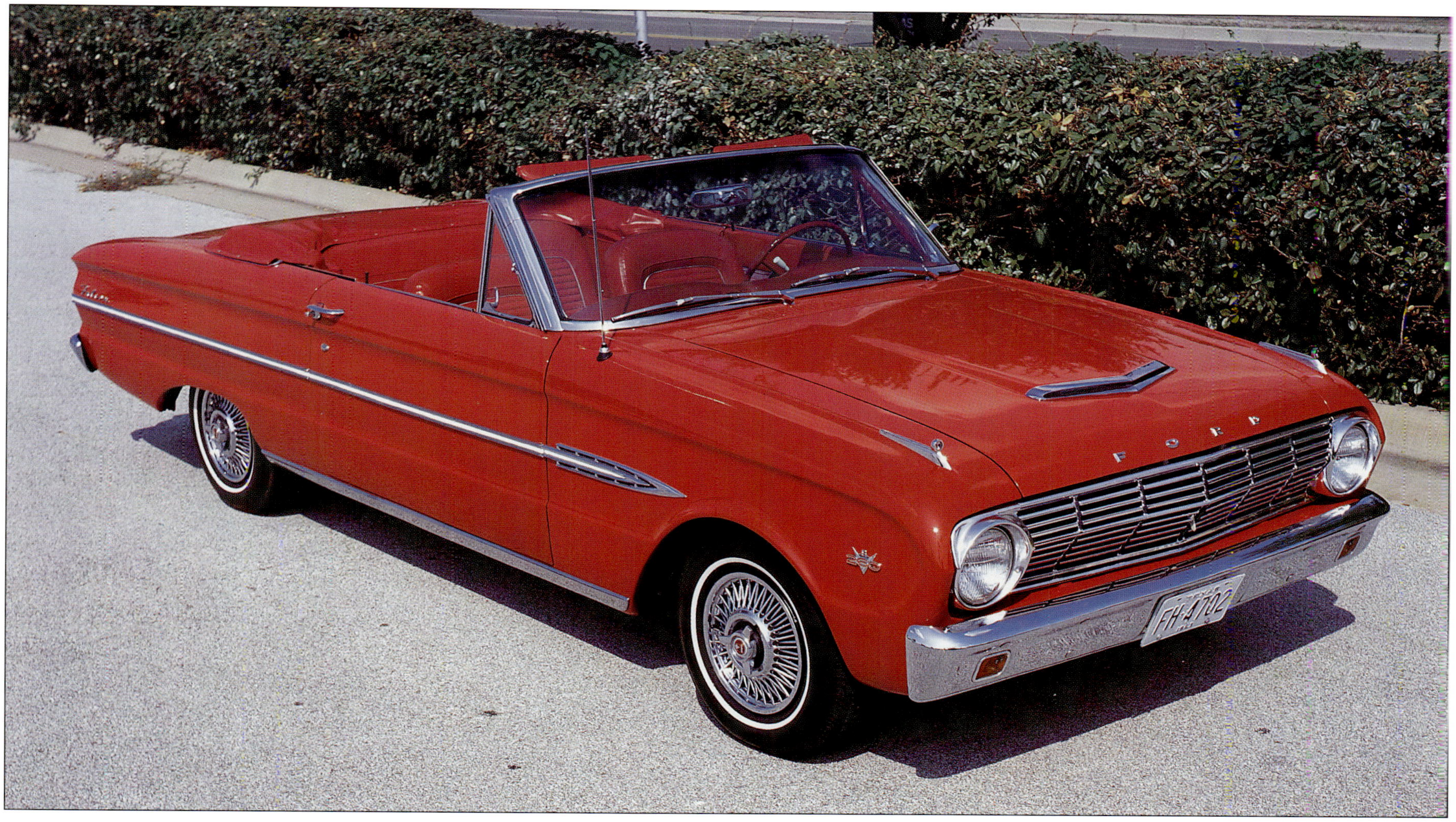

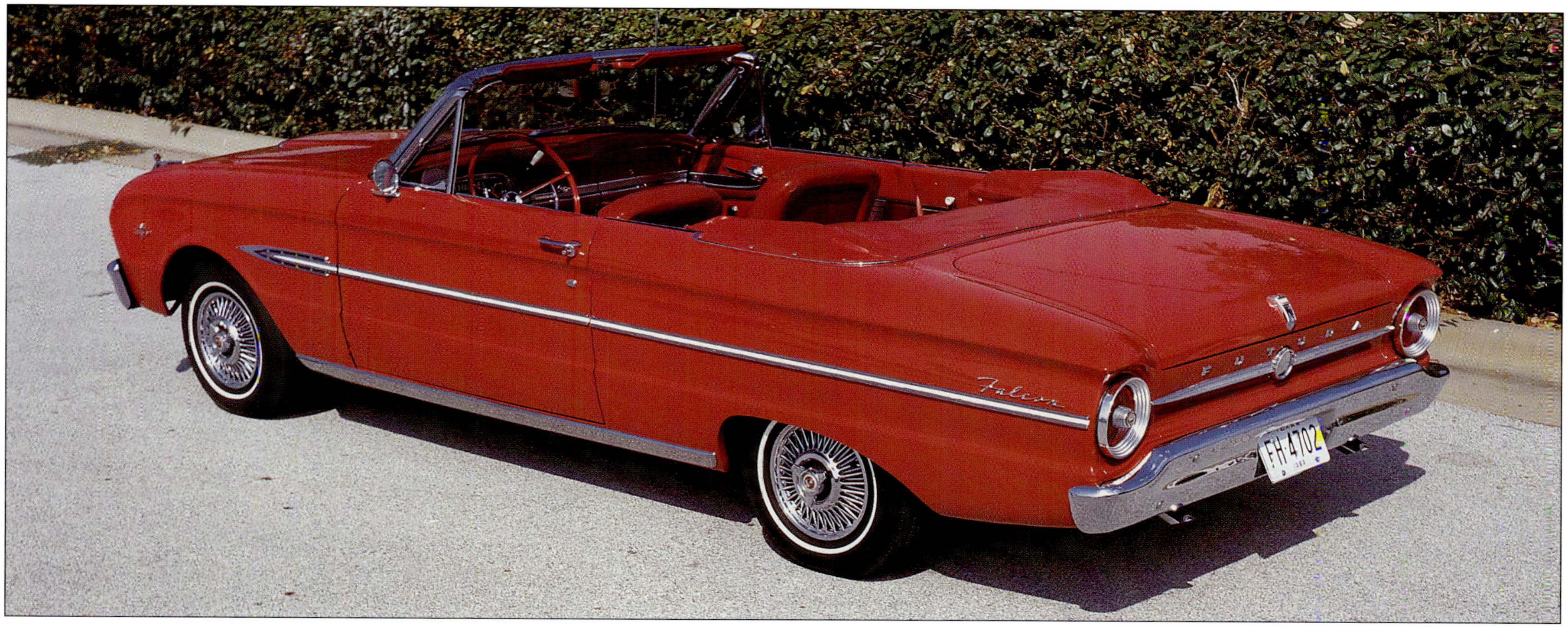

1963 PLYMOUTH SPORT FURY

Like Dodge, smaller big cars with offbeat styling cost Plymouth dearly in '62. Handsome new looks and new big-block power started turning things around for '63.

Plymouth made the same mistake as sister division Dodge by gambling on much smaller 1962 "standard" cars with offbeat Virgil Exner styling. But where Dodge remained ninth in industry production, Plymouth plunged from fourth to eighth.

Fortunately, Chrysler had a new styling chief in Elwood Engel, just recruited from Ford, and his hurry-up efforts produced nicely facelifted '63 standards that helped Plymouth reclaim fourth. Again topping the line was the Sport Fury, which returned from '62 as a convertible and hardtop coupe with standard all-vinyl bucket-seat interior and storming performance potential. Unlike regular Furys, Sports had a standard V-8, a mild 230-horsepower 318. Options ranged from a 265-bhp 361 through three 383s and on to a quartet of newly enlarged 426 big-blocks packing up to 425 bhp with "ram induction."

Plymouth built only 1516 Sport Fury ragtops for '62, so the 3836 delivered for '63 looked like quite a jump. But that's not very many by Detroit standards, one reason you so seldom see one now.

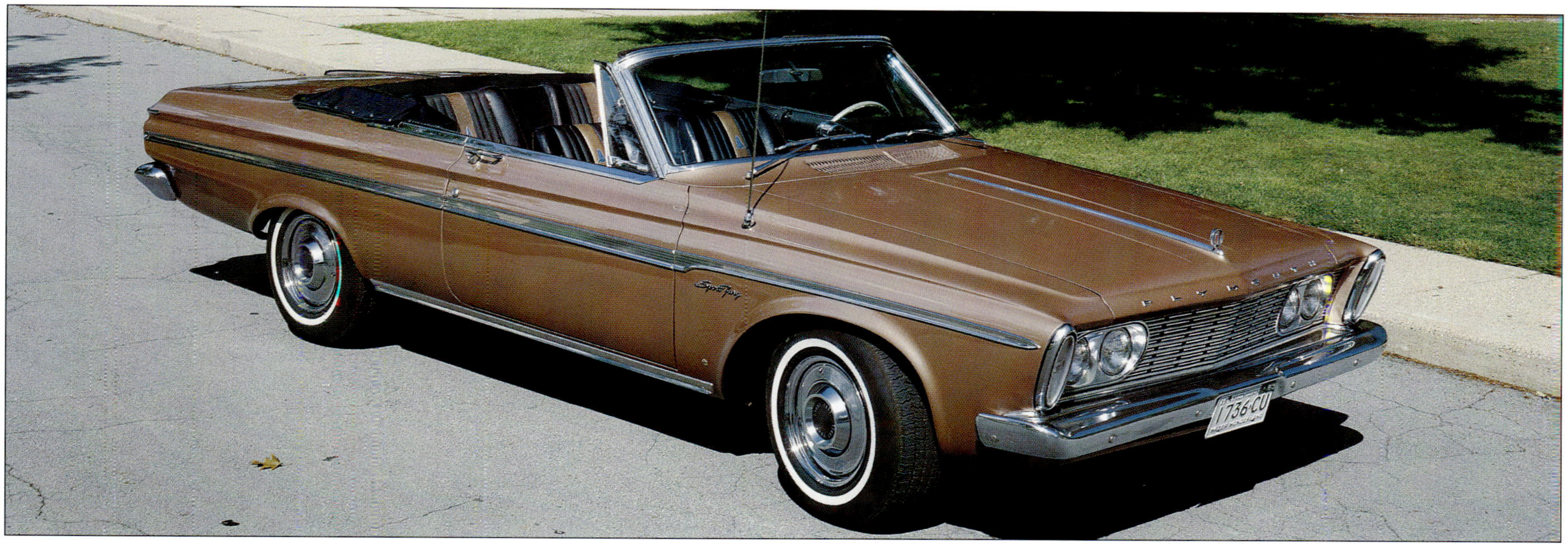

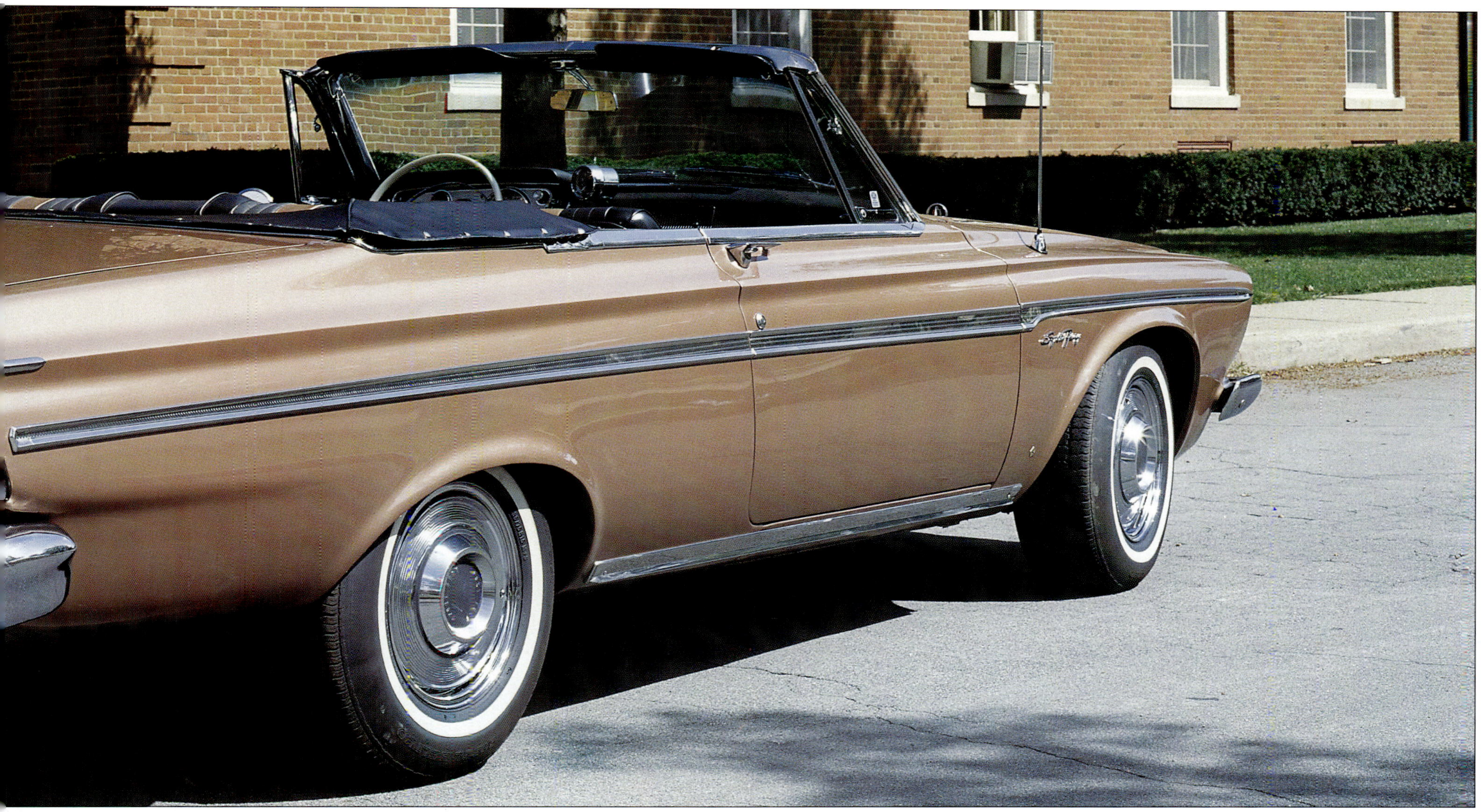

1963 STUDEBAKER LARK DAYTONA

After years of bumbling, Studebaker—by then the oldest surviving American marque—was sinking fast by 1963, and not even sporty cars like the Lark Daytona convertible could save it.

Studebaker was fighting for its life by 1963, but the end was already in sight. Even that year's daring new Avanti sports coupe couldn't save the venerable South Bend company after too many years of misguided management. Though the pert, cleverly conceived 1959 Lark compact provided a hopeful sales upturn, Studebaker began sliding again with the advent of Big Three compacts for 1960. A squarish '61 facelift didn't help. Nor did a more extensive Lark restyle for '62, bolstered by new bucket-seat Daytonas, including a $2679 convertible.

Prices were little changed for '63. So were the cars, which was the basic problem. Even the sporty Daytonas had an ancient low-power 169-cubic-inch six as standard, though Studebaker's trusty 259 V-8 was available with 180 or 195 horses, and there were 289s with 210, 225, and 240 bhp, the last achieved with "R1" supercharging.

But all this was just gilding on an elderly lily. Three years later, Studebaker finally faced reality and left the car business to the Big Three—and a growing pool of imports.

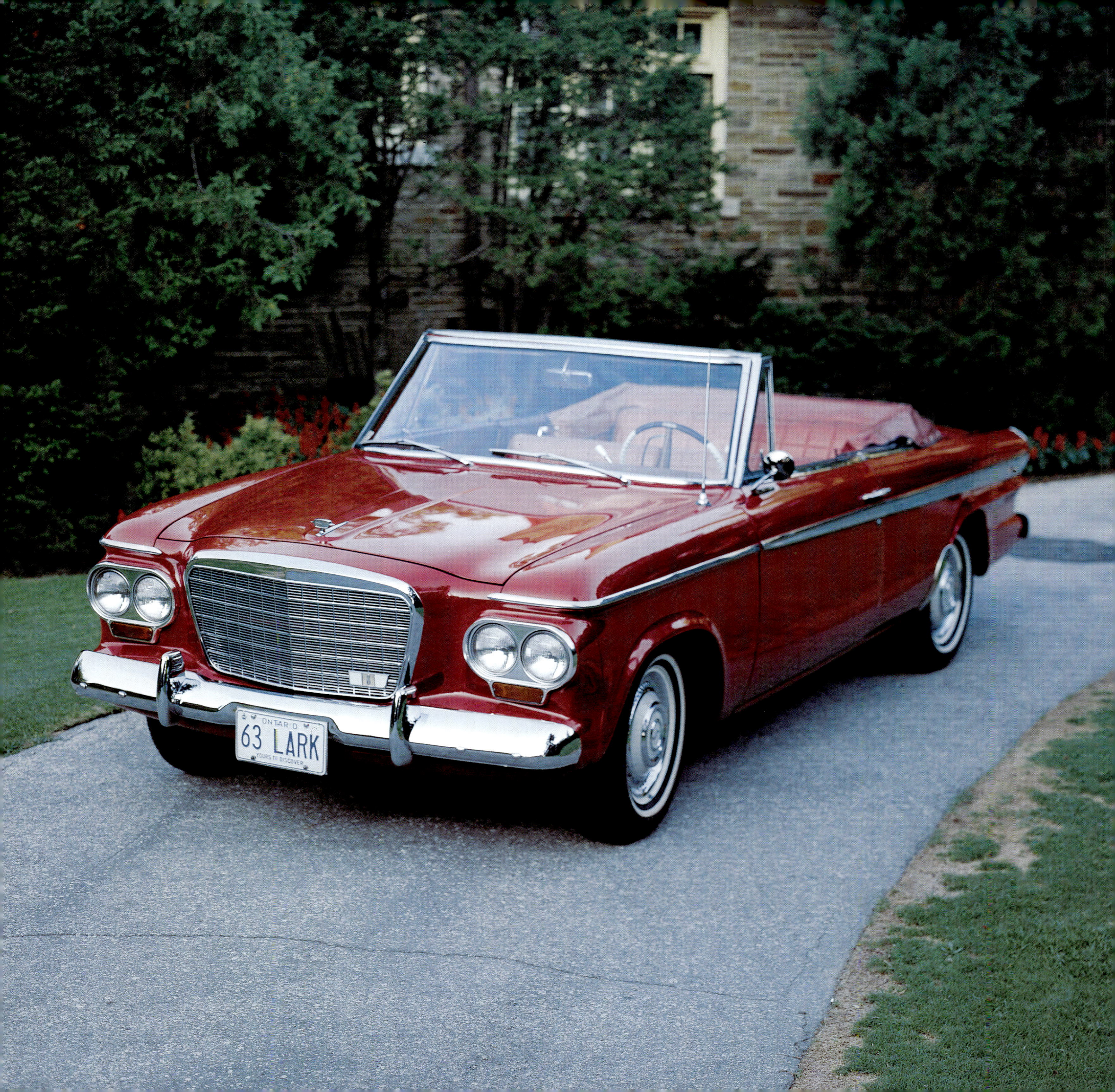
ONTARIO
63 LARK

1964 PONTIAC GTO

If not the absolute first "muscle car," Pontiac's hot, handsome 1964 GTO made the term a household word. And it offered amazing value: less than $4000 even for the ritzy ragtop.

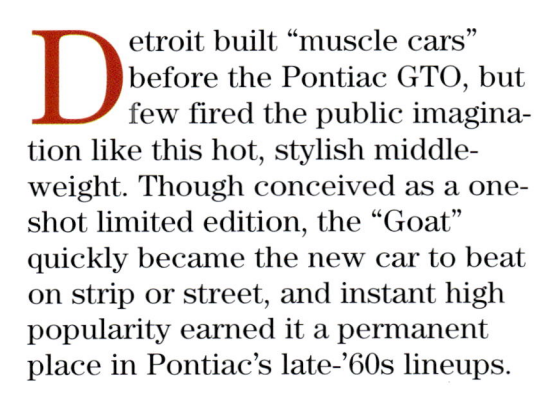

Detroit built "muscle cars" before the Pontiac GTO, but few fired the public imagination like this hot, stylish middleweight. Though conceived as a one-shot limited edition, the "Goat" quickly became the new car to beat on strip or street, and instant high popularity earned it a permanent place in Pontiac's late-'60s lineups.

The GTO debuted as a $300 option for Pontiac's 1964 Tempest coupe, hardtop, and convertible, which grew that year from compacts to handsome mid-sizers on a 115-inch wheelbase. Included were a 325-horsepower dual-exhaust 389 V-8 with three-speed manual floorshift, quick steering, stiff shock absorbers, and premium tires. From there you could order a 348-bhp Tri-Power engine, four-speed gearbox, limited-slip differential, metallic brake linings, and extra instruments. Starting at just $3500, a GTO convertible was cheap considering the performance potential.

Pontiac built only 6644 "Goat" ragtops for '64. We know a lot of folks who wish there'd been more.

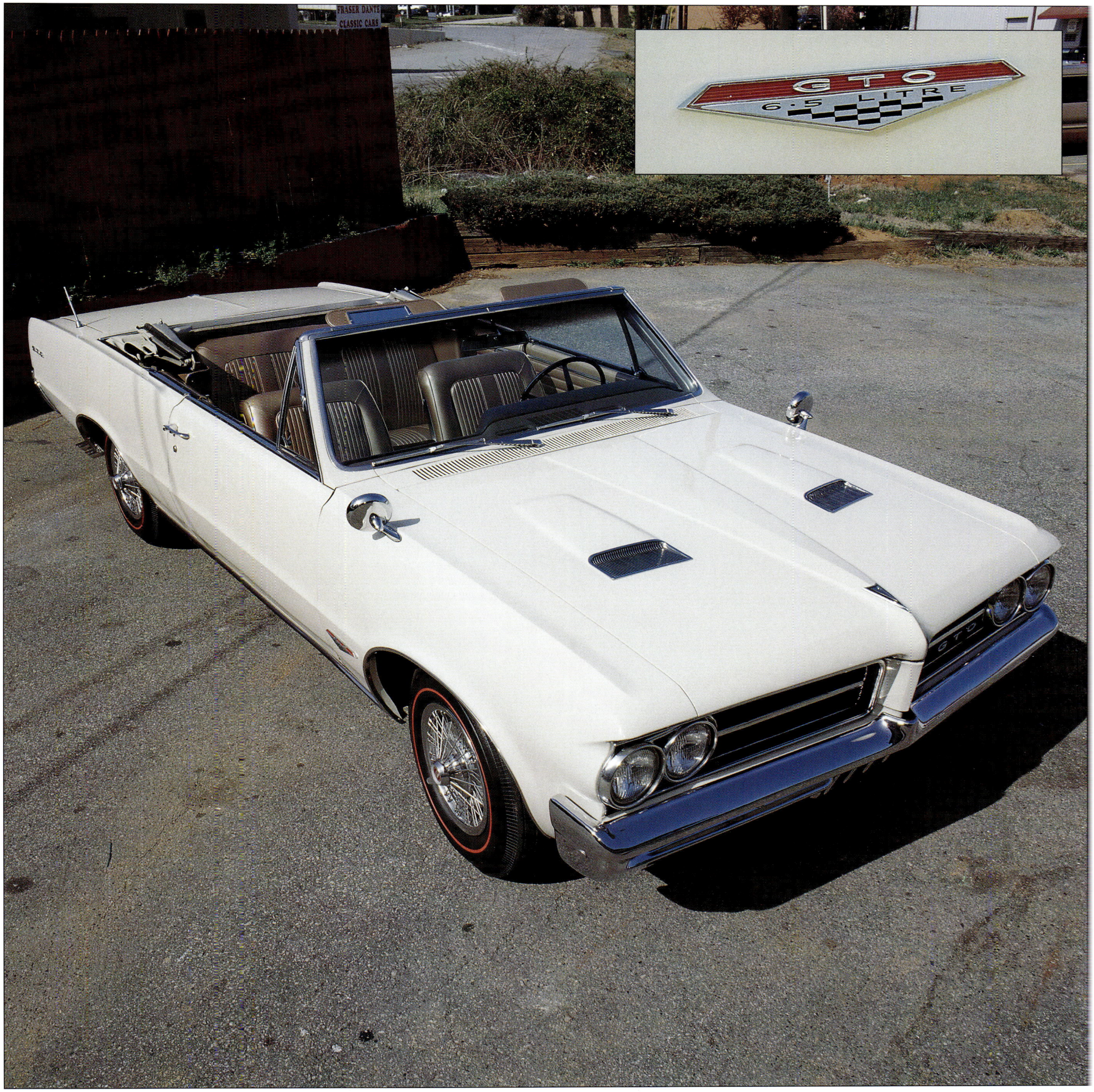
GTO
6.5 LITRE

1965 CHRYSLER 300L

Chrysler's legendary "letter-series" performance line ended with the 1965 300L—or so we thought. Today there's a new 300, but the thrill of a convertible isn't part of the resurrection.

For 34 years, the 300L was the last of the great performance Chryslers that began with the 1955 C-300, but that changed with the introduction of the 1999 300M. Is the M worthy of the great letter-series tradition? If you like V-6 "cab forward" sedans with front-wheel drive, yes. Otherwise, it's nothing like its burly V-8 predecessors.

The same might be said for the 300L hardtop and convertible. In 1965, Chrysler was into a fourth successful year peddling "standard" 300s that were barely sportier than low-line Newports. But that, plus fast-waning demand for sporty big cars, had made letter-series superfluous, so the L was the least special of the original line. Still, it had the same clean new styling and long 124-inch wheelbase as other '65 Chryslers, plus a 360-horsepower 413 V-8 that cost extra in plain 300s. But at $4618 for the convertible, the surcharge for an L amounted to over $700—a lot to pay for little more than distinct badging and the bigger engine—so sales totaled just 440 ragtops and 2405 hardtops.

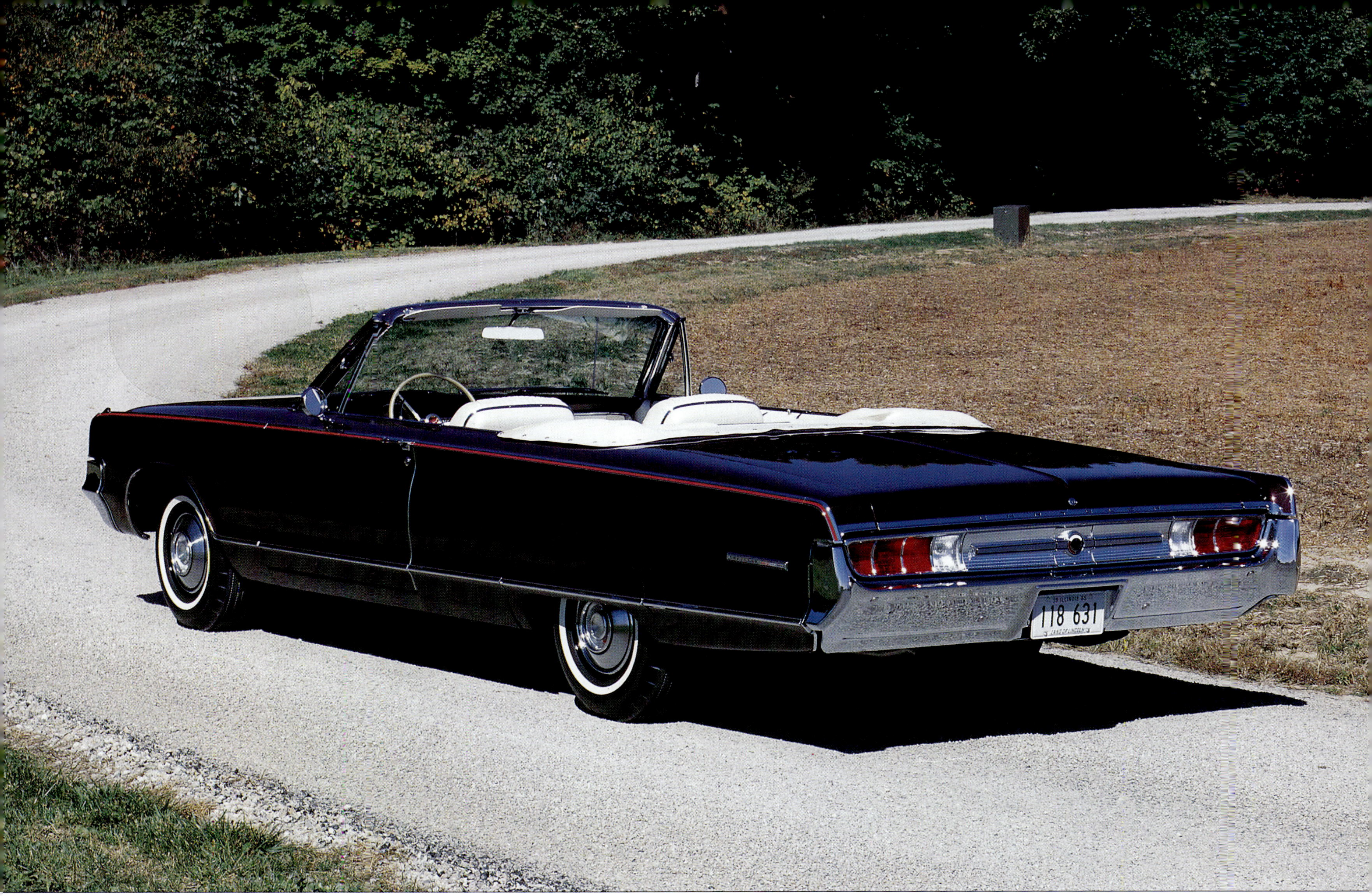
118 631

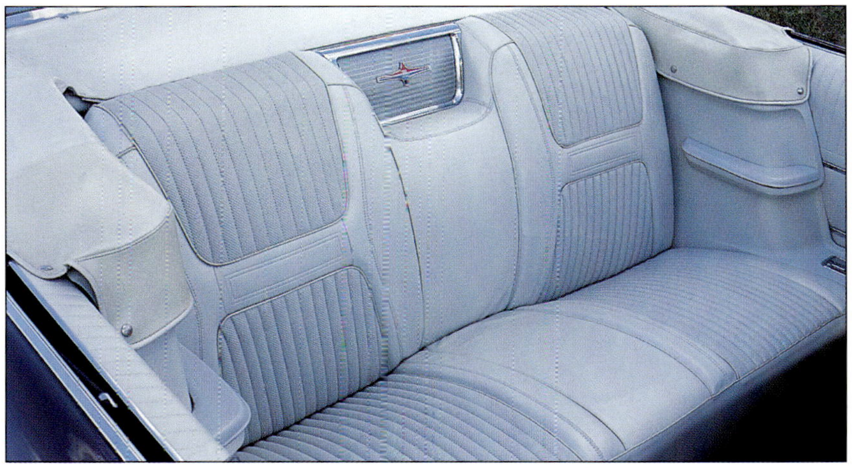

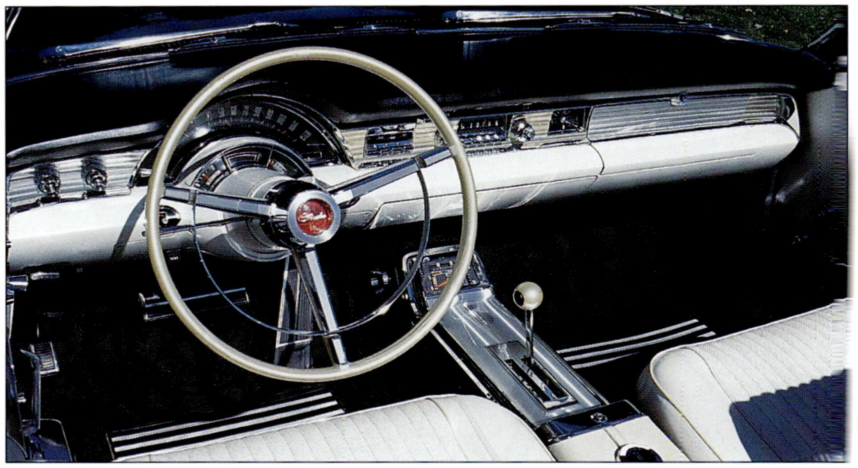

1965 FORD MUSTANG

A lot of people—including some 102,000 fliptop fans—happily succumbed to "Mustang Mania" in 1964-65. No wonder Ford's sporty new compact quickly became the hottest selling car in history.

Is there any self-respecting car lover who doesn't know about the original Mustang? Doubtful. Though just a humble Falcon in a sporty long-hood/short-deck suit, Mustang started a sales stampede to become the biggest success of the '60s. In the first extra-long model year, close to 681,000 found homes—a Detroit record—including nearly 102,000 convertibles. Everyone loved Ford's new "ponycar," and competitors rushed to copy it.

Besides lean good looks, Mustang appealed greatly for its low price. Even the rakish ragtop was an affordable $2614 to start, and the hardtop coupe was just $2368 advertised on Mustang's April 1964 debut. A "2+2" fastback arrived in September for the formal '65 model year.

Equally important was the mile-long options list that enabled buyers to personalize Mustangs any way they wanted. All models came with a lowly six-cylinder engine, but also three-speed floorshift transmission, full wheel covers, carpeting, and all-vinyl bucket-seat interior. Then you could add Cruise-O-Matic or four-speed manual; 260 and 289 V-8s with up to 271 lively horses; heavy-duty springs and shocks; power brakes; "Rally-Pac" tachometer and clock; center console; "Pony" interior trim; a GT package with foglights and firm suspension—the choices were almost limitless.

So is the enthusiasm for early Mustangs, which is why you still see so many of them today. "Mustang Mania," it seems, just can't be cured.

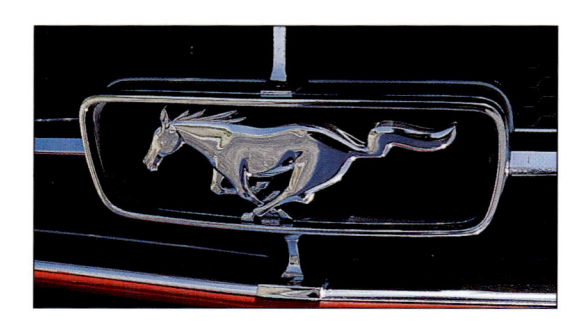

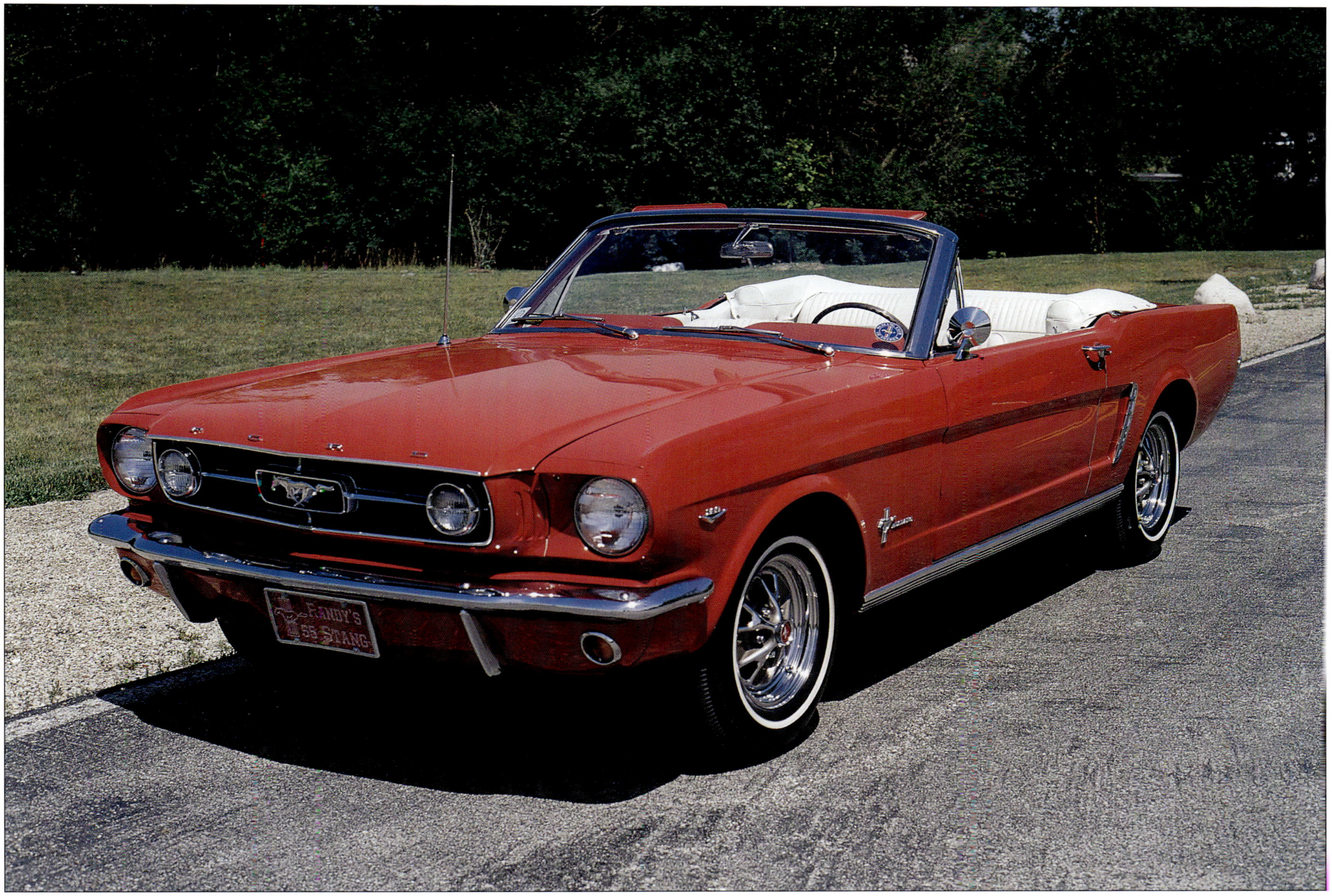

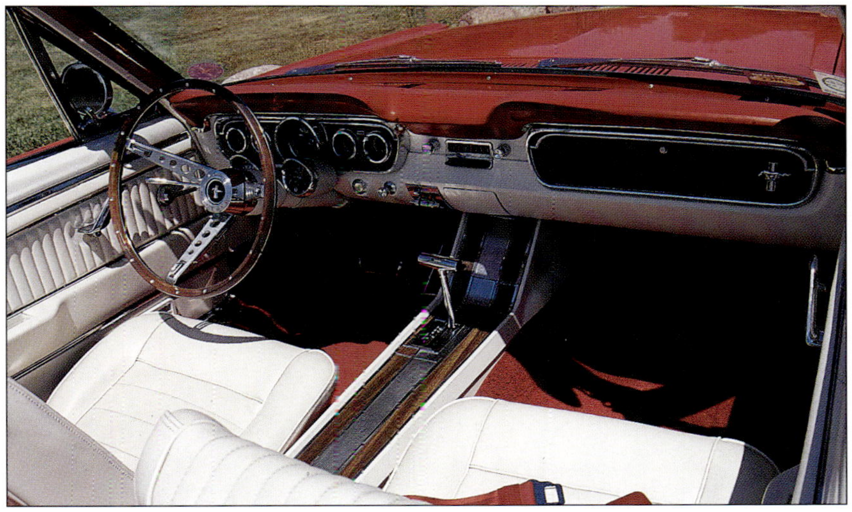

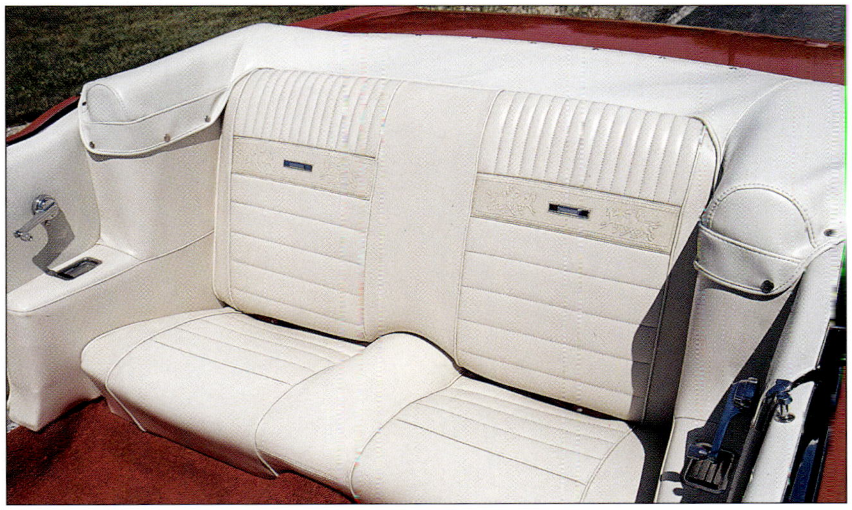

1965 RAMBLER AMERICAN 440

Ragtop Ramblers are few and far between, but the '65 American was one of the best. Too bad it lacked some sporty features that buyers craved, the reason sales were few and far between, too.

Nash bought Hudson to form American Motors in 1954, the year it built just 211 Rambler convertibles. The next ragtop Rambler didn't arrive until 1961, but it was much like that '54 model apart from much blockier styling.

For 1964, however, all Rambler Americans became much prettier thanks to a six-inch-longer wheelbase (now 106) and all-new unit bodies with simple, well-tailored lines and curved side glass. Led by the top-line 440-series convertible, they were arguably the year's most attractive Detroit compacts, and sales soared to a record 160,000-plus.

The '65 Americans were little changed, which meant another year for Rambler's old 195-cubic-inch six making just 90 or 125 horsepower. Nevertheless, all '65 Ramblers were breathlessly advertised as "The Sensible Spectaculars," and the 440 convertible was Detroit's most affordable ragtop at just $2418 to start. Even so, it wasn't yet available with V-8 power and sporty features like bucket seats, which likely explains why only 3882 of the '65s were delivered, down from 8907 for '64.

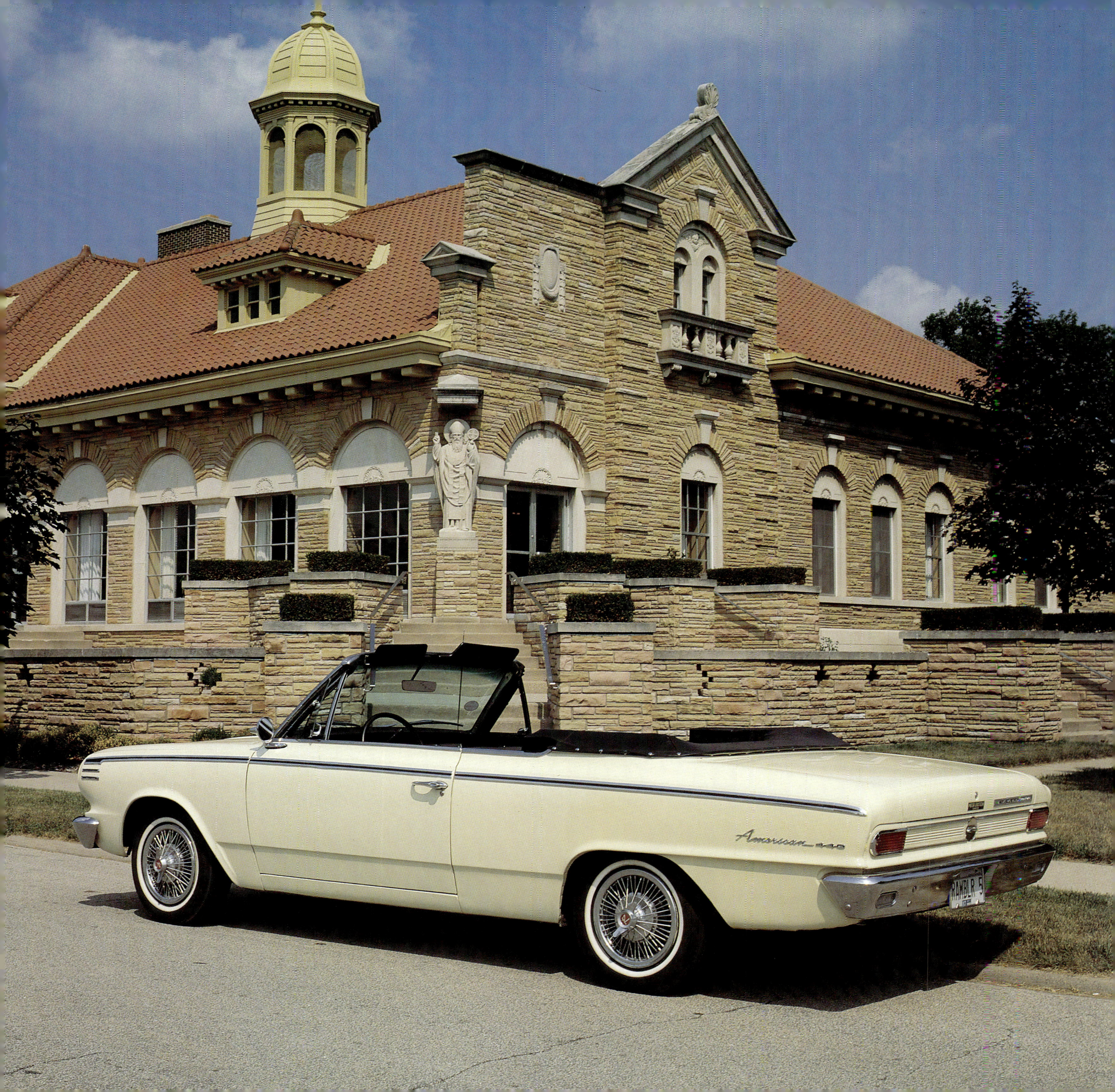
American
RAMBLR 5

1966 CHEVROLET CORVAIR MONZA

Chevrolet's Corvair failed as an economy car but succeeded as a sporty compact with the popular Monza model. The lovely 1965-69 models still look great—especially the seldom-seen ragtops.

As an economy compact, Chevrolet's rear-engine Corvair was too radical to sell well against Ford's conservatively designed Falcon. What saved Corvair's hide was the mid-1960 Monza coupe, which uncovered a vast new market for affordable cars with bucket seats, floorshift, and other sporty features.

Though Ralph Nader branded early Corvairs "unsafe at any speed," the odd handling of the tail-heavy swing-axle design was largely banished by 1964. The following year brought an even more effective independent rear suspension, plus gorgeous new styling. Coupes and sedans became pillarless hardtops, and the Monza convertible (new for '62) looked better than ever. A new Corsa hardtop coupe and convertible (replacing previous top-line Monza Spyders) carried a 140-horsepower version of Corvair's latest 164-cubic-inch air-cooled flat-six; a 180-bhp turbocharged version was optional. Other 'Vairs had either 95 standard horses or 110 optional.

The '65s sold quite well, but Corvair was now under attack by Ford's wildly popular new Mustang as well as Mr. Nader. Worse, Chevy decided to halt Corvair development to concentrate on a true Mustang-fighter, the eventual 1967 Camaro. With all this, the Corvair was doomed, and it departed after 1969. At least the jaunty Monza convertible hung on to the end, though in fast-diminishing numbers: 10,345 for '66, 2109 for '67, 1386 for '68, and a mere 521 for '69.

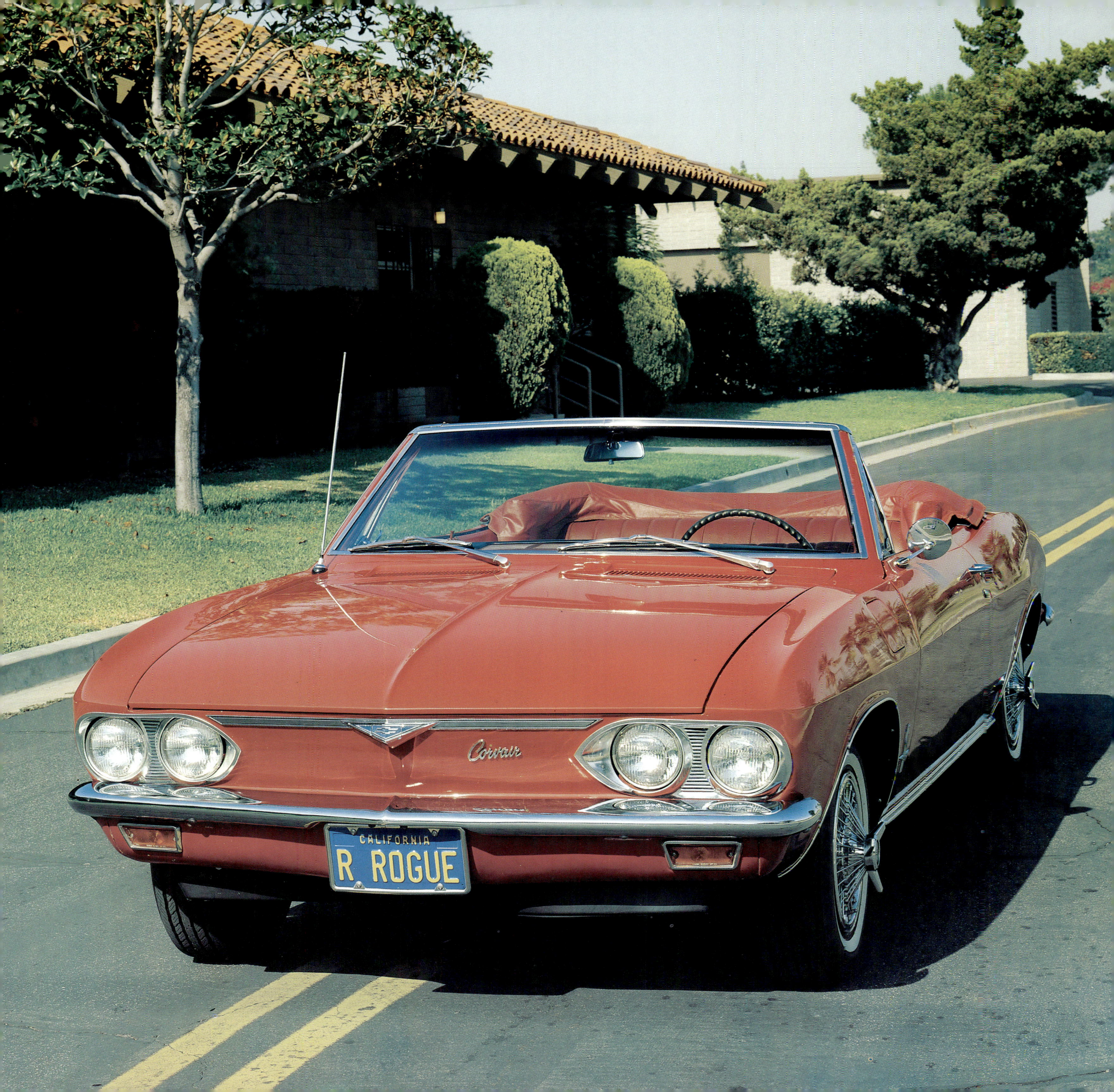

Corvair
CALIFORNIA
R ROGUE

1968 MERCURY PARK LANE

Mercury's lush Park Lane convertible hit the deck with a new 1968 option called "Yacht Paneling." Though an appliqué, it was a nice, nostalgic nod to the real woodies of the late 1940s.

Full-size late-'60s Mercurys were what we'd now call "near luxury" models, yet they were typically big, smooth, feature-laden machines. The all-new '65s were even grandly trumpeted as being "In the Lincoln Continental tradition," especially their square, formal styling. A more fulsome look arrived for '67, when Mercury billed itself "The Man's Car." How times have changed!

Mercury's big '68s were not much changed, still riding a 123-inch wheelbase and offering V-8s up to 428 cubic inches, but there was an interesting new option called "Yacht Paneling." Restricted at first to the top-line Park Lane fastback and $3822 convertible, this involved woody-look side trim like that on Colony Park wagons. As a full-length decal, Yacht Paneling wasn't structural like the real wood on Mercury's 1946 Sportsman convertible, but it was no less distinctive. However, it was none too popular either, lasting only this one year. Of the 1112 Park Lane ragtops built for '68, just a handful were Yacht Paneled, and a mere 15 are known to exist today. Sometimes, it just doesn't pay to go "retro."

114

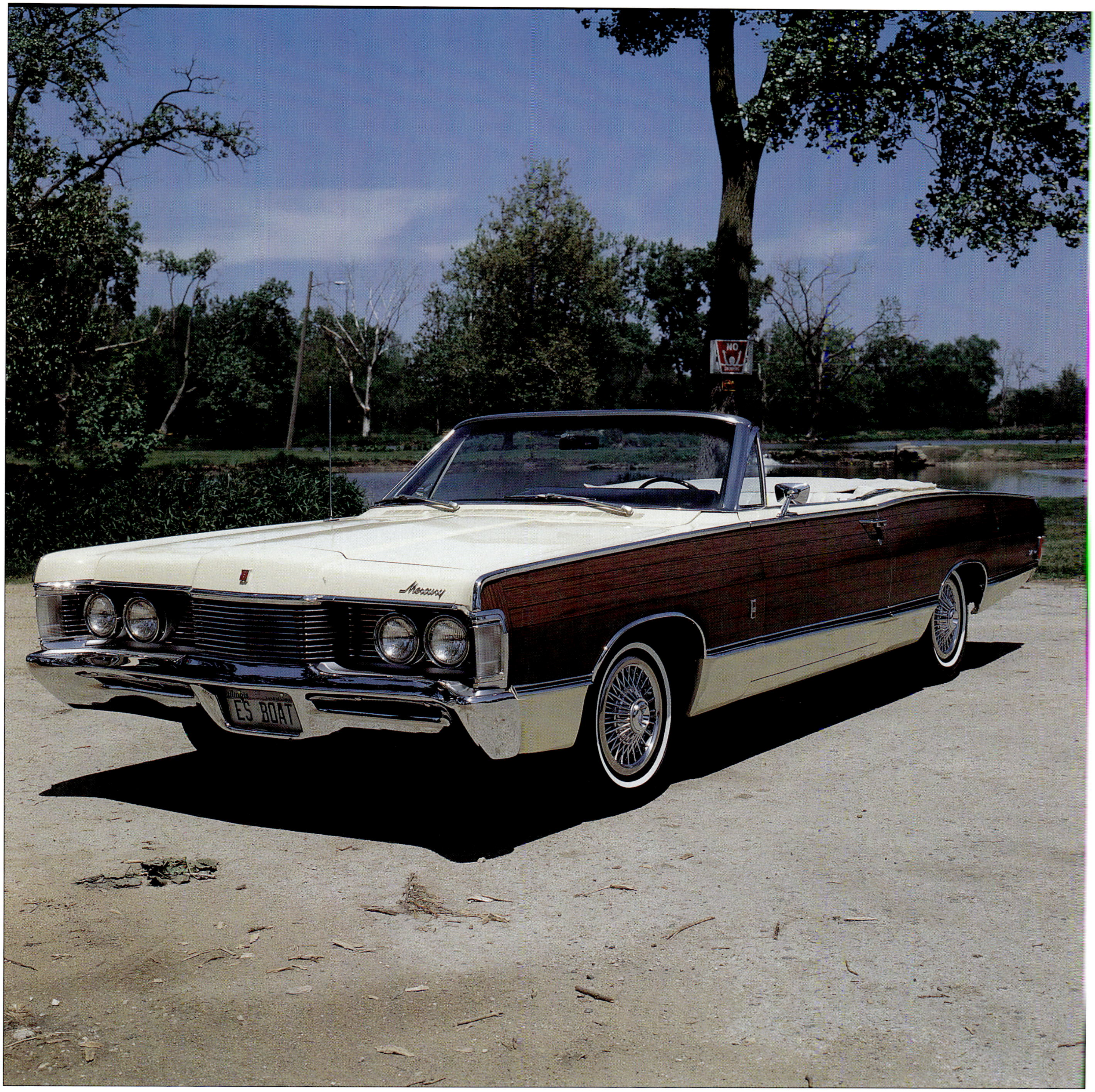
Mercury
ES BOAT

1969 PLYMOUTH ROAD RUNNER

Plymouth's new Road Runner was as quick as the cartoon bird and far cheaper than other muscle cars. Convertibles were the only thing fans might have wanted. Plymouth obliged for 1969.

Plymouth's new 1968 Road Runner was the first "budget" muscle car and an instant hit. A "Beep-Beep" horn and Warner Bros. cartoon-bird insignia identified it. So did a refreshing absence of costly, speed-robbing frills. Instead you got a 335-horsepower 383 V-8, four-on-the-floor, big boots, and firm suspension. A testosterone-packed 426 Hemi was optional. Taxi-plain interior? Who cared? The starting price was just $2896.

But success tends to breed excess in Detroit, and some plushing up occurred for 1969. Among the additions was a $3313 convertible that attracted only 2126 leadfoots versus some 82,000 coupes and hardtops. Today, the '69 ragtop Runner is an even rarer bird, and collectors pursue it like Wile E. Coyote.

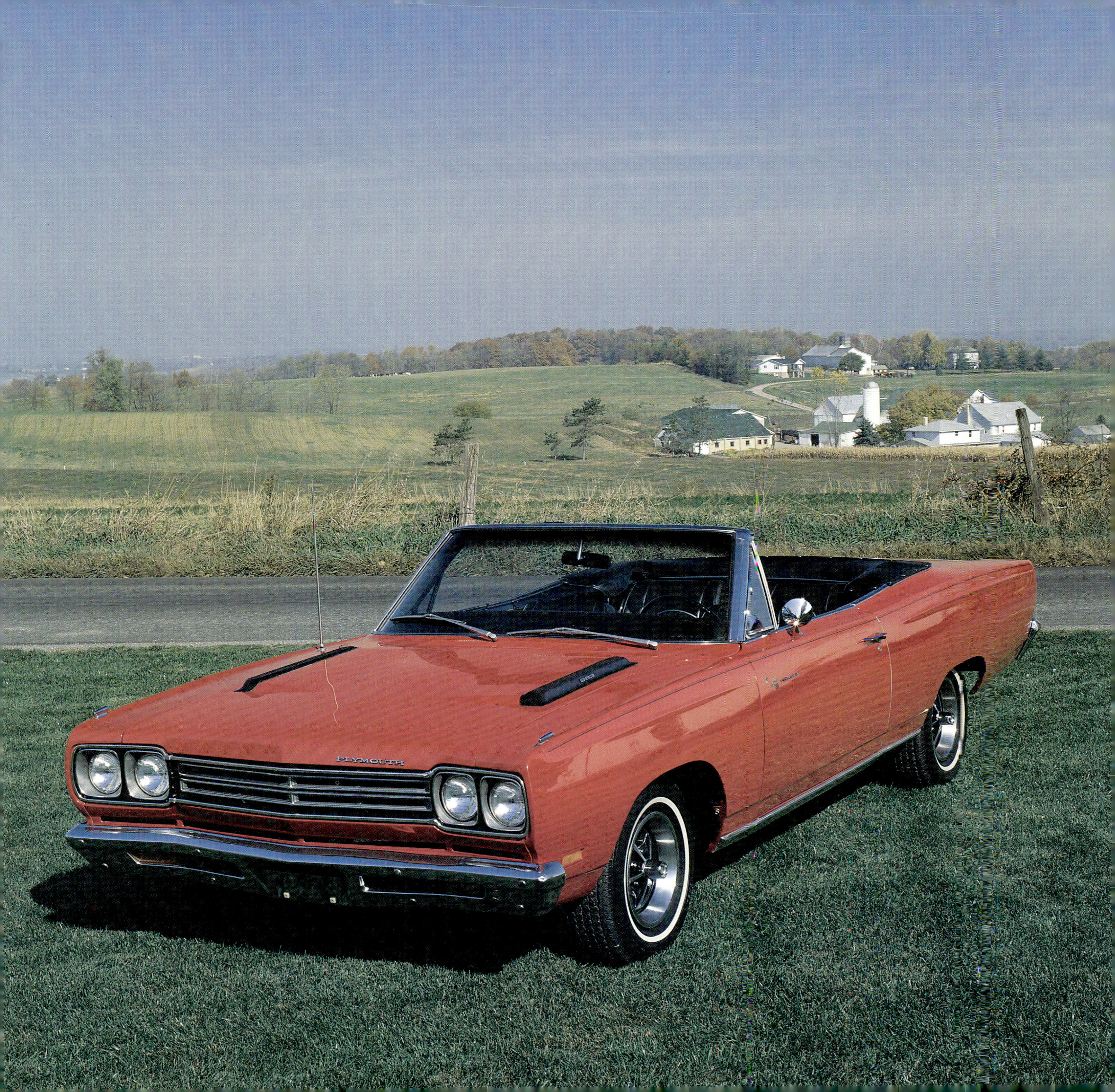
PLYMOUTH

1969 SHELBY GT-500

The rare Shelby Mustangs not only looked racy but had performance to match. Even the relatively posh '69 GT-500 convertible was a force to reckon with in a stoplight drag race.

Take a Mustang, heat up the engine, mix with an artfully race-tuned chassis, then add more "competition" features inside and out. That was Carroll Shelby's recipe for turning Ford's new low-priced "ponycar" into a credible track performer. The result was more than credible, as Shelby's GT-350 Mustangs won most every sports-car race around in 1965-66.

Yet the no-compromise flavor of those first fastbacks was quickly watered down with extra size and fluff. The restyled '67 GT-350 was not only heavier but gained a burly big-engine brother, the GT-500.

The following year introduced convertible versions of both. By 1969, the Shelby GTs were just limited-production custom Mustangs. They were even built by Ford.

Still, a '69 GT-500 turned heads like nothing else, and though its 428-cubic-inch V-8 was available in Mustangs, it made at least 65 more horsepower in Shelbys, a mighty 400 advertised. But this tasty confection cost a steep $5027, so only 335 ragtop 500s were sold for '69, plus a spoonful of reserialed "1970" models. The GT-350 was even scarcer at only 194, plus a dollop of carryovers. It was the last of a great line.

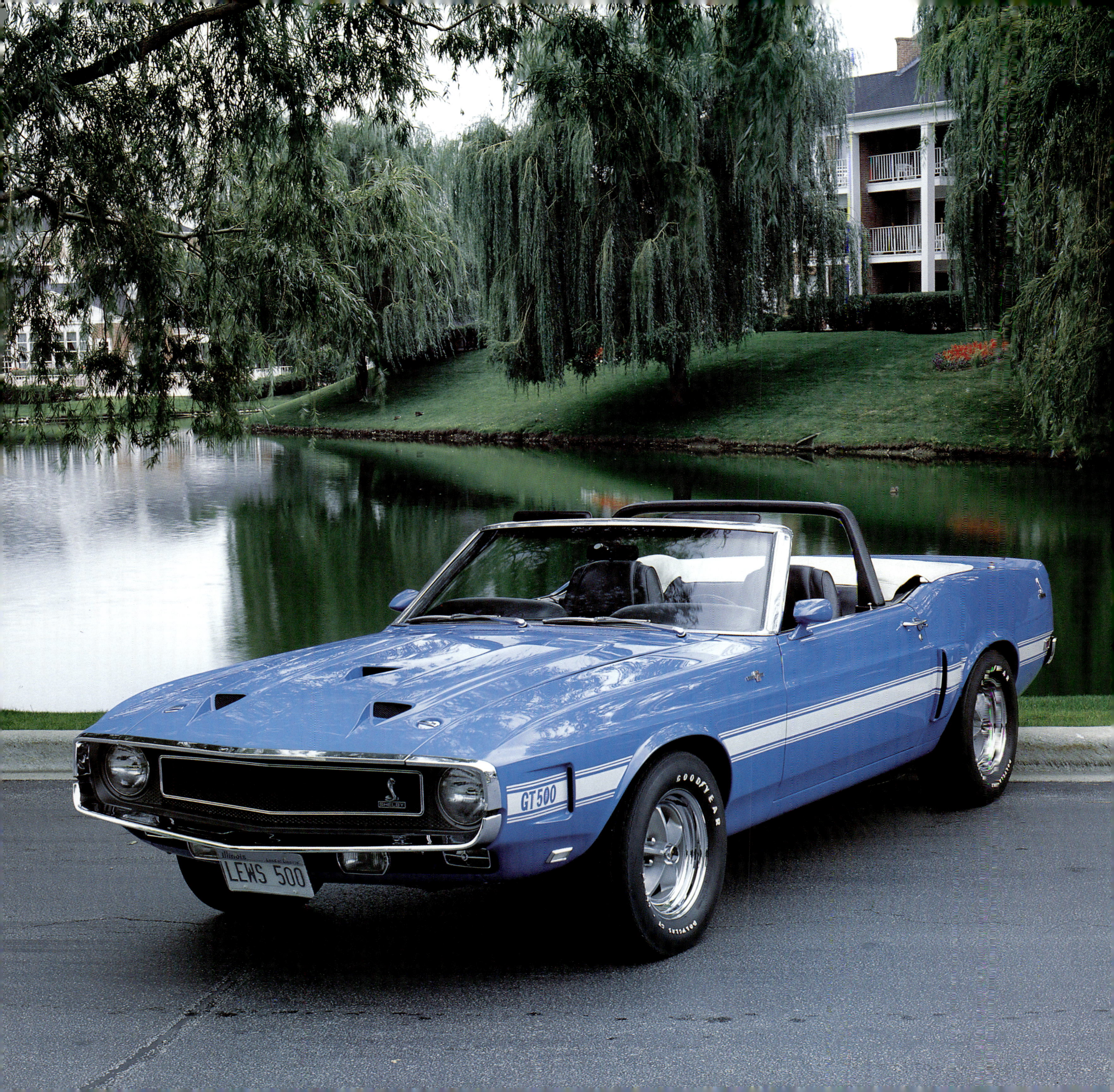
GT500
LEWS 500
GOODYEAR

1973 BUICK CENTURION

Buick's short-lived Centurion fought a brave battle in the early '70s to keep the convertible alive. That it did—but not for long.

As the '70s dawned, convertible sales had already fallen sharply from their peak in 1965. That must surely have been on the minds of Buick execs as they approved plans for the redesigned full-size cars that appeared in 1971.

But that wasn't the only reason to balk. Though ever glamorous, convertibles would be costly to produce for the small anticipated volumes, and there were rumors that Washington might enact accident rollover standards that would effectively outlaw ragtops.

Nevertheless, Buick continued full-size convertibles in the new generation, though the best-seller of the bunch, the big Electra, didn't renew its offering. Slotted in as the top droptop was the new Centurion, replacing the venerable performance-oriented Wildcat nameplate that was evidently deemed a liability in an era when "performance" was becoming a dirty word. Continuing as the "entry-level" full-size Buick was the LeSabre, which also offered a convertible at about $350 less than the similar Centurion.

Centurion's campaign proved brief. Available in upscale convertible, hardtop coupe, and hardtop sedan body styles, the name lasted only through 1973. By then it contained Buick's only ragtop offering, a $4534 luxo-cruiser with standard 175-horsepower 350 V-8. Optional was a massive 455 with 225 bhp. In both cases, clean air dictated mild tuning, though the horsepower figures reflected the new net measure, not the inflated gross quote of old.

Sales of 5739 Centurion convertibles in 1973 were higher than those of any single Buick ragtop model since 1970—and higher than they would ever be again. With the death of the Centurion name, the convertible was adopted by the LeSabre line through '75. After that, Buick abandoned convertibles until 1982, when the first-ever ragtop Riviera sought to regain the company's past glories.

21

1973 MERCURY COUGAR XR-7

Mercury's new-for-'67 sports-luxury Cougar took two years to get into ragtops, then quickly bailed out after 1973. Cougar has been many different things since, but not a convertible.

The Cougar name has graced more different cars over the years than "Save the Whales" bumper stickers: dragstrip demons, Ford Thunderbird clones, even station wagons. In 1973, however, Cougar was in the seventh and final year of its original concept as "Mercury's Mustang," a more luxurious and "mature" version of Ford's popular ponycar.

But times were a-changing, and Mustang had ballooned to heroic new proportions for 1971. Accordingly, Cougar did too, adopting an even grander 113-inch wheelbase and decidedly big-Merc styling. Though a mighty 429 V-8 was available that year with 370 gross horsepower, rising insurance rates and a withering performance-car market reduced '73 Cougars to a trio of detuned 351s with a maximum of 264 net bhp.

Cougar's first convertibles were '69s. The last were '73s: a $3726 base model and an upscale $3903 XR-7 (as shown here). Few were built—1284 and 3165, respectively. Sadly, there's not been another one since.

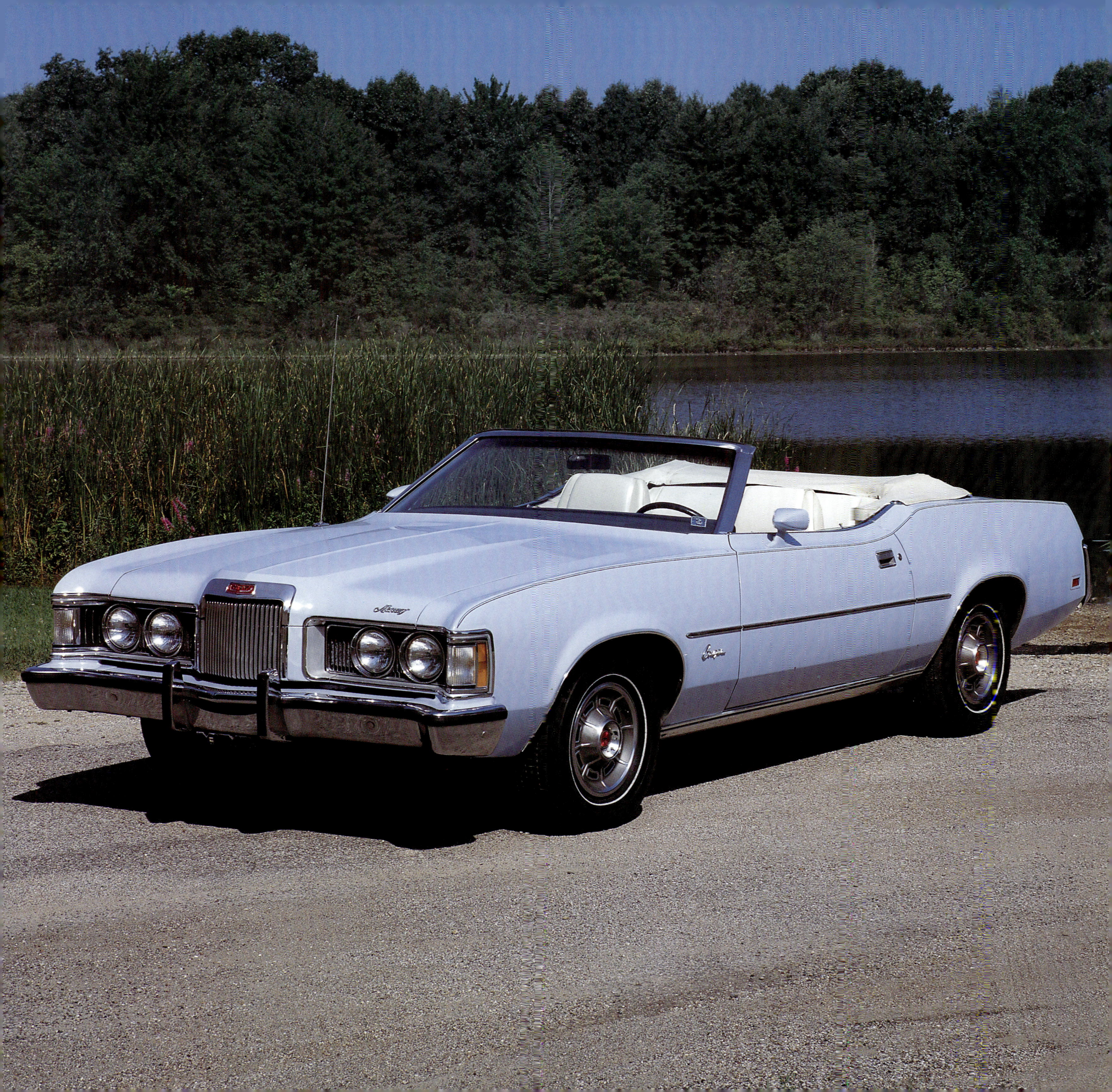

1975 CHEVROLET CAPRICE CLASSIC

Chevy actually built more of its "last" 1975 Caprice convertibles than it did '74s. No matter. As a final fling with flamboyant fliptops, the '75s are now too precious and few.

Here's a funny thing: Many of Detroit's "last convertibles" were more numerous than earlier models. Take Chevrolet's last big ragtop, the '75 Caprice, which saw 8349 copies versus 4670 for the similar '74. Well, that's what happens when people hear that something is endangered and rush to buy before it's all gone.

Chevy's full-size convertible had long been an exclusive member of the top-line Impala series when the Caprice bowed in 1965 as an even finer, more luxurious big bow-tie that eventually overtook Impala in sales. The ragtop belatedly migrated to the Caprice camp for '73, allowing Chevy to clear more money on each one. Still, the '75 was reasonably priced for the day at $5113, which included rich upholstery, major power assists, and a smooth (if thirsty) 175-horsepower 400 V-8 linked to Turbo Hydramatic transmission.

Of course, there have been other ragtop Chevys since, but none as sumptuous as this Caprice. And sadly for convertible lovers, there probably won't be again.

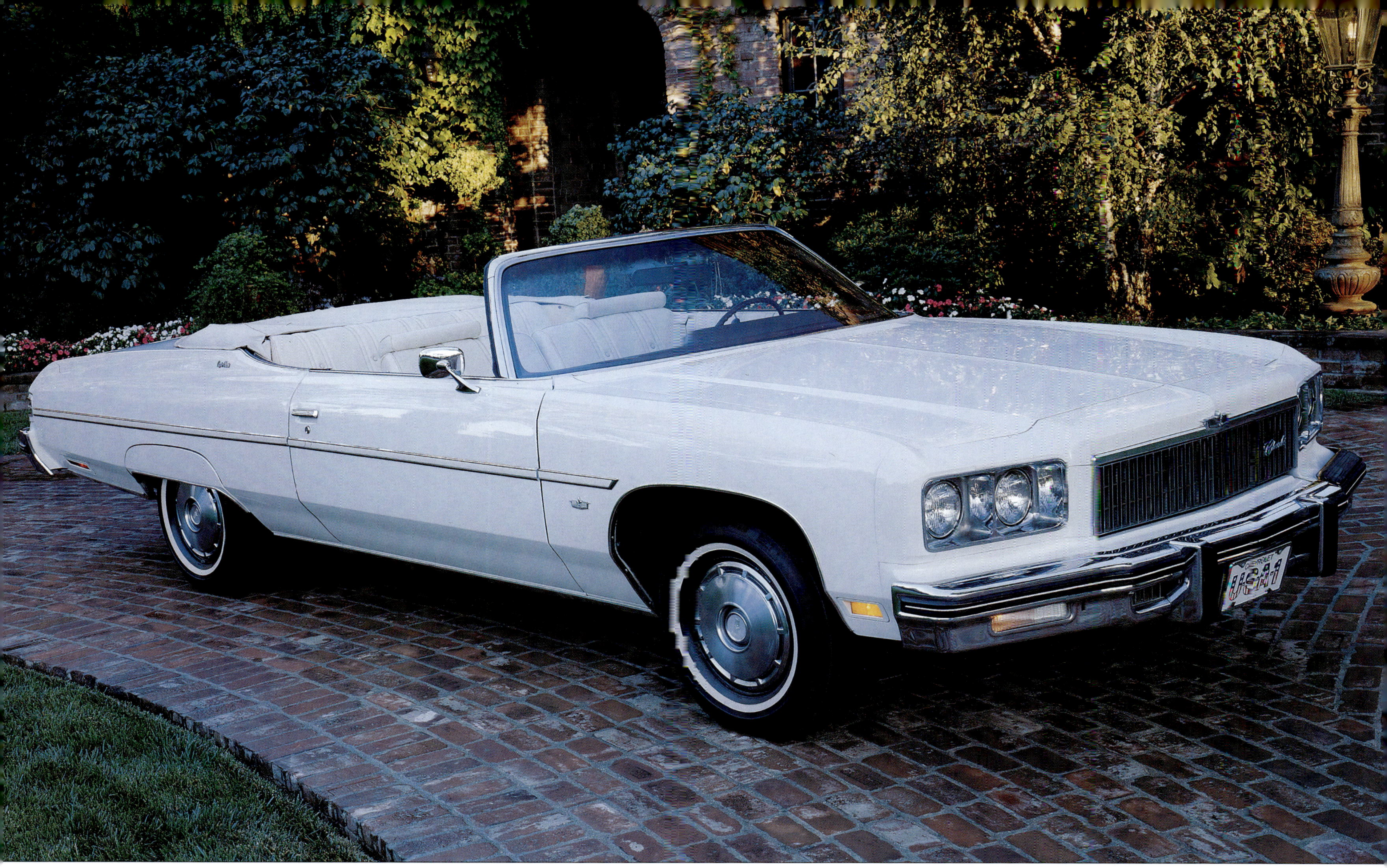

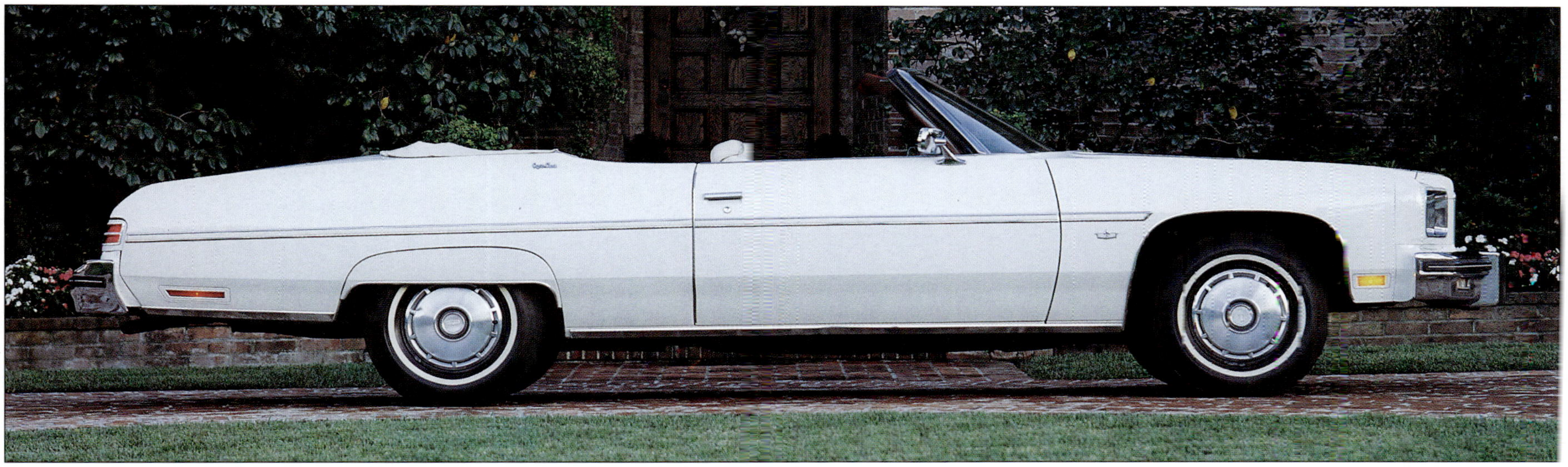

1975 OLDSMOBILE DELTA 88 ROYALE

Oldsmobile was down to one ragtop by 1975, a big, opulent Delta 88 Royale. Amazingly for those times, its sales soared by nearly six-fold over '74.

Detroit droptops dwindled to a precious few by 1975, and the betting was that even those would soon go the way of the dodo. That they did, though some would be reincarnated a decade or so later (albeit in a reduced scale). But buyers couldn't know that at the time, so ragtops like Oldsmobile's 1975 Delta 88 Royale actually enjoyed one last sales hurrah, as top-down enthusiasts and fools with money rushed to buy what looked like surefire "collectibles." As a result, the big Olds attracted 21,038 orders as a '75 model, versus just 3716 as a '74.

Olds was at its zenith in the '70s, with the mid-size Cutlass Supreme consistently at or near the top of the sales charts. The big Deltas and Ninety-Eights were also quite popular, especially for medium-price cars not very different from cheaper full-size Chevrolets. True, the ragtop Delta had a longer 124-inch wheelbase and more "important" Olds styling, but its standard '75 engine, a 170-net-horsepower 350 V-8, was similar to Chevy's. So was the available

185-horse 400. But many, perhaps most, of the big '75 Oldsmobiles were ordered with the top power option, a burly, mildly tuned 455 with 190 bhp.

At $5200, the ragtop '75 Delta 88 cost some $400 more than the '74. Add in an unprecedented gas crunch that had many buyers scurrying to smaller, thriftier wheels, and it's amazing the model scored a near six-fold sales increase. But then, a few buyers were thinking "collector car," hoping to make a killing. With this Olds at least, they didn't.

1975 PONTIAC GRAND VILLE

Pontiac had its troubles in the '70s, but they weren't obvious in the big, lush '75 Grand Ville convertible. It was no '60s "Wide-Tracker," but it would be the last open Poncho for a dozen years.

The full-size 1975 Pontiacs were not the eye-opening "Wide-Trackers" of the '60s. A decision to outproduce and "out-price" Chevrolet took a toll on workmanship, and luxury took precedence over performance when Grand Ville replaced Bonneville as the top-line series for 1971.

In fairness, Pontiac was struggling like all of Detroit with a rash of government rules that resulted in bulky "crash" bumpers and poor-running, vastly detuned engines that remained quite "fuelish." Meantime, convertible ranks were fast thinning, thanks partly to threatened accident rollover standards. Pontiac thus abandoned droptops after 1975 and a final 4519 open Grand Villes.

As Pontiac's only '75 convertible, the $5858 Grand Ville was fairly tasteful for the Disco Age, and a 185-horsepower 400 V-8 or optional 200-bhp 455 provided decent scoot. But while most "last convertibles" scored much higher sales than the year before, this one added only 1519. Pontiac would soon recapture past glories, but not with Grand Villes.

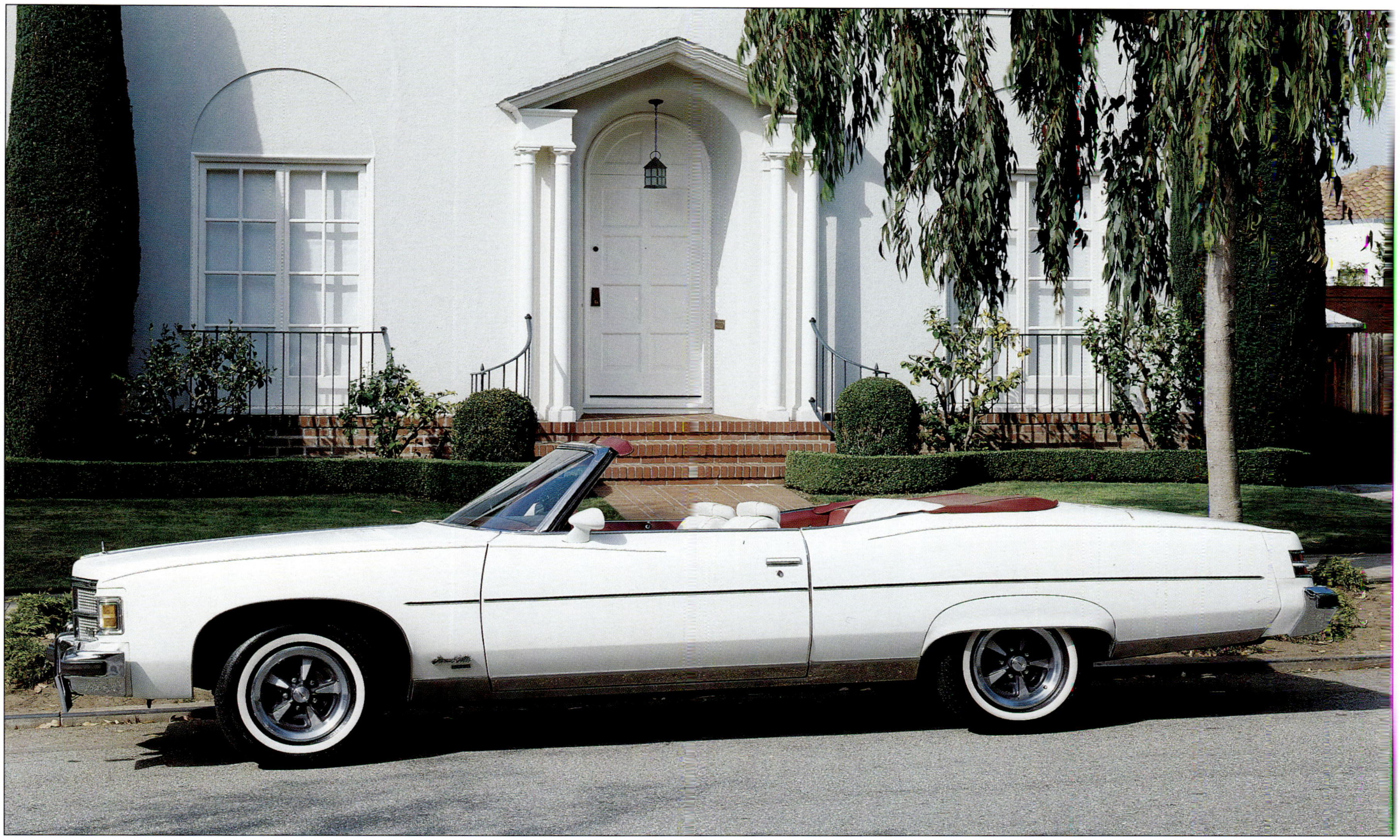

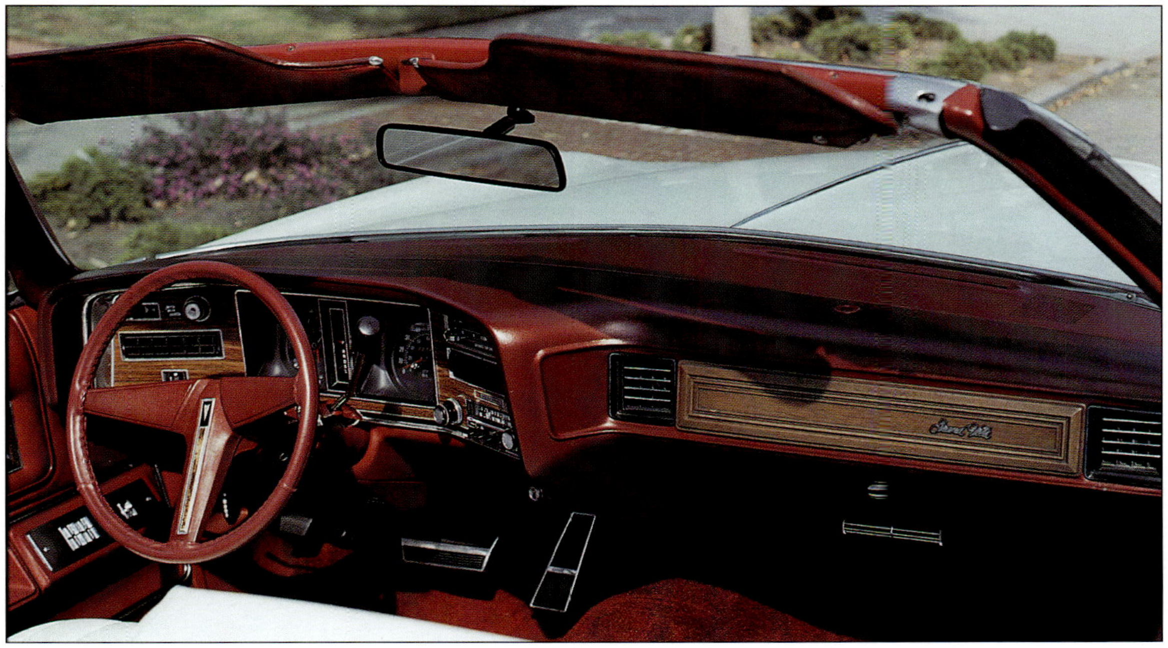

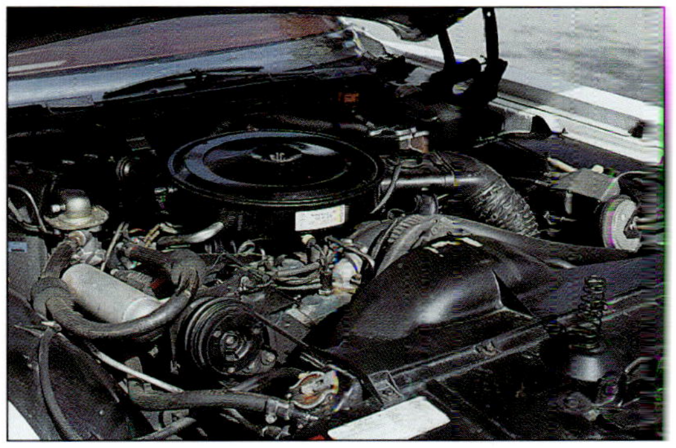

1976 CADILLAC ELDORADO

The 1976 Cadillac Eldorado was America's "last convertible," but not for long. Speculators rushed to buy, only to lose big once ragtops returned in the '80s—including a new Eldorado.

The 1976 Eldorado is the most famous "last convertible," mainly because it wasn't. Cadillac's personal coupe had been redesigned in a new jumbo size for '71, when a convertible returned for the first time since Eldorado went front-wheel drive four years earlier. The convertibles attracted 7000-9500 yearly sales, but Cadillac wanted more for '76, knowing ahead of time that it would own Detroit's only remaining ragtop.

Accordingly, Cadillac announced "no more convertibles" while upping the '76 run to 14,000 from the previous year's 8950. Included were a final 200 "last convertibles" with white paint and top, red pinstripes, and white leather upholstery with red piping. Though any '76 Eldo convertible cost $11,049 base, some sold for up three times as much in the "instant collectible" buying frenzy created by all this carefully calculated PR.

Come 1984, however, Cadillac introduced a new Eldo convertible that not only prompted a lawsuit (for deceptive advertising) but lost a bundle for those who overpaid for '76s. So much for clever marketing.

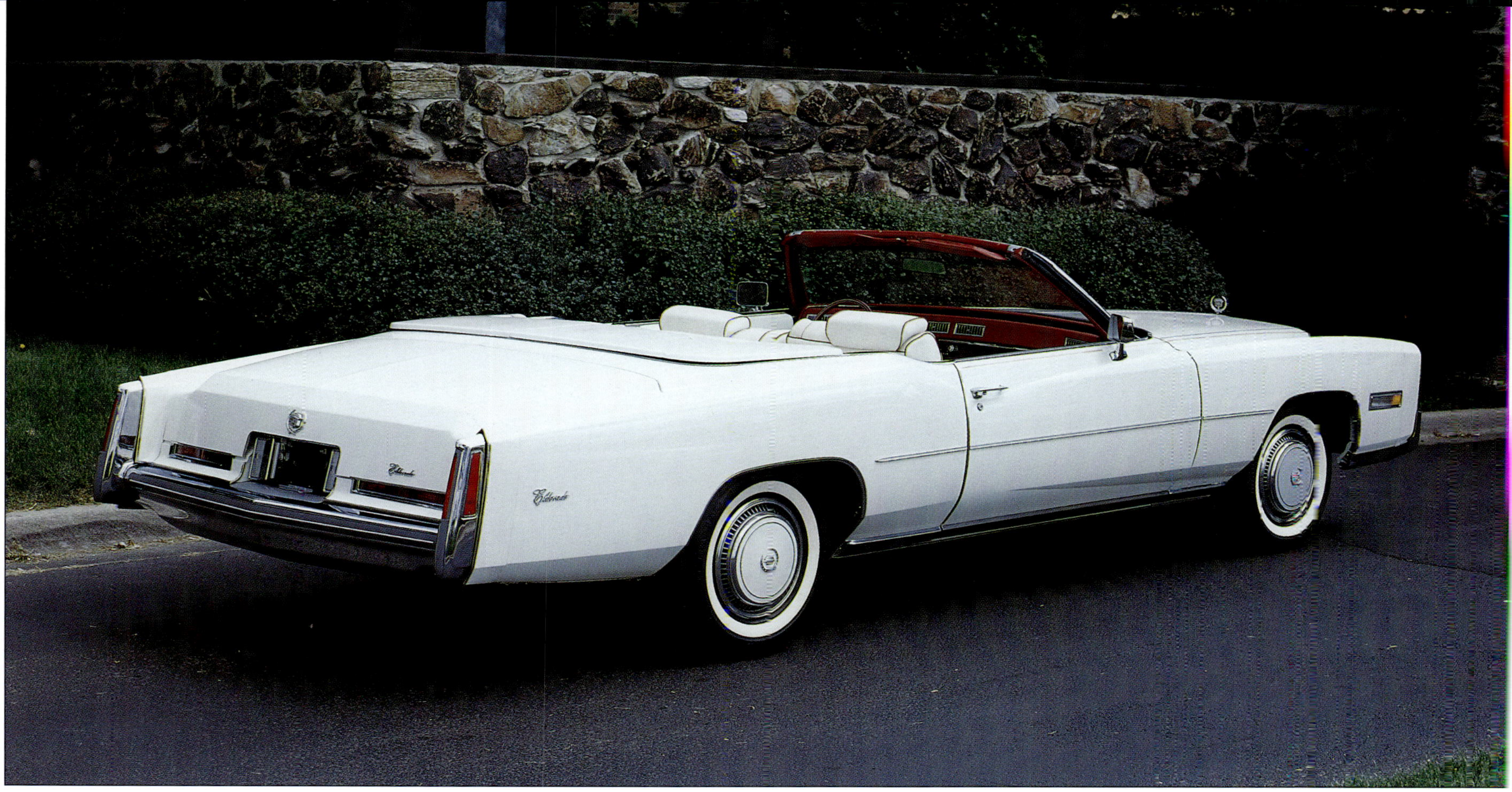

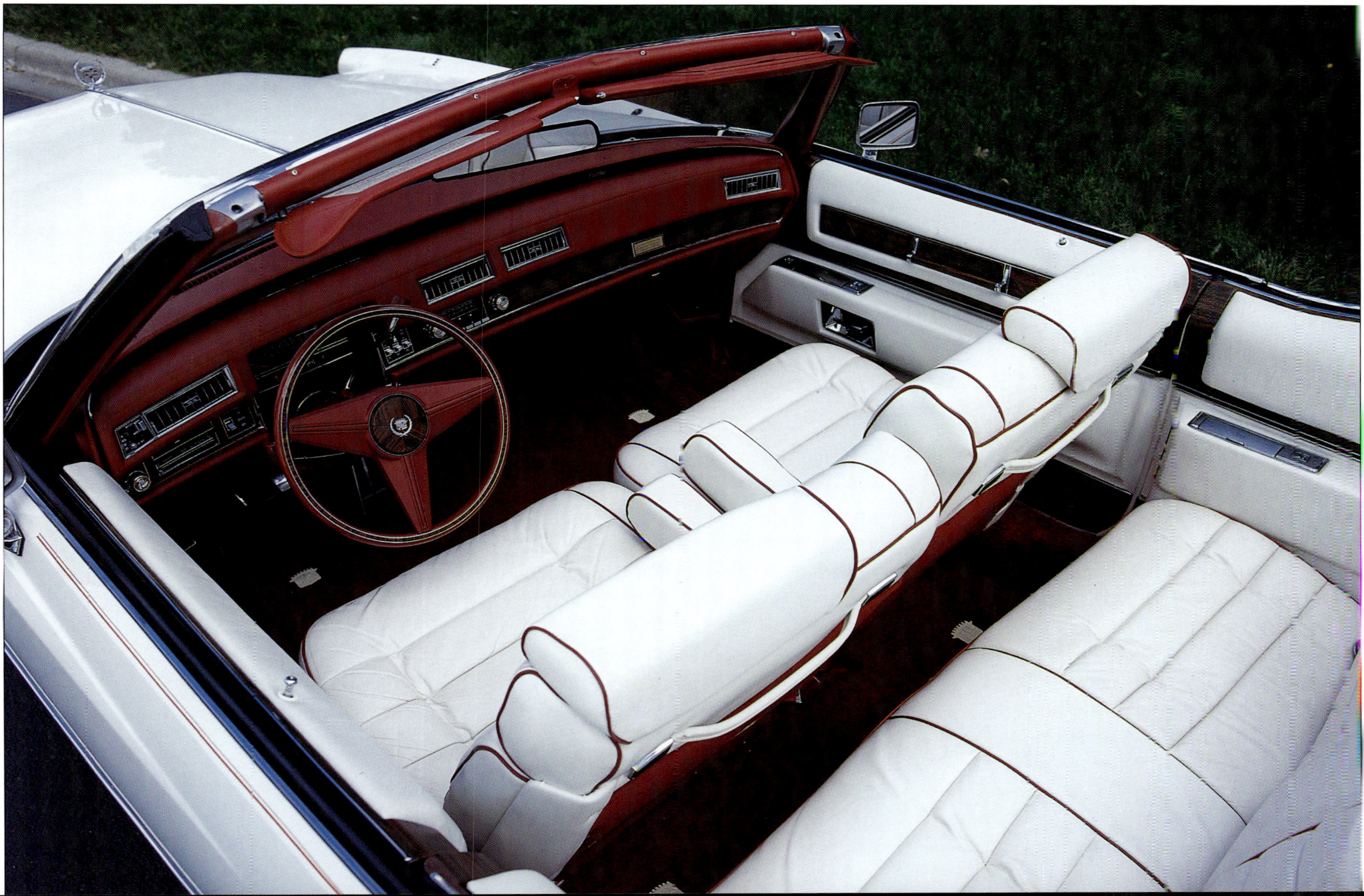

1983 BUICK RIVIERA

Though originally eyed for a convertible and even a convertible sedan, Buick's posh Riviera did not go topless until 1982. The ragtop didn't last long, but it's a coveted rarity today.

In the '40s and '50s, "Riviera" meant "hardtop coupe" at Buick; from '63 on it named a personal-luxury hardtop, Buick's Ford Thunderbird-fighter. But in mid-1982, the Riv flipped its lid. Though Buick's motives remain unclear, the new open Riviera provided welcome proof that the Big Three hadn't abandoned convertibles in the '70s, just put them on furlough.

Like some other reborn ragtops of that time, the Riviera was an outside conversion. ASC Incorporated did the job, and also assisted with body and top engineering. Little structural strengthening was required, as Riviera's new-for-'79 General Motors E-body was already pretty stiff as a hardtop coupe. That redesign also introduced the first Riviera with front-wheel drive and all-independent suspension, plus crisp new styling on a trim 114-inch wheelbase, the shortest in Riviera history. The convertible naturally benefited from all this, and looked even more distinctive than coupes because it didn't share a roofline with stablemates Olds Toronado and Cadillac Eldorado.

Though Riviera coupes came in regular and sportier turbocharged T Type editions, the convertible was a well-equipped solo offering, initially base-priced at $23,994. Buick's new 125-horsepower 4.1-liter V-6 was standard, with a 140-bhp 307 Olds-built V-8 a no-cost option. Buick's 175-bhp turbo 3.8 V-6 was allegedly available, but few if any ragtops were so equipped. Even with the V-8, a hefty 3800-pound curb weight gave the convertible only adequate performance at best.

Not so the twin-turbo V-6 ragtop that paced the 1983 Indianapolis 500. Alas, that honor did nothing for soft-top sales. Nor did few changes through 1985, after which an even smaller Riviera debuted and the convertible was cancelled. Buick built 1750 open Rivieras in 1983, followed by just 500 in '84 and a mere 400 in '85. A modern collector car? You better believe it.

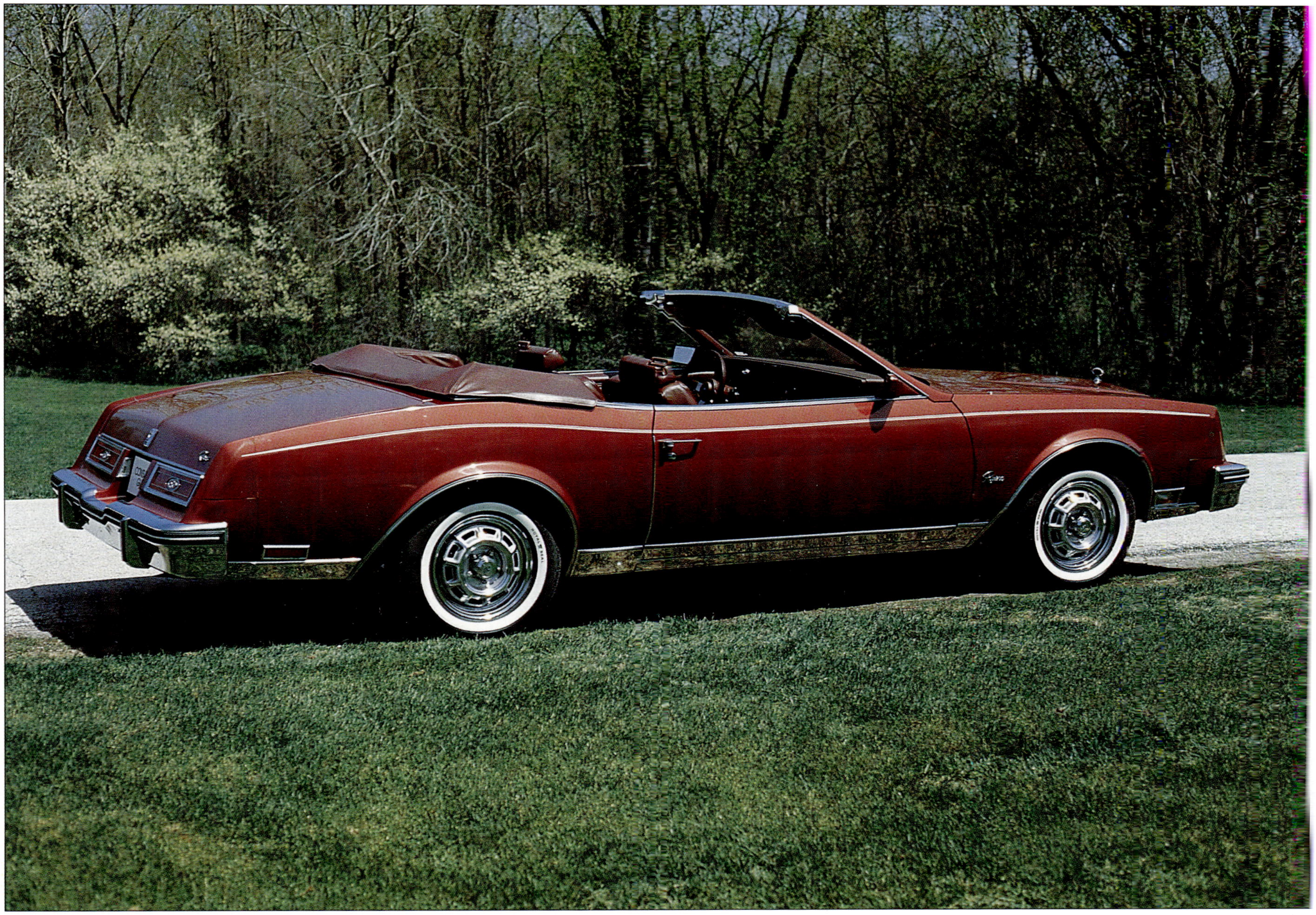

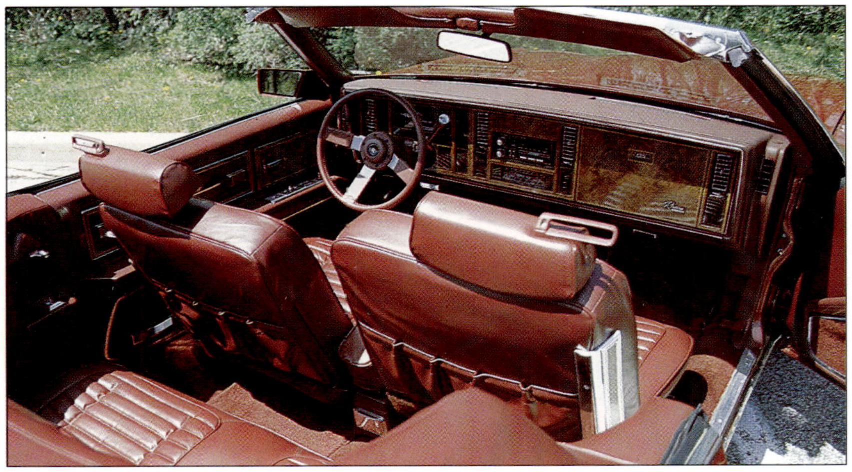

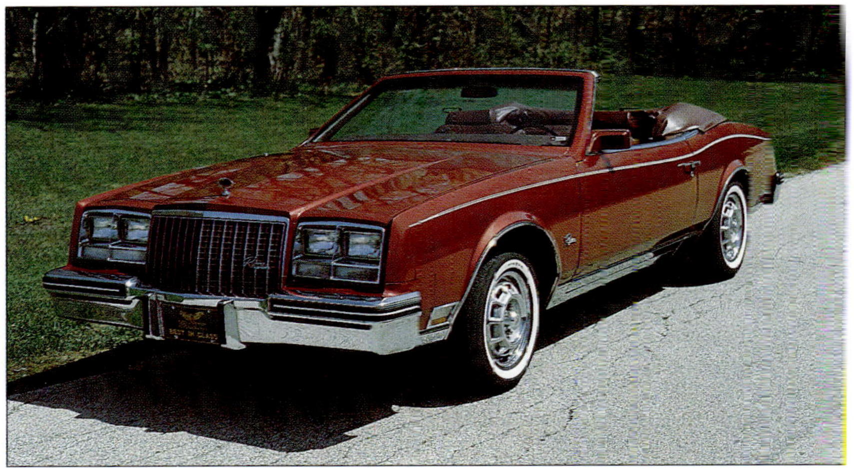

1986 FORD MUSTANG GT

Ford's Mustang was reborn for 1979, once more a genuine ponycar in the spirit of the great mid-'60s original. Ragtops were absent at first, but enthusiasts cheered their return for 1983.

The thrifty, affordable Mustang II was perfect for the gas-short, inflation-wracked '70s, but it was more "econocar" than genuine "ponycar." Ford changed that with a brand-new 1979 Mustang with the spirit of the legendary original. Enthusiasts cheered, especially when a GT version returned for 1982 with an updated 302 V-8 and a decidedly handling-oriented chassis. The nostalgia continued for '83 with the first Mustang convertible in 10 years.

By 1986, Mustang's V-8 had switched from carburetors to fuel injection exclusively; combined with other interim improvements, the result was 200 strong horsepower and real '60s-style go. Though Ford also offered quieter-looking LX droptops with four-cylinder or V-8 power, the racy $14,523 GT was the one to have.

Mustang scored over 224,000 total 1986 sales, a far cry from the mid-'60s perhaps, but more than respectable considering how much times had changed. Ragtops were fairly numerous that year, and are thus easily obtained today. If you decide to buy one after looking at the pictures here, we'll understand.

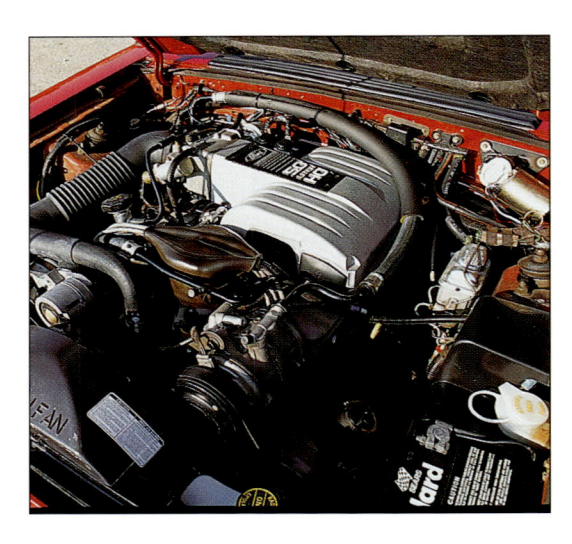

134

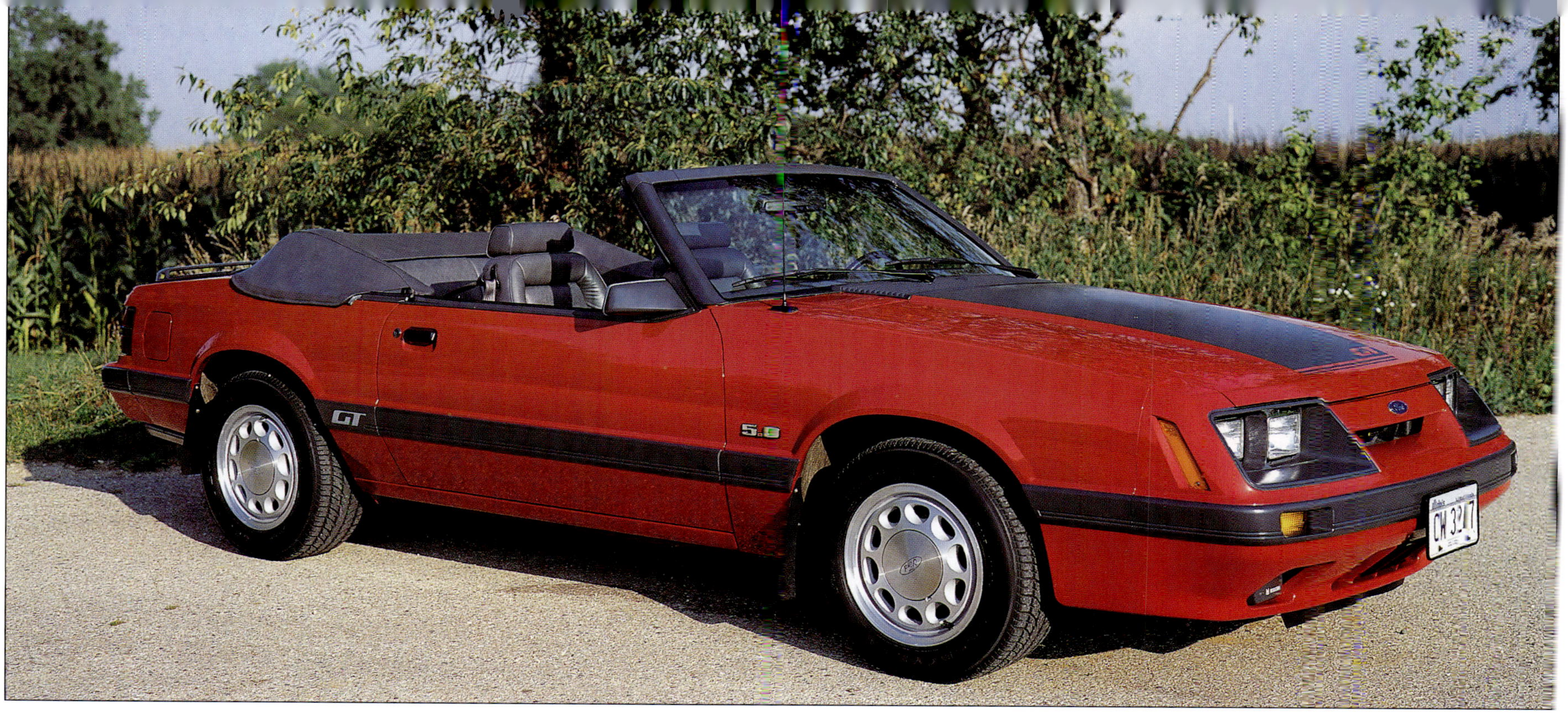
GT

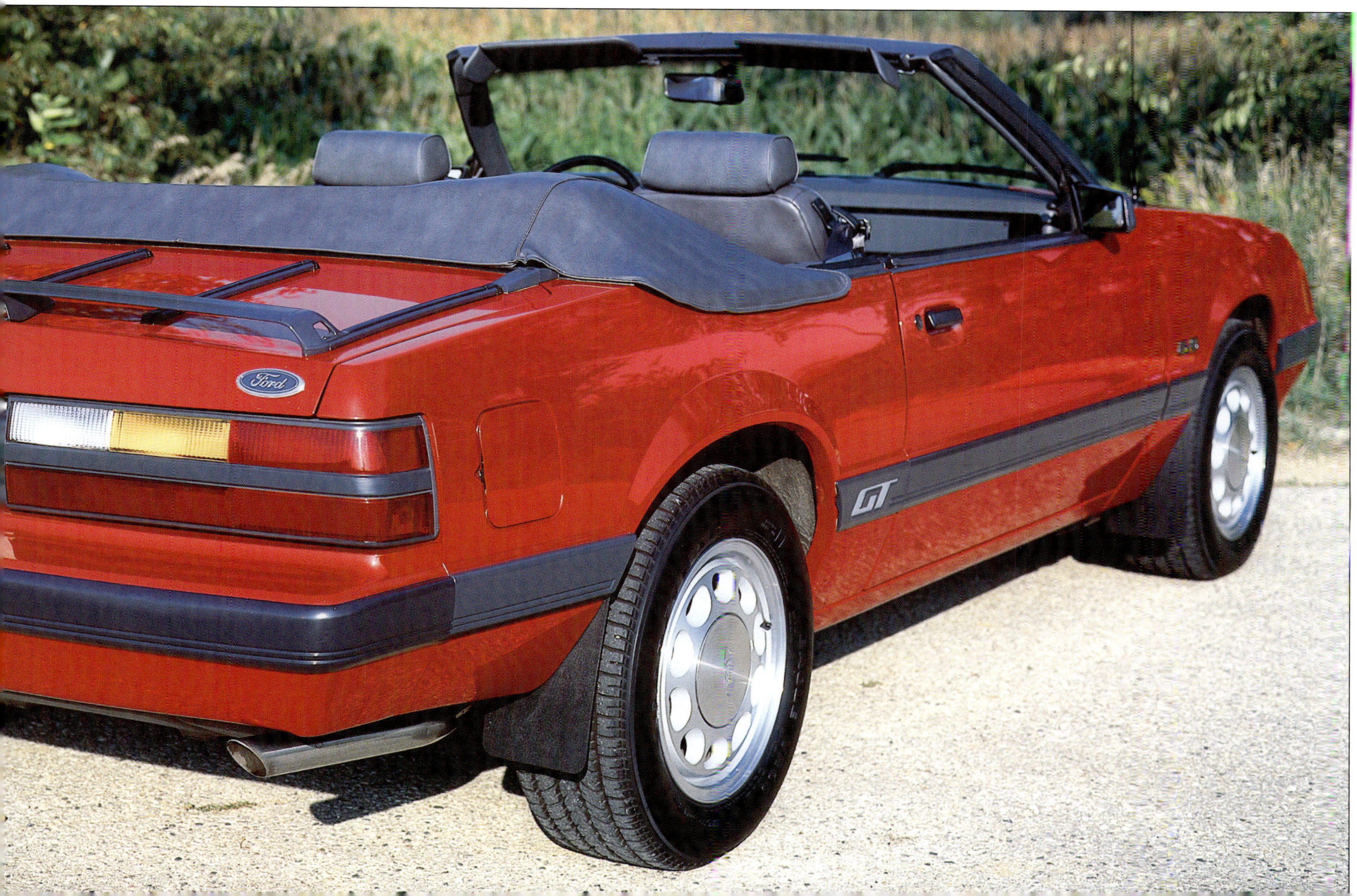
GT

1988 CHRYSLER LeBARON GTC

The little K-car helped save Chrysler in the '80s, but it was dull stuff even as a convertible. That all changed with 1987's glamorous new droptop LeBaron that later spawned a sporty GTC variant.

After going to the brink in 1980, Chrysler Corporation roared back with the unassuming front-drive "K-car" compact and its many clever spinoffs. Chrysler's pioneering minivan was the most wildly successful derivative, but convertibles played their part in the company's resurgence by generating showroom traffic that dealers hadn't seen in years. Indeed, Chrysler led Detroit's ragtop renaissance with LeBaron and Dodge 400 models previewed well before their 1982 debut.

Trouble was, the small, boxy K-car made a rather dull convertible, even those LeBarons decked out in pseudo-wood side trim, Town & Country-style. But the new 1987 LeBaron was something else: still K-car inside, but curvy, clean, and balanced outside. Buyers responded, and Chrysler moved over 38,000 ragtops for 1988, the highest number in five years.

Helping that figure were a handful of "spring special" GTC models introduced at mid-year. Power came from a choice of turbocharged fours: a 174-horsepower 2.2-liter with five-speed manual shift or a 150-bhp 2.5 with Torqueflite automatic. Firm suspension and lacy-spoke aluminum wheels were included, and all sported monochromatic white exteriors, though buyers had a choice of interior hues. Starting price? A bargain $16,495. No wonder this LeBaron line maintained Chrysler's position as maker of America's best-selling convertible by far.

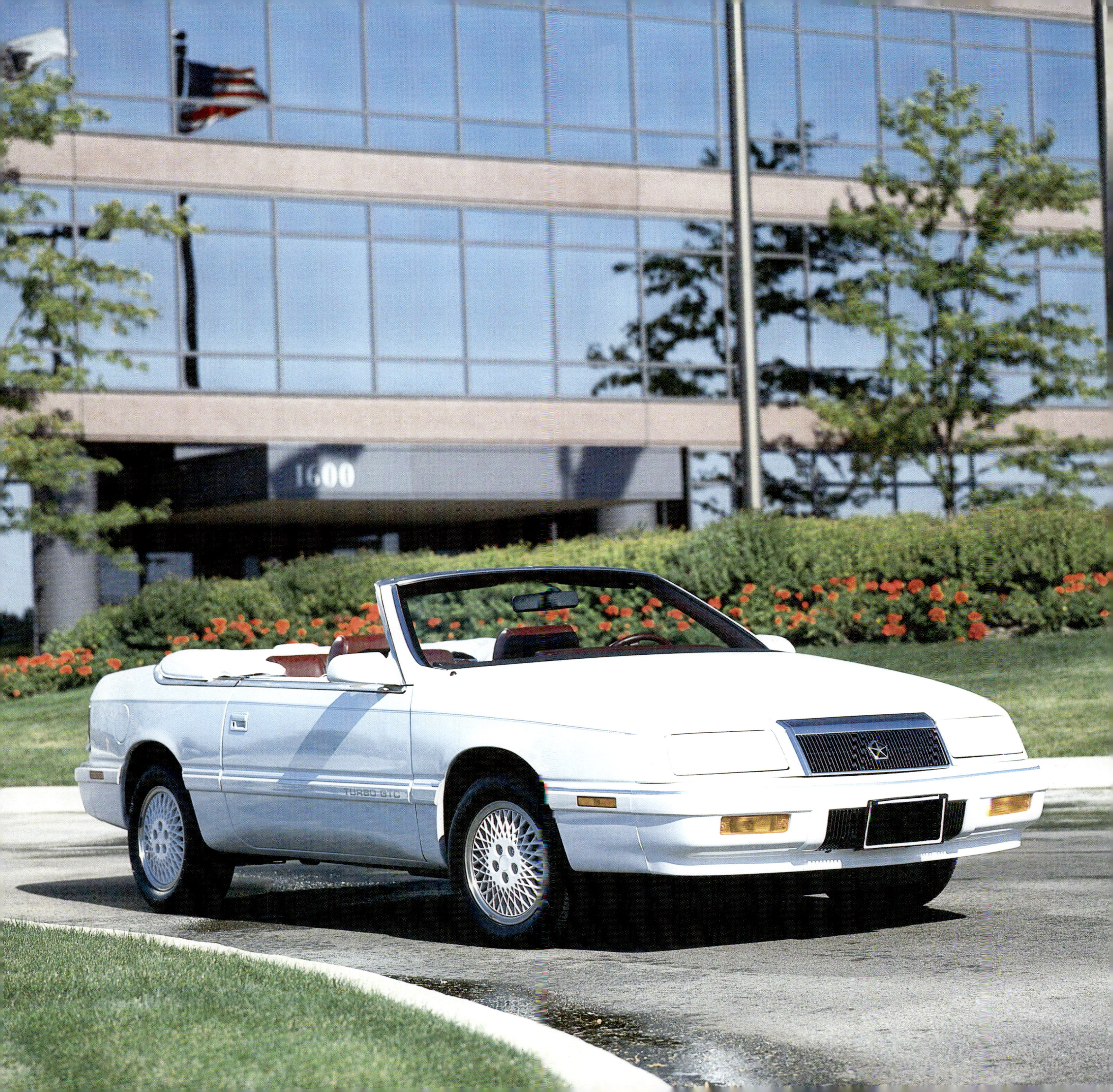
1600
TURBO GTC

1990 BUICK REATTA

Buick's only production two-seat convertible was a here-today, gone-tomorrow misfire. Only 2437 were built, so the ragtop Reatta has already become a prized collector car.

Buick's only production two-seater died after just four years (1988-91) and 21,850 copies, which was about what Buick expected to sell every year. Most Reattas were coupes, but the 1990-91 convertibles are now prized rarities with respective runs of 2132 and just 305.

The Reatta was basically Buick's "redownsized" 1986 Riviera cut to a 98.5-inch wheelbase. It was just as heavy, however, thanks to numerous standard luxuries and an identical front-wheel-drive powertrain comprising a 3.8-liter V-6 and four-speed Turbo-Hydramatic. Styling was unique and clean, but also quite conservative, and the convertible's manual top (with no power option) seemed mean for the initial $34,995 base price.

What sealed Reatta's fate was a fast-worsening cash crisis that forced General Motors to dump slow sellers, including Cadillac's similarly conceived Allante (1987-93). Happily, the Reatta has already carved a secure niche as a modern collectible Buick, and there's justice in that.

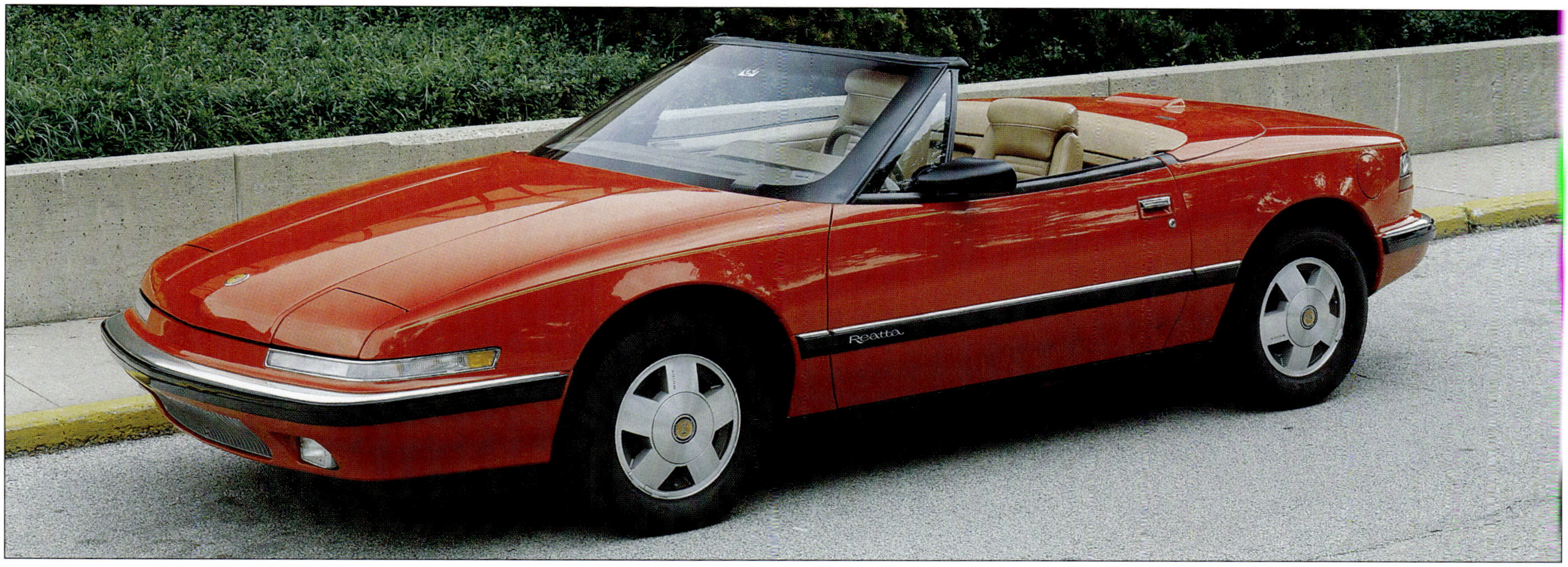
Reatta

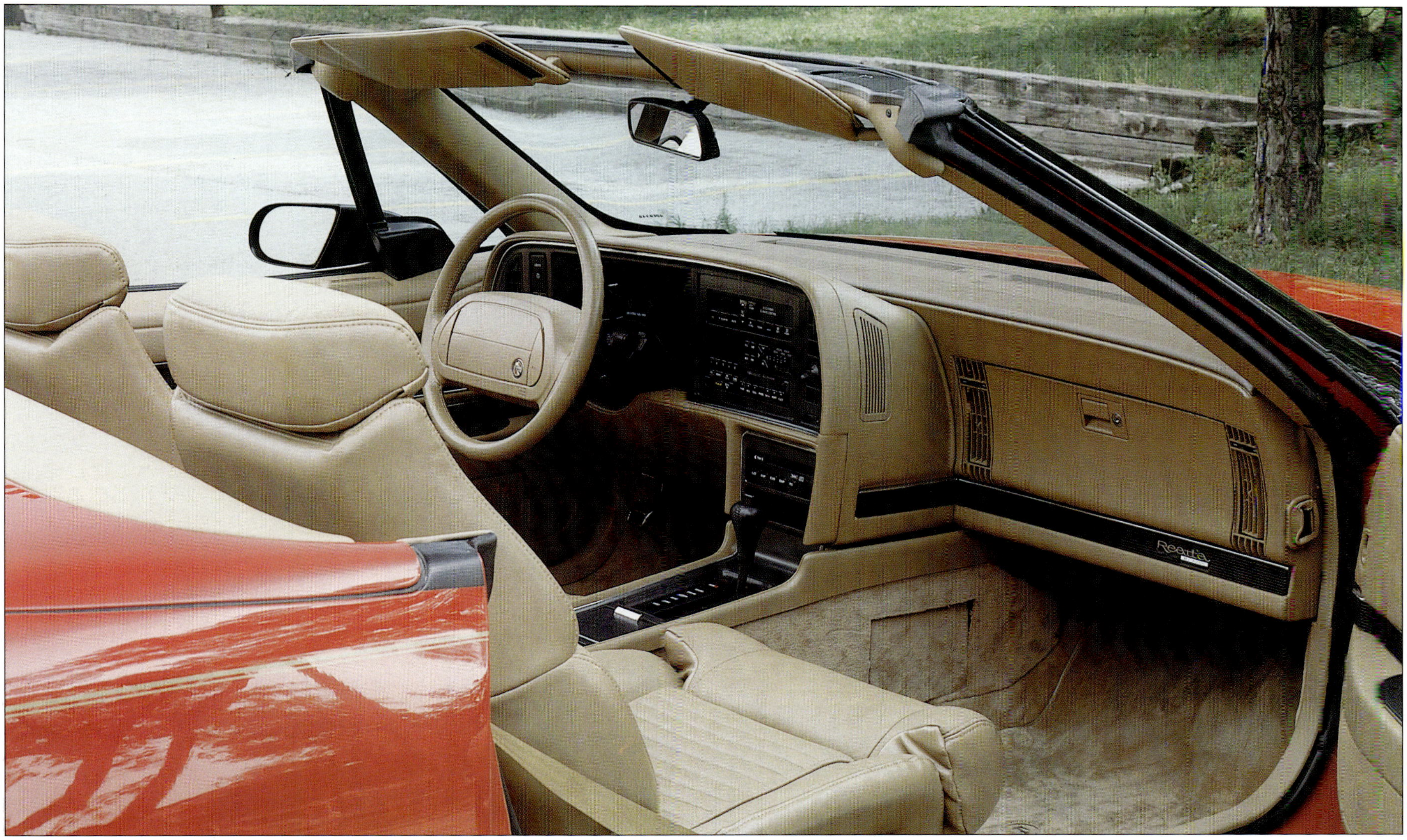
Reatta

1996 CHRYSLER SEBRING JXi

It was America's best-selling convertible, just like the LeBaron it replaced, but the slick new "Cab Forward" Sebring was a far better car—arguably Chrysler's best all-around ragtop yet.

As one of Chrysler's "Cab Forward" generation, the dashing Sebring convertible bowed for 1996 without a trace of K-car in it. Yet like its LeBaron predecessor, it was America's best-selling ragtop—not to mention the "rent-a-vertible" of choice in playgrounds from South Beach to Palm Springs.

There was certainly lots to like about this Sebring. For starters, it was a four-passenger convertible that actually seated four adults in real comfort, helped by a relatively long 106-inch wheelbase and a wide stance that also contributed to secure handling. And though loosely based on Chrysler's Cirrus sedan, the ragtop Sebring was engineered to be a convertible, so it's pleasantly rigid. Acceleration? Decent with the JX model's 150-horsepower 2.4-liter four-cylinder, almost lively with the 163-bhp 2.5 V-6 in the upscale JXi (shown here).

Add standard power top, automatic transmission, and other essential amenities at low-to-mid-$20,000 prices, and it's little wonder the ragroof Sebring sold at a 50,000-plus annual clip. In terms of popularity, nothing else even came close.

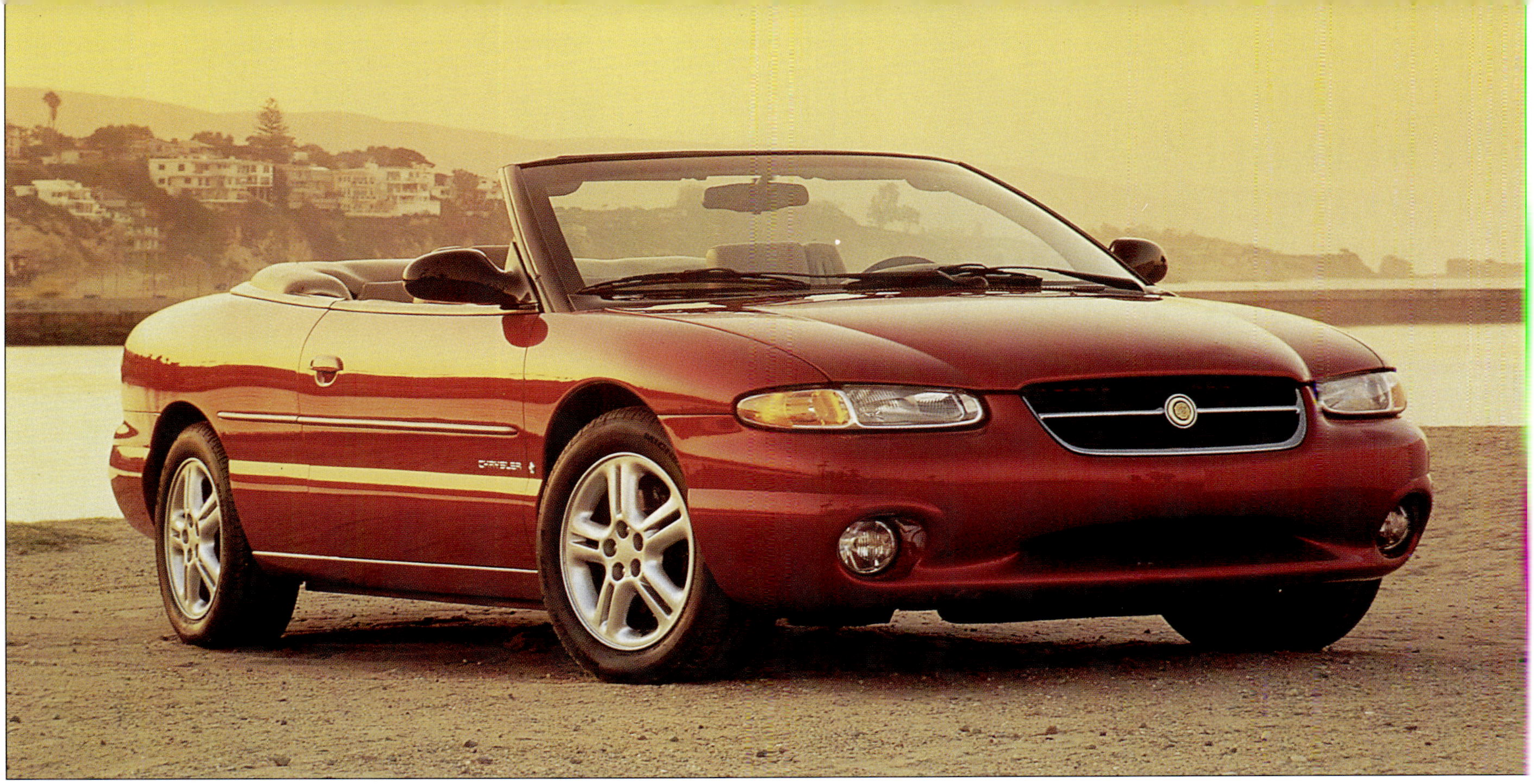

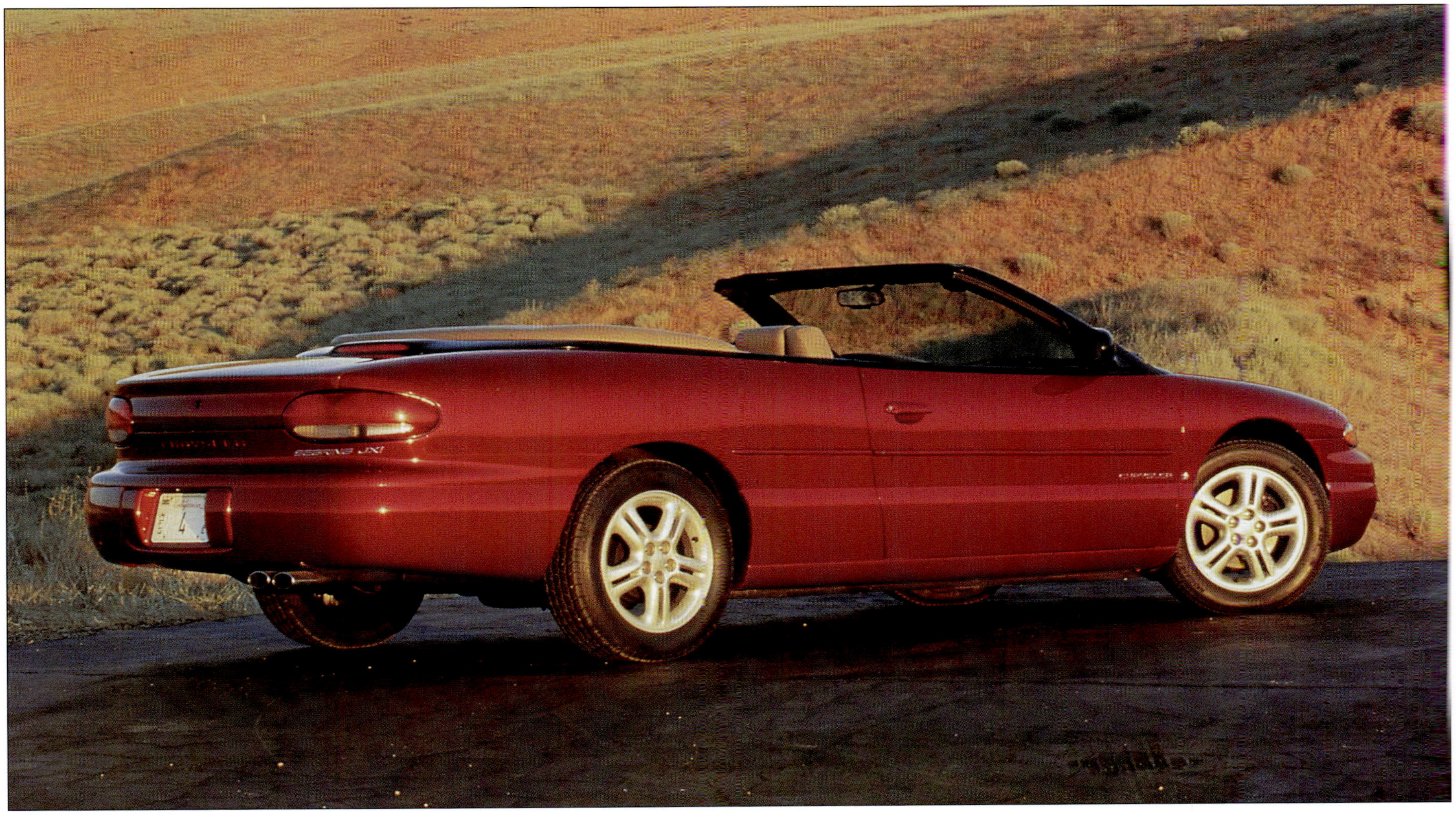

1998 CHEVROLET CORVETTE PACE CAR REPLICA

If not the rarest Corvette Pace Car Replica, the striking 1998 edition is unquestionably one of the most desirable 'Vettes ever made—all but identical to the actual pace cars.

Corvettes had paced the legendary Indianapolis 500 race four times by 1998, and Chevrolet observed each occasion by selling a limited-edition replica. The '98 shown here is one of just 1158 built. Only the 1995 edition is scarcer at 527. In short, this is an unusually collectible Corvette.

Aside from lacking race-required strobe lights, rollover bars, and onboard fire extinguishing system, the '98 Pace Car replicas were identical to the actual pacers, a claim none of the previous Replicas could make. It also differs in having its Indy 500 livery applied by the factory, not the owner (save the windshield name decal). And striking it was, especially the wild flag logos, yellow wheels, and eye-popping yellow/black interior. It's the main attraction of a package that added $2800 to the $44,900 base price of a fifth-generation or "C5" convertible.

Naturally, the Replicas inherited all the sterling features of the regular ragtop. To wit: an all-aluminum LS1 V-8 with 345 potent horsepower, rear-mounted automatic or available six-speed manual transmission, the stiff 'Vette structure, anti-lock brakes, and a chip-controlled Active Handling stability system that helped keep the car on course and out of trouble in the twisty bits.

With all this, plus sub-five-second 0-60 performance, the '98 Replica was a guaranteed sellout, and a certain future collectible.

Indianapolis 500
OFFICIAL PACE CAR

Indianapolis 500
OFFICIAL PACE CAR

1998 FORD MUSTANG COBRA

Cobra was the hottest modern Mustang, not to mention the most sophisticated. And with only a few thousand built each year, Cobra convertibles have already become prized keepsakes.

For 1998 the hottest Mustang was called Cobra, introduced for 1993 as a very limited-edition coupe. Though never intended to make real money, Cobra continued in the new-for-'94 Mustang line as an image-building step up from the sporty V-8 GT coupe and convertible. It was built by Ford's Special Vehicle Team (SVT), the in-house performance operation that turned out a few thousand each year for determined leadfoot Mustangers.

At $28,430 to start, the '98 Cobra convertible was a bargain in top-down thrills. Sophisticated too, with a twincam 4.6-liter V-8 delivering 305 horsepower, anti-lock brakes, and big 17-inch wheels mounting wide Z-rated tires to go with a unique handling suspension. Standard traction control, dual exhausts, and leather interior were shared with GTs, but not white-face gauges or the trademark snake emblems recalling the great Shelby Mustangs of the '60s.

Collectors have already started reeling in late-'90s Cobras, especially the ragtops. That's smart, as these cars can only become more scarce and valuable as time passes.

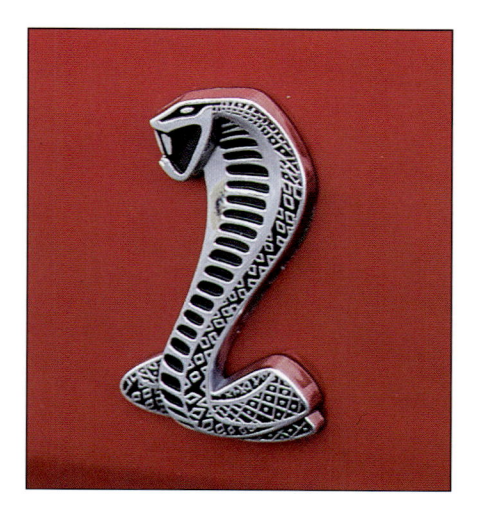

144

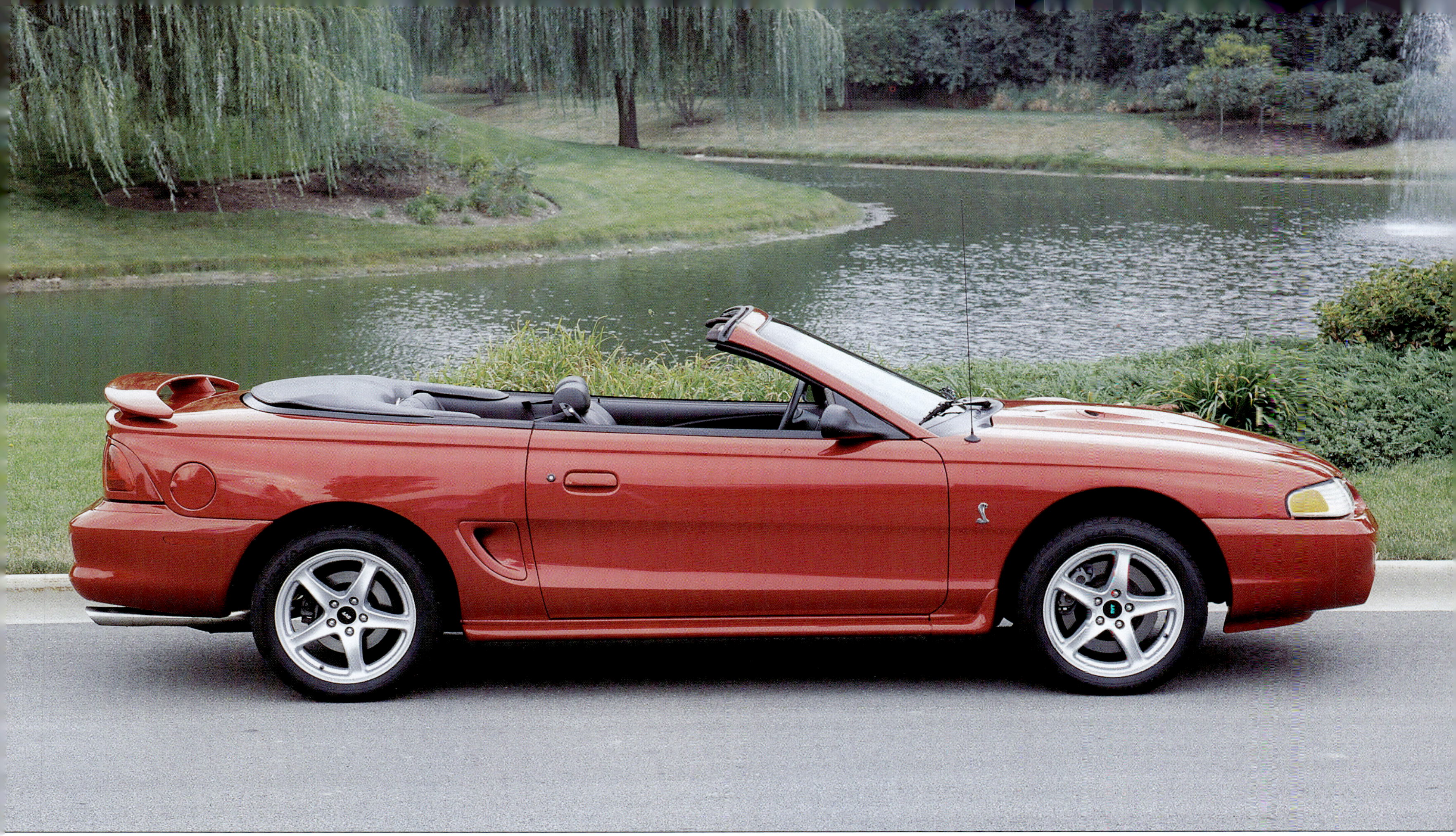

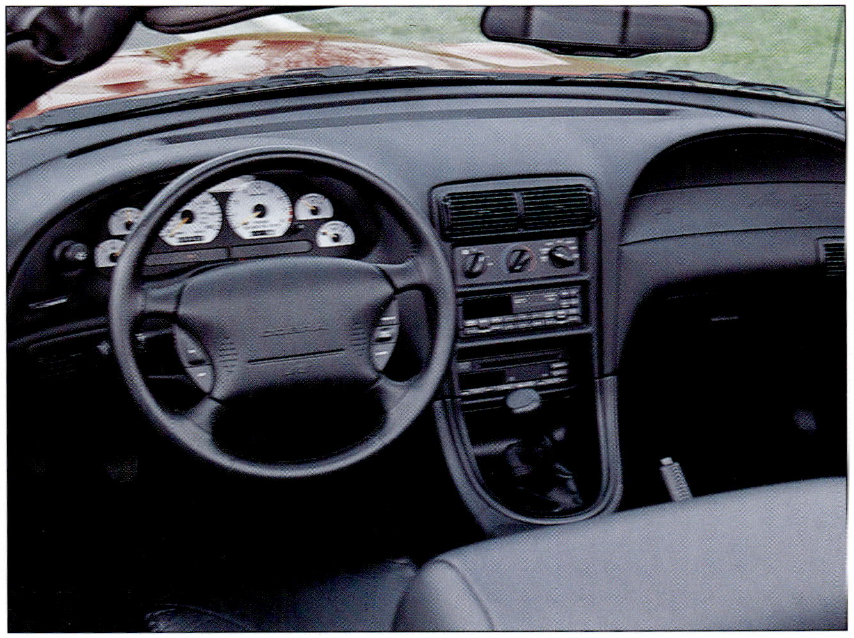

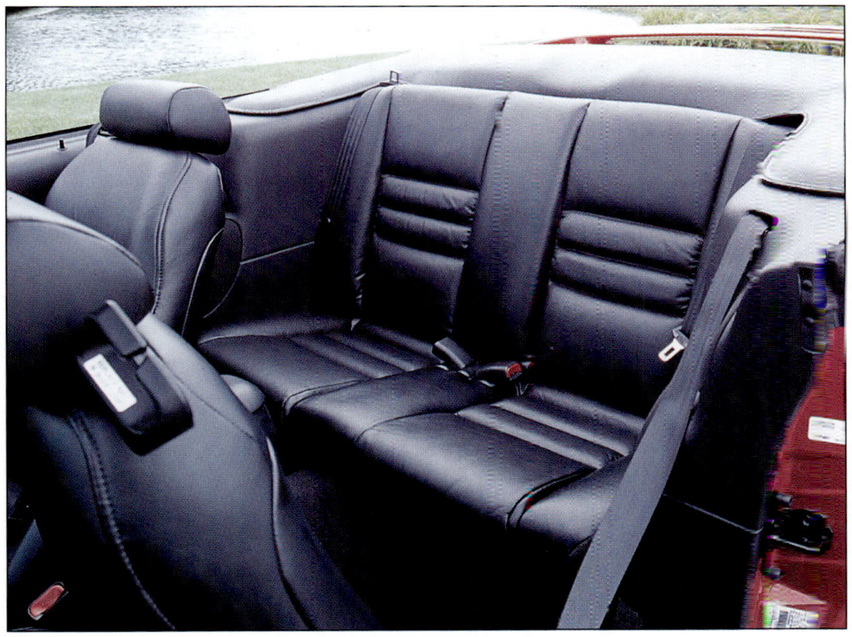

1999 PONTIAC TRANS AM 30TH ANNIVERSARY SPECIAL EDITION

Pontiac made a point of celebrating the anniversary of its Trans Am, but few would have guessed the 30th would be the last for this ponycar legend.

After a 36-year run, the final Pontiac Firebird rolled off the assembly line in 2002. For 34 of those 36 years—it wasn't offered the first two—the Trans Am headlined the Firebird line and was arguably America's most outrageous combination of muscle-car style and speed.

While others came and went, Trans Am was not only consistently among the very best performing ponycars, it was the only one among its ilk to never skip a year of production. So celebrating its milestones was all the excuse Pontiac needed to build something special. Starting with the 10th anniversary of the 1969 original, Pontiac marked Trans Am anniversaries at five-year intervals. And as the last anniversary edition, the 30th was special indeed.

Like the first-ever Trans Am, the 30th Anniversary Special Edition came only in white with a white interior and blue hood and rear-deck stripes. The 30th was also the first anniversary edition since the original Trans Am to have ram air, in this case, the 320-horsepower WS6 version of the Corvette's 5.7-liter V-8. It was good for 0-60 mph in about 5.5 seconds. The WS6 package also included a stiffer suspension and 17-inch wheels and tires, even larger than those of the standard Trans Am.

Only nine 1969 Trans Am convertibles were produced, ranking them among the rarest of all 'Birds. The 30th was considerably more common, with convertibles accounting for 535 of the 1600 built. That's still a small run, but while its looks and performance were anything but common, the 30th Anniversary Special Edition—being the last of the anniversary flock—was special far beyond its numbers.

146

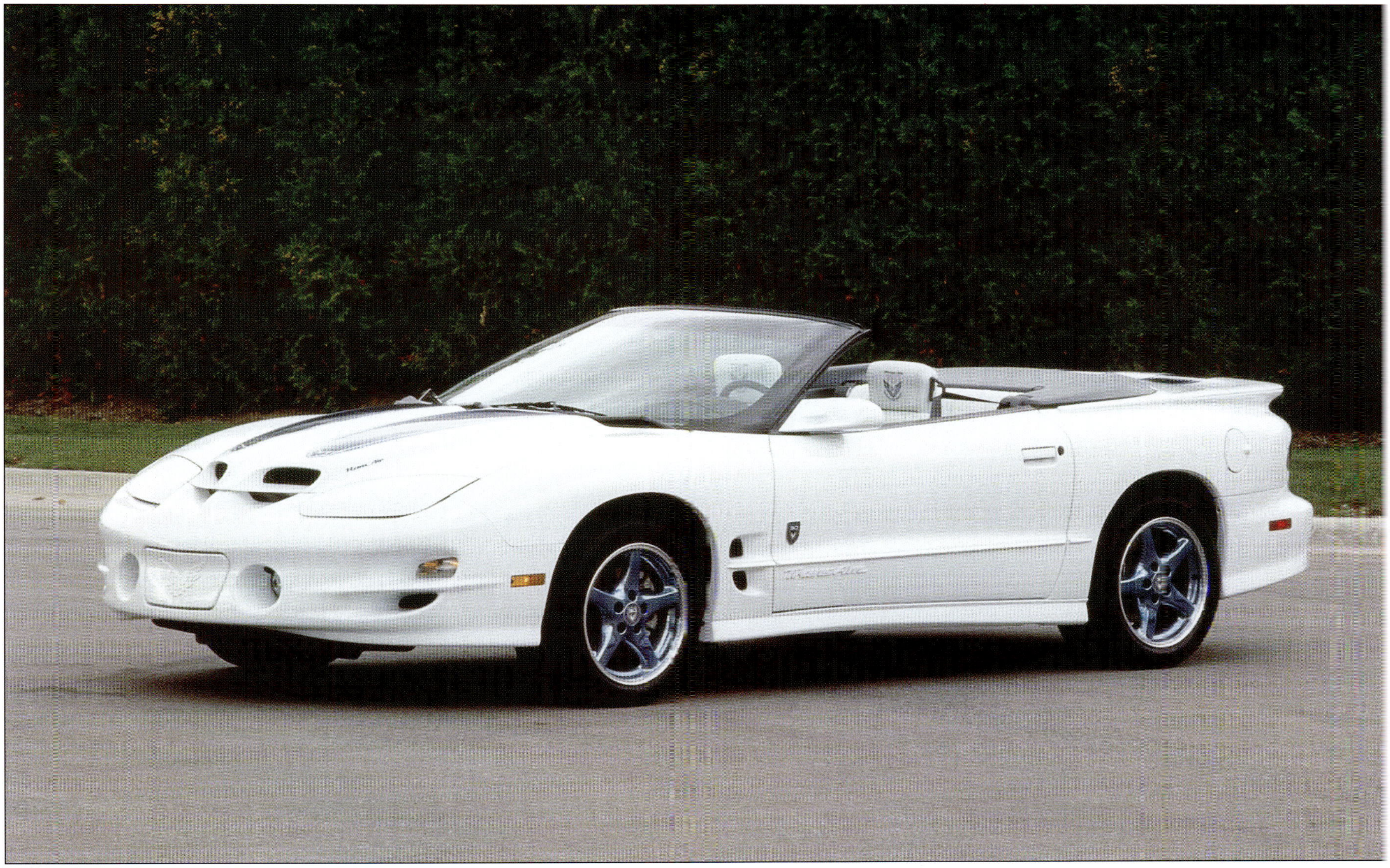
Ram Air

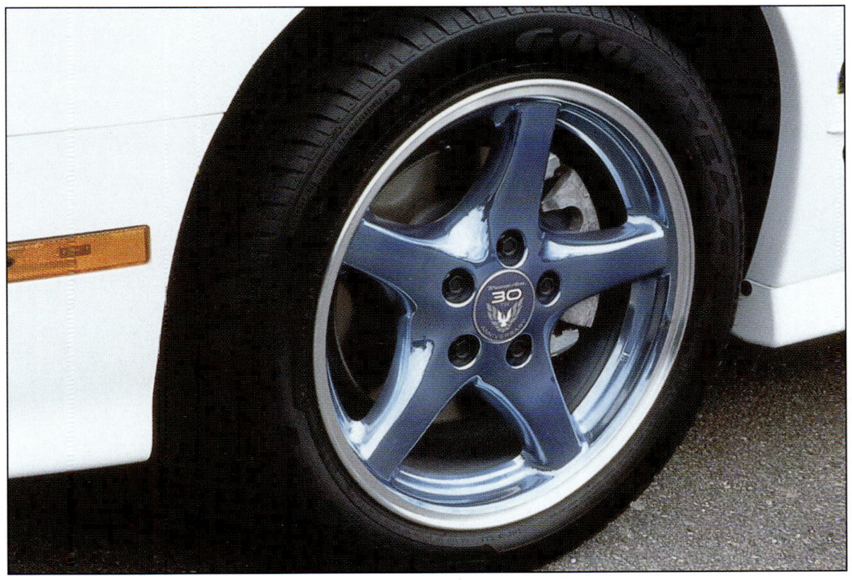

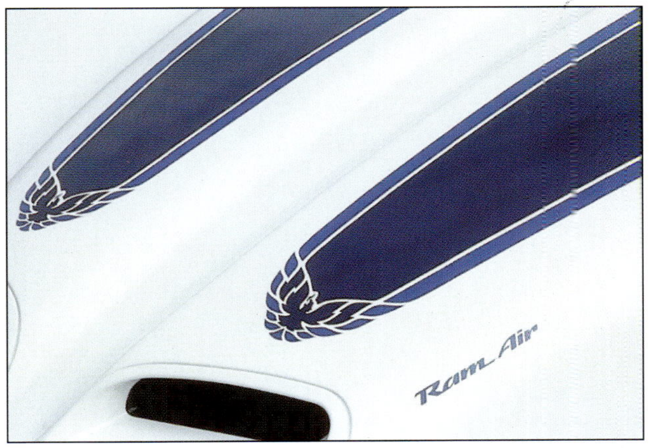
Ram Air

2000 PANOZ ESPERANTE

An Irish chassis, a Mustang engine, and an upstart factory in suburban Atlanta combined with surprising results: a new American car company and an exciting convertible.

By the time the Esperante was introduced in 2000, it was clear that Danny Panoz had managed to do something that hadn't been accomplished since Chrysler was incorporated in 1925, start a successful American car company. Using a race-bred aluminum chassis designed by an Irish engineering firm known for its work with Lotus and Maserati, and a rumbling American V-8, Panoz Auto Development Company created the AIV Roadster. Despite its impressive performance the roofless, windowless Roadster appealed only to hard-core driving enthusiasts. Responding to demand for a more practical car, the luxurious Esperante was added to the eleven-year-old Panoz line. With its roll-up windows, leather interior, and power top, Esperante appealed to drivers that craved performance as well as daily drivability.

The lightweight Esperante featured an all-aluminum body and an engine purchased from Ford. The double overhead-cam 4.6-liter engine is the same V-8 used in 2001 Mustang Cobras and produces 320 horsepower. At a modest 3400 pounds and with its strong engine, Esperante sprints from 0-60 mph in about 5 seconds.

Panoz hand assembled about 100 $80,000 2000 Esperantes at its Hoschton, Georgia, factory. At the end of the assembly line Panoz employees that worked on a car etched their signature on an aluminum plate mounted under the hood.

Fast and rare, each Esperante is a tribute to the American institutions of top-down motoring and entrepreneurial spirit.

2000 PLYMOUTH PROWLER

Plymouth hoped to evoke the past and brighten its future with the Prowler. The aluminum-bodied sportster was a hit with drivers and collectors. Plymouth was less fortunate, however, and Prowler rode out its last season wearing a Chrysler badge.

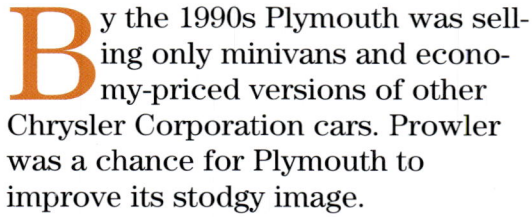

By the 1990s Plymouth was selling only minivans and economy-priced versions of other Chrysler Corporation cars. Prowler was a chance for Plymouth to improve its stodgy image.

The show-stopping Prowler appeared in 1997, almost identical to the 1993 concept car. Prowler was an immediate hit. Limited supply and early demand fueled reported selling prices in excess of $100,000 over the Prowler's $39,000 sticker price. Just under 400 1997 Prowlers were built, all in any color you wanted, as long as it was purple.

Early problems at the factory resulted in a shortened 1997 production run and an extended 1999 season, skipping 1998 completely.

Prowler's appeal was more than skin deep. The chassis was formed of precision-welded aerospace-quality aluminum alloy and most of the body was aluminum as well. Use of lightweight materials helped keep the nimble Prowler under 2900 pounds.

All Prowlers came with Chrysler's 3.5-liter V-6. Transversely mounted in other Chrysler cars, the V-6 was turned "North-South" to accommodate the Prowler's rear-wheel-drive drivetrain. Prowlers featured a unique one-piece transmission/axle "transaxle" set back in the car for excellent weight distribution. All Prowlers were equipped with Chrysler's AutoStick automatic transmission with manual-shift feature.

Horsepower was 214 for 1997 models and 253 for later versions. Prowlers were quick, with the higher-output cars running from 0-60 mph in about 7 seconds.

After the all-purple first season, Plymouth had fun with color, rolling out much-anticipated new hues, one at a time. Limited-run editions included the red and black "Woodward" and the black and silver "Black Tie."

Plymouth folded in 2001, but Prowler enjoyed a brief run badged as a Chrysler for the 2002 model year. Fewer than 1500 "Chrysler" Prowlers were built. The last Prowler, the only one painted High Voltage Blue, was sold at a charity auction for $175,000.

151

2002 35TH ANNIVERSARY CHEVROLET CAMARO SS

Born to do battle with Mustang, Camaro fought the good fight. Thirty-five years later Chevy says goodnight to its legendary ponycar with the best "'Maro" yet.

For 2002 Chevy bid farewell to Camaro with a special 35th Anniversary edition available only on SS-package-equipped Z28s. On top of the SS's 325-horsepower Corvette-derived V-8, anniversary editions added exclusive hood, roof and rear-deck striping, 35th Anniversary badging, and a hot-rod inspired painted rear differential.

It was a fitting finish to one of America's proudest nameplates. Camaro was born in the late 1960s out of Chevrolet's desperate need for something sporty and youthful to battle Ford's successful Mustang. With the much-maligned, rear-engine Corvair on the way out, General Motors design chief Bill Mitchell oversaw development of a more conventional replacement. From its 1967 debut, Camaro had the long-hood, short-tail look that would define the line for almost four decades.

Like Mustang, Camaro was initially offered in versions ranging from 6-cylinder basic to V-8 exciting. Equipped with the standard 140-horsepower engine, the $2466 base Camaro provided stylish transportation on a budget. Buyers looking for more excitement could opt for the Super Sport, or SS, edition with V-8s ranging from 295 to 375 horsepower. Nineteen sixty-seven also gave birth to the Z28, a race-ready Camaro based on the car that won 18 out of 25 Trans-Am races that year.

A convertible was part of Camaro's magic right from the start, and usually was available with even the most-powerful engines and in both SS and Z28 trim. Camaro's convertible disappeared from the line in 1970, and didn't appear again until 1987. The ragtop would remain a part of the Camaro lineup until the end, skipping only 1993.

Of 3000 35th Anniversary Chevrolet Camaro SSs built, just 1398 were convertibles, assuring that this last of the breed would also become one of the most coveted.

SS
CHEVROLET CAMARO

35th ANNIVERSARY
SS
CHEVROLET CAMARO

CAMARO
4PWA007

2002 FORD THUNDERBIRD

After a four-year absence, Thunderbird returned without rear seats and without a roof—replacing substance with style.

Arguably the best-loved Thunderbirds were the first. The tidy dimensions and understated style of the original 1955-57 two-seaters have made them among the most coveted of all drop-top T-Birds.

Ford recalled the charm of the original "Little Bird" for 2002 with the first two-seat Thunderbird since the first generation. More than an updated copy of the original, the 2002 borrowed styling elements from several generations of Thunderbirds. The resulting design was both new and nostalgic, and very much Thunderbird. And like the original, the new Thunderbird was only available as a convertible.

Thunderbird owed much mechanically to the Lincoln LS with which it shared both drivetrain and chassis components. Thunderbird's 3.9-liter double overhead-cam V-8 boasted 252 horsepower, enough to propel the sprightly ragtop from 0-60 mph in 7 seconds.

More sporty than sports, the 2002 Thunderbird was a touring car in the tradition of the original two-seater. With a suspension tuned for ride instead of handling Thunderbird was about taking in the scenery instead of carving up the curves.

In 2002, demand for the $36,000-$40,000 Thunderbirds exceed the 25,000-car supply, proof perhaps that modern design can evoke the spirit of classic top-down motoring.

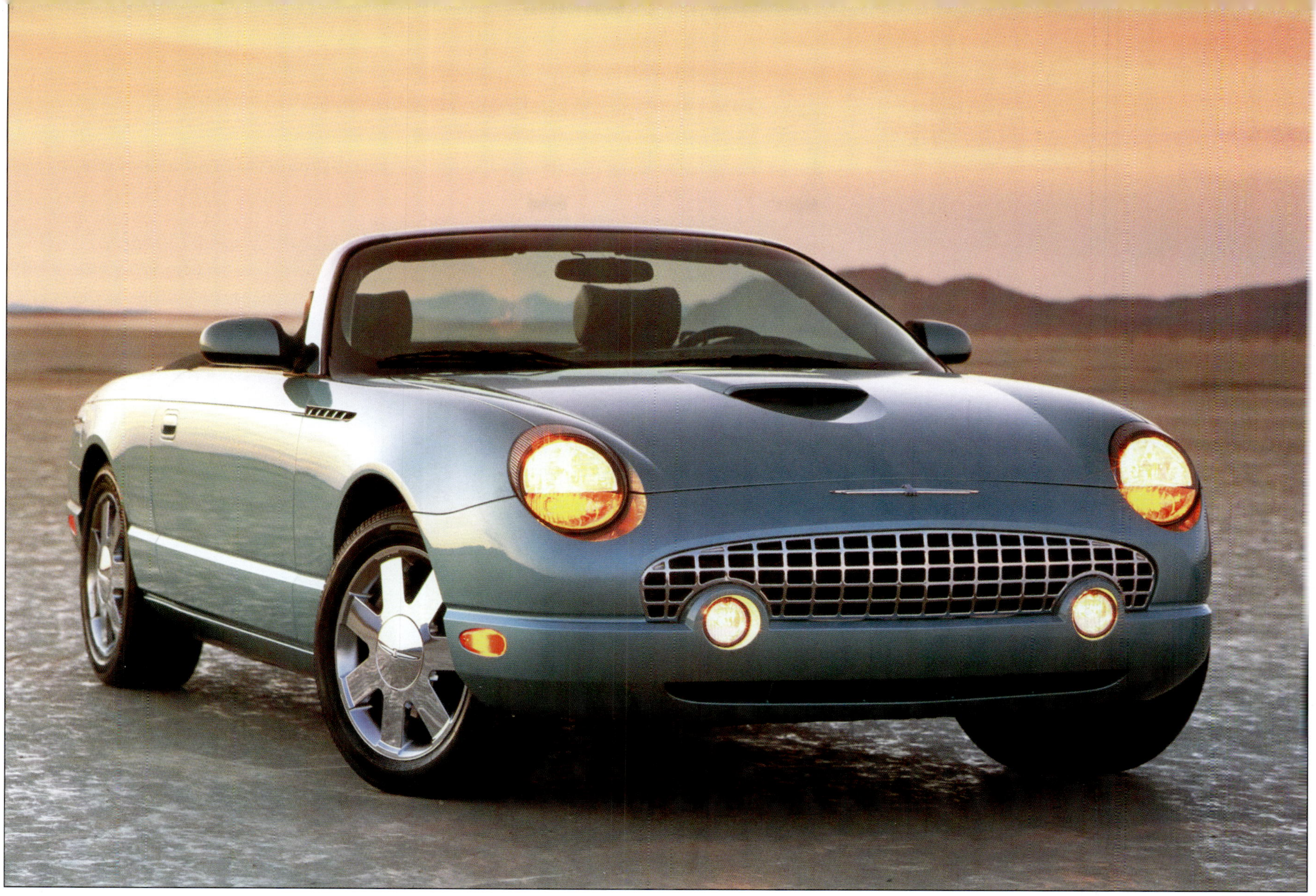

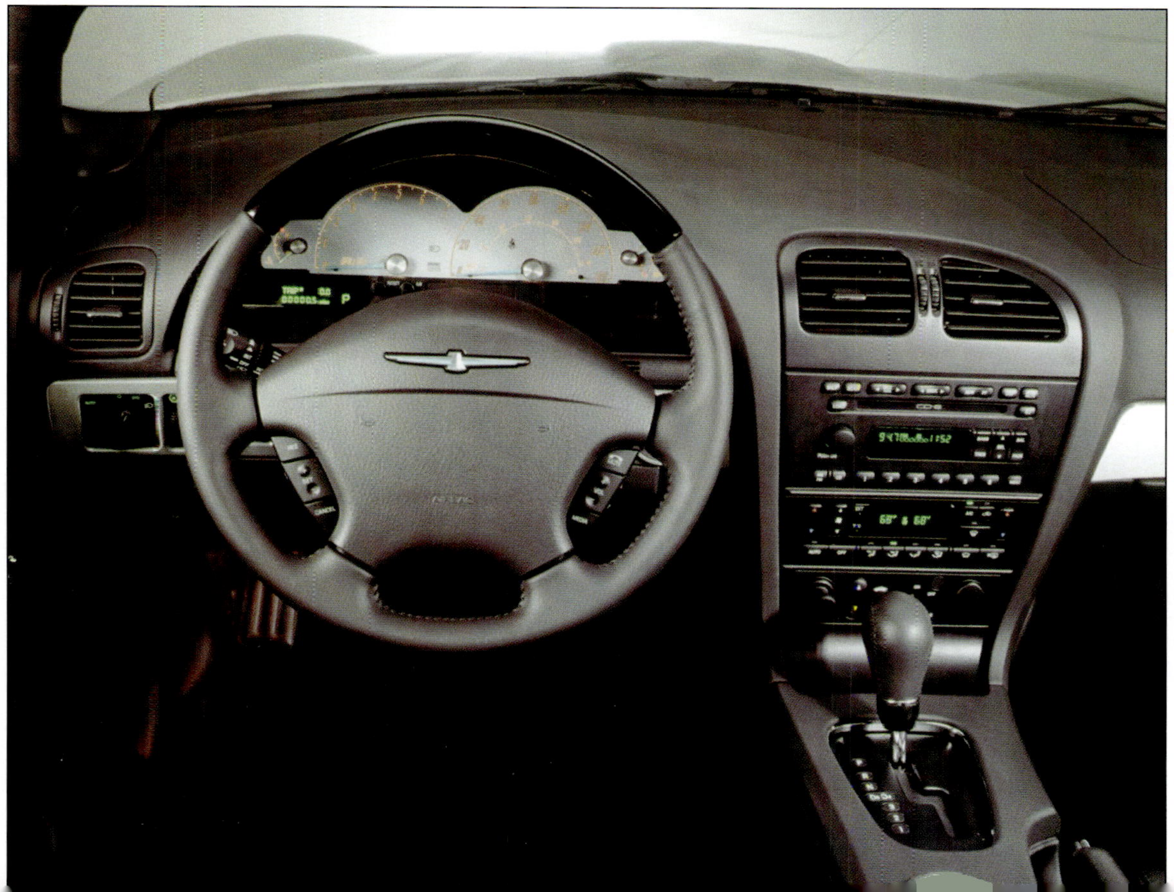

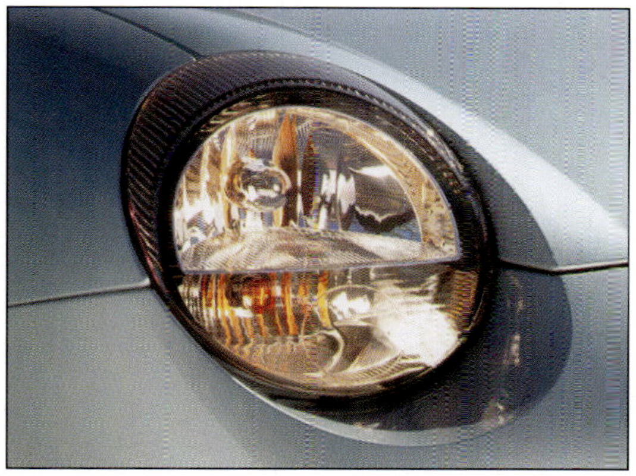

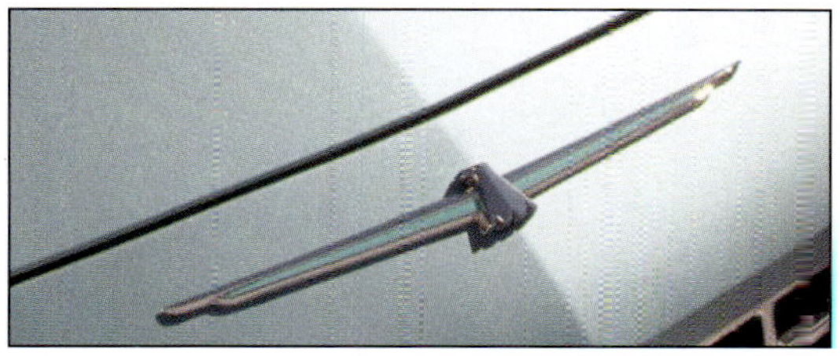

2003 DODGE VIPER

To keep Viper ahead of Corvette, Dodge applied the first rule of hot rodding: "There is no substitute for cubic inches."

American car lore is full of great rivalries. Camaro and Mustang fans never tire of boasting about their ponycars. And when Dodge rolled out the first Viper in 1992, the Corvette faced its first American competition in decades.

The 2003 Viper picked up where the 1992-2002 original left off. At 8.0 liters, the first-generation Viper engine was huge, and for 2003 it got bigger. The thundering Viper V-10 was bumped to 8.3-liters—505 cubic inches.

With 500 horsepower, Viper bested Chevy's fastest drop-top 'Vette by 150, and defended its position as the most-powerful production car in America. Viper blasted from 0-60 mph in well under 4 seconds and topped out around 190 mph.

Still a raucous ride, with every bit of its he-man personality in place, Viper was more civil than the original. Part of its taming was that it was now a true convertible with a well-engineered folding top. This design replaced the original's roof-hoop structure and cumbersome snap-on lid.

Viper could now continue its speed war with Corvette, while matching it with classic convertible style.

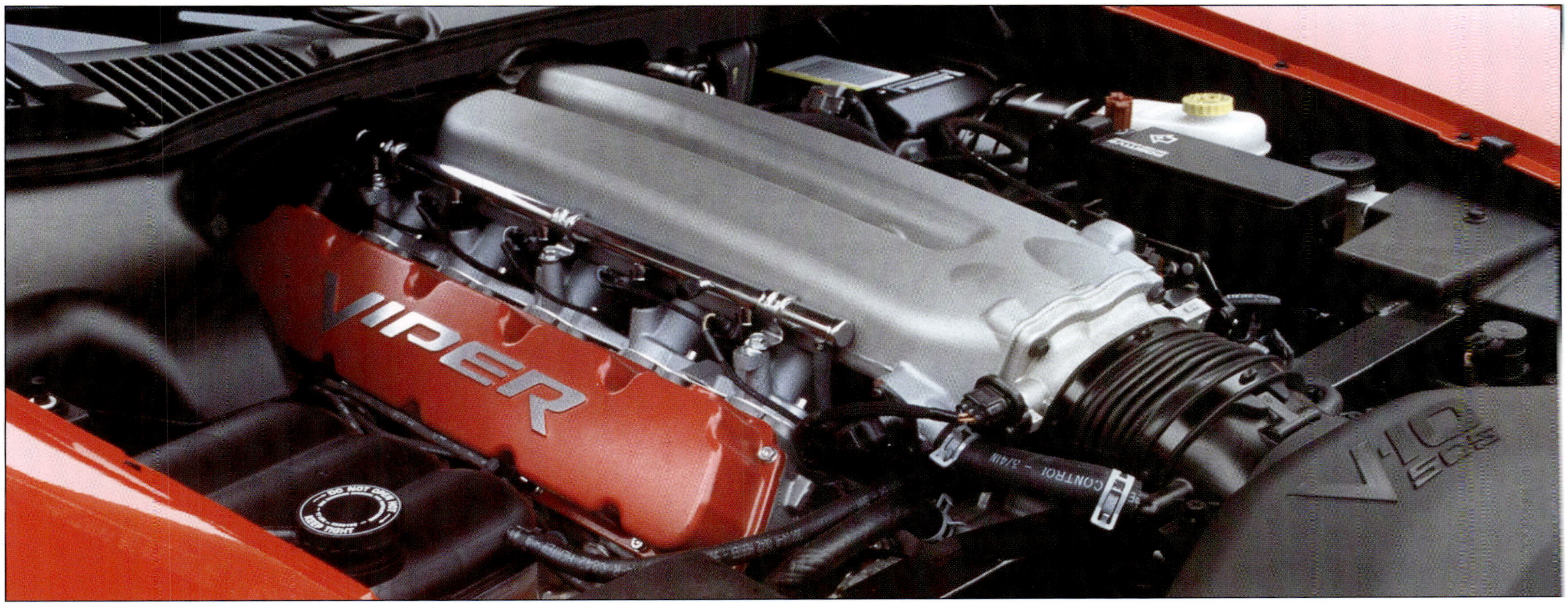
VIPER

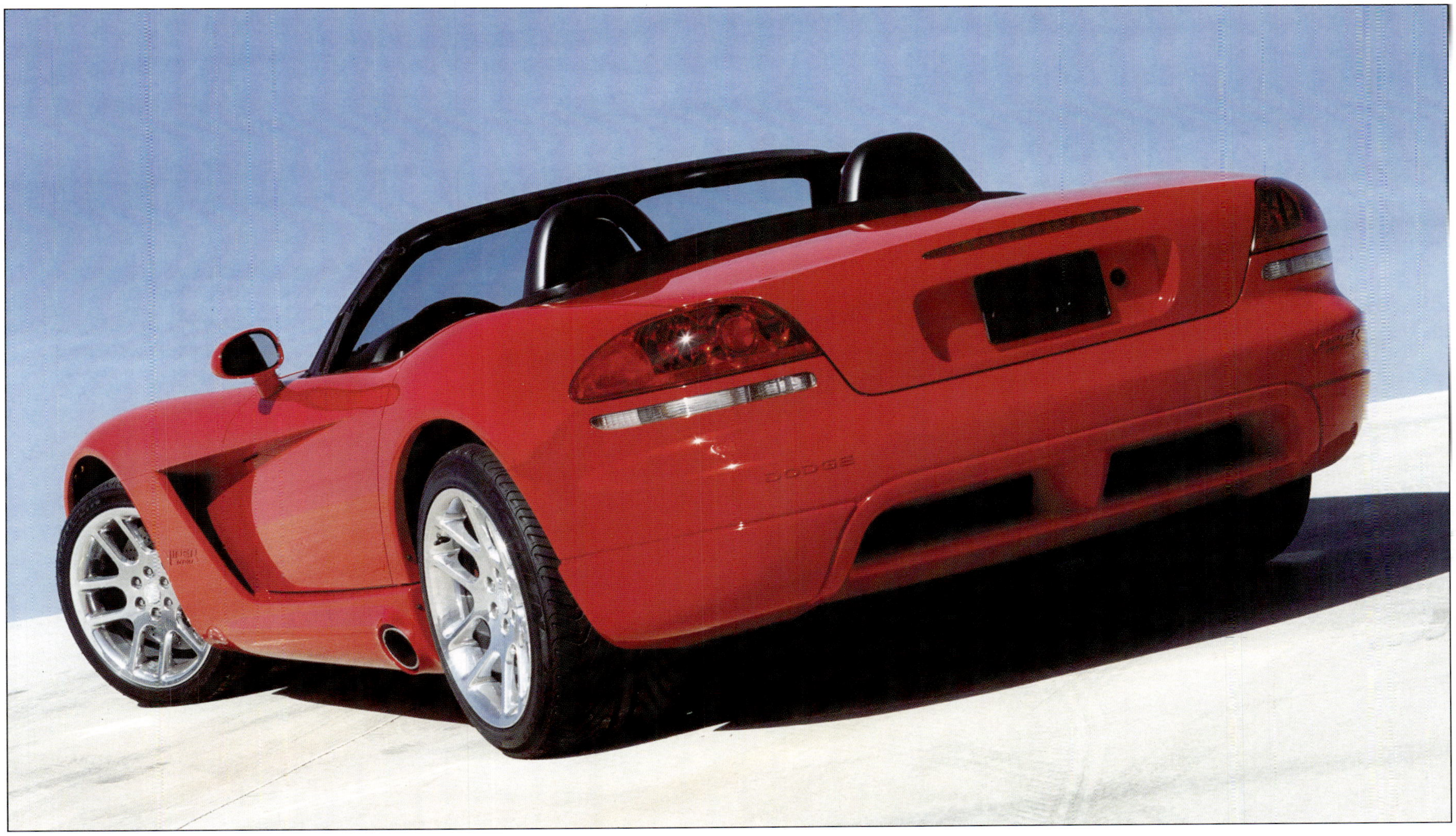

2004 CADILLAC XLR

With the XLR, Cadillac came one step closer to forgetting past mistakes and reclaiming its title of "Standard of the World."

XLR was Cadillac's chance to get it right. Its previous foray into the two-seat luxury-performance realm fell embarrassingly short with the 1987-93 Allante, an American-Italian amalgam of front-wheel drive, quiet styling, and undistinguished performance.

For the XLR, Cadillac reached straight for GM's best performance platform, that of the 2004 C6 Corvette. With a state-of-the-art chassis, rear-wheel drive, and more than 300 horsepower, it was well prepared for battle. And its controversial, edgy "Arts and Science" design guaranteed XLR distinction from its Lexus, Mercedes, and Jaguar competition.

XLR was first seen on auto show stands as the Evoq concept car in 2001. Its champion was swashbuckling auto executive Bob Lutz, who joined GM in 2001 to breathe excitement into the company. The production version debuted in spring 2003, the boldest example yet of Cadillac's edgy styling theme.

Sharing the Corvette's basic chassis but trading the 'Vette's pushrod V-8 for Cadillac's own "Northstar" double overhead-cam V-8, the XLR secured its upscale performance credentials. Assembled alongside Corvette in Kentucky, XLR featured a longer wheelbase for a better ride, a retractable hardtop for coupe-like comfort, and instruments designed by Italian watchmaker Bulgari.

XLR helped pioneer the move to bolder design and return to rear-wheel drive by GM's flagship division. It was a key element in Cadillac's quest to reclaim its title of "Standard of the World."

INDEX

A
American Motors, 48
ASC Incorporated, 132

B
Buick
   Centurion (1973), 120-121
   Century (1955), 52-53
   Reatta (1990), 138-139
   Riviera (1983), 132-133
   Roadmaster (1948), 32-33

C
Cadillac
   Eldorado (1976), 130-131
   Series 62 (1947), 28-29
   Series 62 (1949), 34-35
   Series 62 (1955), 54-55
   Series 62 (1959), 80-81
   Series 90 (1939), 16-17
   XLR (2004), 158-159
Chevrolet
   Bel Air (1955), 56-57
   Bel Air (1957), 66-67
   Camaro SS 35th Anniversary (2002), 152-153
   Caprice Classic (1975), 124-125
   Corvair Monza (1966), 112-113
   Corvette Pace Car Replica (1998), 142-143
   Impala SS (1963), 94-95
Chrysler
   LeBaron GTC (1988), 136-137
   New Yorker (1951), 40-41
   New Yorker (1957), 68-69
   Sebring JXi (1996), 140-141
   Town & Country (1947), 30-31
   300L (1965), 106-107
Classic Car Club of America, 18
Continental
   Mark III (1958), 76-77

D
Dodge
   Custom (1942), 22-23
   Polara (1959), 82-83
   Polara (1960), 88-89
   Polara 500 (1962), 94-95
   Viper (2003), 156-157

E
Edsel
   Citation (1958), 78-79
   Ranger (1960), 90-91
Engel, Elwood, 100

F
Ford
   Cabriolet (1933), 10-11
   Fairlane 500 Skyliner (1957), 70-71
   Falcon Futura (1963), 98-99
   Galaxie Sunliner (1961), 92-93
   Mustang Cobra (1998), 144-145
   Mustang (1965), 108-109
   Mustang GT (1986), 134-135
   Thunderbird (1956), 60-61
   Thunderbird (1959), 84-85
   Thunderbird (2002), 154-155
Ford, Edsel, 10, 18
Ford, Henry, 10
Frazer
   Manhattan (1949), 36-37
Frazer, Joe, 36

G
Gregorie, E.T. "Bob," 18

H
Hudson
   Hornet Brougham (1954), 48-49
   Super Six Brougham (1946), 24-25

I
Indianapolis 500, 142
   (1951), 40
   (1983), 132

K
Kaiser, Henry J., 36

L
Lincoln
   Continental (1941), 18-19
   Cosmopolitan (1951), 42-43
   Premiere (1956), 62-63
   Premiere (1957), 72-73
Lutz, Bob, 159

M
Mason, George, 44
McCahill, Tom, 58
Mercury
   Cougar XR-7 (1973), 122-123
   Montclair (1955), 58-59
   Park Lane (1968), 114-115
   Sportsman (1946), 26-27
   XM-800 Show Car, 62
Mexican Road Race, 38, 62
Mitchell, Bill, 152
Motor Trend, 52

N
Nader, Ralph, 112
Nance, James, 50
NASCAR, 38

O
Oldsmobile
   Delta 88 Royale (1975), 126-127
   88 (1950), 38-39
   F-30 (1930), 8-9
   Fiesta (1953), 46-47
   L-38 (1938), 14-15
   Super 88 (1957), 74-75

P
Packard
   Caribbean (1954), 50-51
   Caribbean (1956), 64-65
   One Twenty (1941), 20-21
Panoz
   Esperante (2000), 148-149
Panoz, Danny, 148
Petty, Lee, 74
Petty, Richard, 74
Pierce-Arrow
   Salon Twelve (1934), 12-13
Plymouth
   Prowler (2000), 150-151
   Road Runner (1969), 116-117
   Sport Fury (1963), 100-101
Pontiac
   Bonneville (1959), 88-89
   Grand Ville (1975), 128-129
   GTO (1964), 104-105
   Trans Am 30th Anniversary Edition (1999), 146-147

R
Rambler
   American 440 (1965), 110-111
   Custom Landau (1951), 44-45

S
Shelby
   GT-500 (1969), 118-119
Shelby, Carroll, 118
Studebaker
   Lark Daytona (1963), 102-103